FAITH AND KNOWLEDGE

BEACON TEXTS IN THE JUDAIC TRADITION
N. N. GLATZER, EDITOR

FAITH
AND
KNOWLEDGE

The Jew in the Medieval World

EDITED AND INTRODUCED BY

NAHUM N. GLATZER

BEACON PRESS   BOSTON

Copyright © 1963 by Nahum N. Glatzer

All rights reserved

Published simultaneously in Canada by
S. J. Reginald Saunders and Co., Ltd., Toronto

Library of Congress catalog card number: 63-17528

Printed in the United States of America

To Richard and Joyce Stiebel
in friendship

Preface

The intent of this volume is to acquaint the reader with some major currents of thought and belief in medieval, and especially, but not exclusively, in European Judaism. Though issued as a sequel to *The Rest Is Commentary: A Source Book of Judaic Antiquity* (volume I of the series, *Texts in the Judaic Tradition*), published in 1961, it is independent and self-contained. A third, concluding, volume of the series, dealing with the Jew in the Modern Age, is to follow.

Medieval Jewry built its literature upon the foundations of Judaic Antiquity. Certain main themes of antiquity recur in the Middle Ages in new forms and with different emphases. The material in chapters I, II, and IV of the present volume ("God," "The Love for God," and "Man") represents a further development of insights formulated in the section "God-Man-World" of chapter IX in the first volume, *The Rest Is Commentary;* the theme of "Knowledge," chapter V in the present volume, goes back to motives recorded in the first volume's section "Revelation and the Study of the Law" in the same chapter. An interesting comparison can be drawn between "The Community of Israel," chapter VII of the present volume, and the section "Israel" in chapter IX of the first volume, or, between the first volume's chapters III ("The Hope for a New Age") and VII ("After the Fall of Jerusalem") and the present volume's chapter XI ("The Land of Israel, Exile, and Redemption"). It will be noted, however, that not only the literary form and style have changed, but, despite the parallels, much of the substance. One pivotal theme remained outside the scope of this anthology: the Halakha, i.e., the analysis, interpretation, and codification of Jewish law. In the editor's opinion, no selection in translation can pretend to communicate an adequate impression of this branch of learning. Here, silence seemed preferable.

The main spokesmen of the period encompassed in the present volume are the poet and thinker Judah ha-Levi (Spain, 11th-12th cent.), the philosopher and talmudist Moses Maimonides (Spain, Egypt, 12th cent.), Judah the Pious (Germany, 12th-13th cent.), Moses de Leon, the mystic author of the *Zohar* (or, Book of Splendor, end of 13th cent.), and Israel the Baal Shem, founder of Hasidism (Podolia, 18th cent.). But lesser figures, too, speak with authentic voices.

The term Middle Ages is somewhat inexact; in the Jewish realm, the "age between" Antiquity and the modern period stretches beyond the era generally called the medieval. Even within the Jewish realm no clear-cut division can be made. Thus, for example, Hasidism in Eastern Europe can be considered as part of the Jewish Middle Ages, while the West-European Enlightenment of the same period is a chapter in modern Jewish history.

The Introduction will point to certain aspects of the period. And, as in the preceding volume, prefatory notes to the individual selections give the required background information. The translations from the (mostly Hebrew) originals, recorded in the sections "Sources" and "Acknowledgments," have been revised in places and abridged; important abridgments are indicated by brackets.

The editor wishes to express his gratitude to Mr. Edward Darling, director of Beacon Press, and its editor, Mr. Karl Hill, for their enthusiastic interest in this work, and to Mrs. Ruth Alexander for her understanding and gracious aid in the preparation of the manuscript.

N. N. GLATZER

Brandeis University
October 1962

Contents

V. KNOWLEDGE

VI. THE WAYS OF GOOD LIFE

VII. THE COMMUNITY OF ISRAEL

VIII. THE SABBATH

IX. THE WAYS OF THE MYSTICS

X. THE WAYS OF THE HASIDIM

XI. THE LAND OF ISRAEL, EXILE, AND REDEMPTION

EPILOGUE

Notes

Introduction

I

The Jews of Prague used to relate an ancient legend according to which their ancient synagogue, the *Altneushul,* was built with stones which exiles from Jerusalem carried away when the Temple was destroyed by the Romans. They promised themselves to dismantle the synagogue and carry the stones back to the Holy Land once the Messiah came. Style and structure, however, point to the eleventh century as the period in which the synagogue was built and to the twelfth as the time of renovation. Later plans at reconstruction are said to have been stopped by the sages, in order not to disturb the blood of the martyrs that adhered to the walls. At the Torah-reading platform is a lovingly preserved scarlet flag; it was presented to the Jewish community in recognition of its aid in the defense of Prague against the Swedes during the Thirty Years' War.

This is the legend and a few facts about the Prague synagogue. Independent of fact and fiction has been its function, unchanged throughout the ages: to provide the devout with a place to assemble and to offer thanks for the light of day and for the rest of night; to pray for insight, sustenance, and peace; to sanctify the seventh day and to remember, as a community, the great events of the Biblical past and to keep alive, together, the hope for a Messianic future; to repent sins and to pray for forgiveness on the Days of Awe; forever, to utter the praise of the Creator; and, forever to study the classical writings and to grow in knowledge.

The building grew older; the prayers and the studies retained the freshness and immediacy of youth. The building became a quaint relic of the past; but the assembly of the faithful and the studious converted the memories of the past and the hopes for the future into strength to master this day and every day.

The community of Israel in the period after the loss of its land, living among many nations yet separated from them, has these two faces. Symbol of the first is the exterior of an old building, hallowed but often odd to behold and anachronistic to its surroundings; symbolic of the other is a living community, giving voice to what it considers great, enduring, transcending the moment.

To focus on the external aspects of Jewish existence creates a gloomy, rueful picture historically, and a demonically distorted image theologically. Israel, then, would appear to be (or to have been) a ghostlike, weird, arid, rootless, eccentric, marginal group of people, and its faith retarded, present without future, question without answer, missed opportunity; a faith doomed and destined to fail. Only he who ventures to penetrate the surface will become conscious of forces that sustained Judaism and allowed it not only to survive medieval discrimination, persecutions, expulsions, misunderstanding, and hatred, but to keep alive the spirit of trust, of optimism, of cooperation, ready for the dawn of a new day.

At the core of this faith lie the convictions that historical success or failure is not the ultimate measure of things, that might is not necessarily right, and powerlessness and rejection by men is no evidence or sign of divine rejection. Yannai, an early medieval Hebrew poet expressed this in the following lines:

> Not everyone who is loved, is loved.
> Not everyone who is hated, is hated.
> Some are hated below, and loved above. . . .
> Hated we are, for you we love, O Holy One!

Those who, in view of historical realities—the fall of Zion and the rise of Rome in whatever form—doubted the reality of this "love above" left the community of Israel. Those who remained did so in the daily and hourly affirmation of that love; they did so, prepared to bear the paradox of the concluding line of Yannai's poem.

II

Although centuries-old Jewish communities continued to exist in Eastern countries (e.g., Palestine and Mesopotamia), the centers of Jewish life and thought in the Middle Ages were in the West; the most active part of Jewry had become European.

Jews lived in Rome from the second pre-Christian century, and in Spain from the first Christian centuries, first under the Romans, then under the Visigoths, the Moslems, and the Christians, respectively. They were known in France, in Germany, in the Balkans, in southern Russia, long before the barbarian invasions. Economically, the Jews underwent a transition from predominantly agricultural and artisan groups in Antiquity and the early Middle Ages to an even greater concentration in later periods on business, petty trade, and, finally, on moneylending. This concentration resulted from the legislation of the dominant society that excluded the Jew from landownership, from control of a working force, from craft-guilds and merchant guilds. The resolve of the Church to enforce the Biblical prohibition of usury among its adherents, left this economically necessary but morally reprehensible occupation to the Jew, the outsider, if not the outcast, in this society. On a different level, however, many Jews were employed as financial and political advisers by various rulers, especially in Spain, and many others followed the medical profession and were often called to serve at the courts of Spain and Italy. Nevertheless, the total occupational structure was abnormal and unhealthy; its cause was intolerance directed toward a people in dispersion that refused to conform to the dominant religion; its effect was still greater intolerance, deeper hostility.

Yet, despite all this, and despite restrictive laws, periods of pogroms and edicts of expulsion, an important positive aspect must not be overlooked. It is true that a vast gulf separated the Biblical religions: Judaism, Christianity, and Islam. But it was a common ground, and, in the case of Judaism and Christianity, a common document of faith, the Hebrew Bible, on which the religions disagreed. Both disagreement *and* the common source are determining factors in Western Jewish history and in the history of Judaeo-Christian relations; it was the latter that allowed for some measure of communication in the present and an expectation of reconciliation in the hoped-for future. The Jew had a rightful place in the universal scheme of things as seen by the Christian; the aim was not the Jew's annihilation, but his inclusion, for which end he was to be preserved (though in a state of degradation).

In the Jewish view, the Christian's rejection of Israel was temporary, just as the low state of Israel in dispersion was in appearance only and, as such, served a high purpose. In the words of the poet Judah ha-Levi: "God has a wise design concerning us, which may be likened to the seed that falls into the ground and to all appearances is transformed into earth, water, and dirt, retaining none of its qualities—or so it would seem to the ordinary observer—whereas actually it is the seed that transforms the earth and the water into its own substance. . . . And once the pure core appears and is ready to assume . . . the form of the first seed, then that tree produces fruit like that from which its own seed has come. So it is in the case of the law of Moses. All who come after it will yet be transformed to it by virtue of its essential truth, although to all appearances they would seem to reject it. The nations are a preparation and introduction to the awaited Messiah, who is the fruition. And they will all become his fruit once they recognize him, and the tree will be one. Then they will praise the root that they formerly despised."

This parable (*Kuzari* IV, 23) expresses the medieval Jew's belief that, in the final analysis, he lived in a world in which his role as the seed of the divine teaching will be realized, not in spite of, but through, his suffering; a world in which, at present, nation lifts up sword against nation and faith is set against faith, but in which, in the future, the relationship between the "seed" and the "fruit" will be recognized "and the tree will be one."

The philosopher Maimonides, too, saw Christianity and Islam as fulfilling the historical mission of spreading in the world essentially Judaic ideas, thus preparing the world for the Messianic era and for universal and pure monotheism.

Such views had no immediate, practical, institutional implications in the medieval scheme of things. But beneath all antagonism and the attitude of mutual exclusiveness there existed an unspoken, passive awareness of a common ground. It was one of the factors that prevented Judaism from assuming the character of a fossilized sect, a development that would have taken place if Judaism had had to survive, say, in a Far Eastern society.

III

There was one vast area of intellectual endeavor which allowed interaction and open communication between the members of different religious societies. This was the activity of transmitting and interpreting the knowledge and thought of Antiquity to the European West, of bringing Moslem science to the attention of the new centers of learning, of continuing these efforts, an activity through which the Middle Ages advanced into an age of broader scope. In this intellectually immensely important process, the Hebrew language played the role of intermediary between the Greek and the Arabic on the one hand, and Latin, the language of Christian scholarship, on the other. A few examples will illustrate the point.

Abraham bar Hiyya (Spain and Provence, 11th-12th cent.), mathematician and astronomer, together with the Italian Plato of Tivoli, translated Arabic treatises that introduced mathematics to the Latin world. Leonardo Pisano (Fibonacci) used bar Hiyya's work in the field of geometry in his *Practica Geometriae*. The Biblical commentator Abraham ibn Ezra (Spain, 12th cent.) translated philological and astronomical studies from Arabic into Hebrew; some of his mathematical treatises were translated into Latin and edited by Peter of Abano in Padua (13th-14th cent.).

Emperor Frederick II (1211-1250), who has been called the "first modern man," made his court a center of studies for Christian, Moslem, and Jewish scholars; he called Jacob ben Abba Mari Anatoli of Southern France to Naples, where Anatoli translated into Hebrew the Moslem philosopher's, Averroës (12th cent.), commentaries on Aristotle, Averroës' own and al-Farabi's (9th-10th cent.) works on astronomy and logic, and the *Almagest* by Ptolemy, the second-century Alexandrian astronomer and geographer. Among other scholars invited to join Frederick's Italian center was Judah ibn Makta of Toledo, author of a

Hebrew and Arabic scientific encyclopaedia based on Aristotle's works. Charles of Anjou, King of Sicily, commissioned Faraj ben Salim of Girgenti (13th cent.) to render into Latin the *Liber continens*, the great medical work of Rhazes, the Persian-born physician (9th-10th cent.), and other works. Robert of Anjou, King of Naples and patron of scholarship, had Kalonymus ben Kalonymus of Arles, Provence (13th-14th cent.) come to Rome to translate from Arabic into Hebrew some of the works of the philosophers Averroës, al-Kindi (9th cent.), al-Farabi, and Galen, the second-century Greek physician.

Jewish astronomers were invited to compile the "Alfonsine astronomical tablets" and to translate them into Spanish; improved tablets were made by Joseph ibn Wakkar (1396), and again by Abraham Zacuto, court astronomer to King Emanuel of Portugal (1492); the latter work, in a Latin translation, accompanied the expeditions of Vasco da Gama and Columbus. Cresques of Las Palmas, Majorca, drew the first world map (1375), which the King of Aragon presented to Charles VI of France; the map set forth the voyages of Marco Polo. Invited by Henry the Navigator, Cresques assisted in the establishment of an astronomical observatory in Portugal.

Once printing presses were established, major works of the past were made available to the scholarly community. In 1520, Aristotle's *Posterior Analytics* was published in Venice, accompanied by Averroës' "Major Commentary," in a translation by the grammarian Abraham de Balmes, Jewish physician to the learned Cardinal Domenico Grimani. De Balmes also translated (from the Hebrew intermediate version) *Liber de mundo* by the Arab astronomer al-Haytham (10th-11th cent.). A few years later, Averroës' *Destructio destructionis*, a work in defense of rationalism was published in a Latin rendition by the physician Calo Kalonymus, who also translated into Latin Moses ibn Tibbon's Hebrew verison of *Theoria planetarium* by the Arab astronomer al-Bitroji. The great eleven-volume Latin edition of the works of Aristotle, with Averroës' commentaries, published in Venice in the mid-sixteenth century, incorporated the renditions of many Jewish translators and commentators, e.g., Gersonides, Jacob

Mantino, and Jacob Anatoli. Later in the sixteenth century, Aristotle's *De coelo* was issued in a Latin translation by Moses Alatino, a pupil of the philosopher Francesco Piccolomini in Perugia; the translation was based on a Hebrew rendition of an Arabic translation of the lost Greek original.

These examples (they could be multiplied) demonstrate the existence in the Middle Ages of a field of cultural interest in which, guided by Aristotle and his interpreters, many ages, countries, races, religions, and languages were involved. The search for rational knowledge, for rational confirmation of faith, for extension of the limits of the knowable, bridged, on some level at least, the gulf that separated medieval societies.

IV

Dedicated as medieval and early modern Jews were to this work of the transmission of knowledge of Antiquity to, and revival of learning in, the Western world, the main intellectual effort was quite naturally directed toward the cultivation of Israel's law, piety, and wisdom. These studies admitted contacts with extra-Judaic cultures (especially in the fields of philosophy and poetry), but the prime intention of the Jewish thinker and writer was to contribute his share to the instruction, strengthening, and growth of the community of Israel. The present volume does not attempt to cover all, or even most, of the aspects of medieval Jewish life and learning. Many other concerns, in addition to those contained in the title of this book, were characteristic of medieval Jewry: emphasis on community organization and its institutions, which gave the Jewish group the instruments of survival in a predominantly hostile world, and which permitted the preservation of its distinct religious civilization; cultivation of family life as the sacred core of the group organism; discipline of the law and the amenities of custom, which gave life the assurance of a meaningful order and a sense of proportion; cultivation of Hebrew, chiefly as a written language, which provided a means of communication, connecting the communities in various parts of the world and, at the same time, the present with the Hebraic past, thus strengthening the consciousness of continuity and the unity of Israel; and, finally, the Messianic belief, expressed either in the patient hope for redemption, or in activist movements designed to throw off the burden of exile.

Out of the many possible aspects, the present volume concentrates on two major themes: faith and knowledge. In the literature at hand we encounter attempts to correlate the two, to treat the one as the precondition of the other, to interpret the one in the light of the other. Ideally, the aim is the harmony between the realms of spiritual life; in reality, there is tension, crisis, tendency toward onesidedness; occasionally, however, the ideal becomes the real, and thought turns into life.

No attempt was made to idealize medieval Jewry; the selections include harsh self-criticism. But the reader is expected to gain some understanding of that element by which Jews maintained their dignity and sense of purpose in periods of degradation. He will realize, it is hoped, that the external appearance of medieval Jewish quarters, the weird, dreary, relic-like exterior of a house of prayer, or decayed tombstones are no fit symbols for a community that strove to preserve the breath of life in both faith and knowledge. "For you we love, O Holy One!"

Prelude

KNOWLEDGE AND FAITH

Abraham ibn Ezra, Joseph Caspi, and
Solomon ibn Gabirol

That knowledge is a prerequisite of faith, that knowledge of God presupposed knowledge of the physical universe is a frequent theme in medieval Hebrew literature. Equally recurrent is the theme of faith as the summit of the Law. Of the three quotations that follow, the first is from Abraham ibn Ezra's (Spain, 12th cent.) commentary on the Bible, the second from *Sefer ha-Musar* (Treatise on Ethics) by Joseph Caspi (South France, 13th–14th cent.), known especially for his commentary on Maimonides' *Guide to the Perplexed*. The third quotation, on faith, is from the *Choice of Pearls* by the poet Solomon ibn Gabirol (Spain, 11th cent.).

I

"And let us know, eagerly strive to know the Lord, his going forth is sure as the morning" (Hosea 6:3).

This [knowledge of the Lord] is the aim of all wisdom and solely to this end man was created. But man cannot know the Lord unless he has studied many branches of wisdom which are comparable to the steps of a ladder on which man ascends until he reaches the highest rung. The reason [why Hosea uses the image of] "the morning" is that like the morning commences [with but a little] light which grows bigger and bigger, so does the student [only gradually] recognize the Lord out of His works until he [finally] sees the truth.

1

II

How can I know God and that He is one, unless I know what knowing means, and what constitutes oneness? [. . .] No one really knows the true meaning of loving God and fearing him, unless he is acquainted with natural science and metaphysics, for we love not God as a man loves his wife and children, nor fear we Him as we would a mighty man. I do not say that all men can reach this intellectual height, but I maintain that it is the degree of highest excellence, though those who stand below it may still be good.

III

A wise man said, "Everything requires a fence."

He was asked, "What is the fence?" He answered, "Trust." "What is the fence of trust?" he was asked; and he replied, "Faith." To the further question, "What is the fence of faith?" he answered, "To fear nothing." A wise man was asked, "What is the fence of faith?" and his reply was, "Trust in God, acceptance of His decrees, and self-surrender to Him."

There is nothing greater than faith; but few men endure patiently such misfortunes as poverty, sickness and terror. Yet know that all these [can be better endured when aid is derived] form the gates of faith.

O men, supplicate your God that He endow you with faith, for faith is the summit of the Law. Beg also tranquility from Him, for it is the summit of greatness; in cheerfulness seek it in this world and the hereafter. In faith is a sufficiency of riches; and in His service a sufficiency of occupation.

I. God

THE ONENESS OF GOD

Moses Maimonides

Within medieval Judaism, Maimonides (or, the Rambam, as he is traditionally called) made the most determined attempt to do justice to both faith and knowledge. Born in Cordoba, Spain, in 1135, he led a migratory life in Spain from 1148 to 1158; the following years the Maimonides family spent in Fez, Morocco, then established permanent residence in Egypt in 1165 or 1166, first in Alexandria, then in Fostat. Moses, "the marvel of the generation," was a rabbinical scholar, philosopher, leader of Jewry, and physician, and his writings encompass all these fields. For years he was physician at the Court of Saladin, the Sultan who in 1187 reconquered most of Palestine from the Crusaders. Maimonides died in 1204.

His major works include: *A Commentary on the Mishnah,* written in Arabic, concluded in 1168; *Mishneh Torah* (Code of Jewish Law), written in Hebrew, completed in 1180 (the first of the Code's fourteen books, *Sefer ha-Madda* [The Book of Knowledge] is a presentation of the principles of Judaism and a summary of the author's metaphysics and philosophical ethics); and *Moreh Nebukhim* (The Guide to the Perplexed), written in Arabic, completed about 1190, which is an exposition of his philosophy, a conciliation between the Bible and Aristotle, a synthesis of classical Jewish religion and Neoplatonic Aristotelianism. Among his shorter writings *The Epistle to Yemen* (*Iggeret Teman*), a treatise on Jewish persecution and the faith in redemption, should be mentioned. In addition he wrote hundreds of *responsa* and some twenty medical treatises. In his *Mishneh Torah,* Maimonides gave the traditional Jew a systematically arranged, all-comprising *Code* to facilitate both study and practice of the religious laws.

The passage that is here reprinted is from the first chapter and the beginning of the second in his *Code.* What was to become a major

concern in his *Guide,* the oneness and incorporeality of God, is here
stated in a clear, strong outline.

The first edition of the *Mishneh Torah* appeared in Italy about
1480, the second at Soncino in 1490. They were followed by numerous
other editions, mostly with commentaries.

The foundation of foundations and the pillar of all wisdom
is to know that there is a First Being who caused all beings to be.
All beings from heaven and earth, and from between them, could
not be save for the truth of His being.

If it could be supposed that He did not exist, nothing else
could possibly exist.

If, however, it were supposed that all other beings were non-
existent, He alone would still exist. Their non-existence would
not involve His non-existence. For all beings are in need of Him;
but He, blessed be he, is not in need of them nor of a single one
of them. Hence, the truth of His being is incomparable to the
truth of any other individual being. [. . .]

This God is one. He is not two nor more than two, but one;
so that none of the things existing in the universe to which the
term one is applied is like unto His oneness; neither such a unit
as a species which comprises many [individual] units, nor such
a unit as a body which consists of parts and dimensions. His oneness is such that there is no other oneness like it in the universe. [. . .]

That the Holy One, blessed be he, is incorporeal is clearly
set forth in the Torah and in the Prophets, as it is said, "(Know
therefore) that the Lord, He is God in heaven above, and upon
the earth beneath" (Deut. 4:39); and a corporeal being is in-
capable of being in two places at one time. Furthermore, it is
said, "For ye saw no manner of form" (Deut. 4:15).

Since this is so, what is the meaning of the following expressions found in the Torah: "Beneath his feet" (Exod. 24:10);
"Written with the finger of God" (Exod. 31:18); "The hand of
God" (Exod. 9:3); "The eyes of God" (Gen. 38:7), "The ears
of God" (Num. 11:1), and similar phrases? All such terminology
is adapted to the conception of sons of man who have a clear perception of corporeal things only. The Torah speaks in the language of men. All these phrases are metaphorical. [. . .]

Since it has been demonstrated that He is incorporeal, it is clear that none of the accidents of matter can be attributed to Him; neither joining nor separation, neither place nor dimension, neither ascent nor descent, neither right nor left, neither front nor back, neither sitting nor standing. Nor does He exist in time, in the sense that either a beginning or an end or number of years can be attributed to Him. Nor does He change, for there is nought in Him that would cause any change in Him. He is neither subject to death nor to life like to the life of a living body. Folly cannot be attributed to Him, nor can wisdom, like that of a wise man; neither sleep nor awakening, neither passion nor frivolity; neither joy nor melancholy; neither silence nor speech like that of human beings. And so the sages have said, "Above, there is neither sitting nor standing, neither rigidity nor relaxation." [1]

This being so, the expressions in the Torah and in the words of the Prophets and others similar to these, are all of them metaphorical and figurative, as for example, "He that sitteth in the heavens shall laugh" (Ps. 2:4), "They have provoked me to anger with their vanities" (Deut. 32:21), "As the Lord rejoiced" (Deut. 28:63), etc. To all these applies the saying "The Torah speaks in the language of men." So too, it is said, "Do they provoke Me to anger?" (Jer. 7:19); and yet it is said "I am the Lord, I change not" (Malachi 3:6). If God could sometimes be angry and sometimes rejoicing, He would be subject to change. All these states exist in physical beings that are of lowly and mean condition, dwelling in houses of clay, whose origin is in the dust. Blessed and exalted above all this, is God, blessed be he.

This God, honored and revered, it is our duty to love and fear; as it is said, "Thou shalt love the Lord, thy God" (Deut. 6:5), and it is further said, "Thou shalt fear the Lord, thy God" (Deut. 6:13).

And what is the way that will lead to the love of Him and the fear of Him? When a person will contemplate His great and wondrous works and creatures and will behold through them His wisdom which is incomparable and infinite, he will spontaneously love Him, praise Him, glorify Him, and long with an exceeding longing to know the Great Name. And when he ponders these matters, he will be taken aback in a moment and stricken with awe, and realize that he is an infinitesimal creature, lowly and humble, endowed with slight and slender intelligence, standing in the presence of Him who is perfect in knowledge. In harmony with these matters, I shall explain some large, general aspects of the works of the Lord of the universe, that they may serve the intelligent individual as a door to the love of God, even as our sages have remarked in connection with the theme of the love of God, "Observe the universe and hence you will recognize Him who spoke and the world was called into existence." [2]

KNOWLEDGE OF GOD

Moses Maimonides

In Biblical thought the will of God is expressed in His laws and especially in the moral commandment; man worships God by fulfilling the commandment. Maimonides, while retaining the Biblical view, points to a higher form of communion between man and God: Knowledge. Knowledge of the physical world is the basis for the purely theoretical knowledge, which, in turn, culminates in the knowledge of God. In taking this position, Maimonides follows the lead of Aristotle, who considered the faculty of knowing to be man's supreme achievement, just as God, the highest mind, exists in the apprehension of Himself. And, again following Aristotle and his Moslem interpreters, Maimonides explained human reason and thought as becoming actualized by their contact with the cosmic source of all knowledge, the so-called "Active Intellect" which originates in God. Man, in developing his faculty of reason, is in contact with God. Knowledge of God is the road to God; in this knowledge, too, originates the love for God.

The excerpt below is from *Moreh Nebukhim* (The Guide to the Perplexed). To the intellectual, conscious of the rationalist trends in some parts of the Islamic and Christian world, and perplexed about the validity of revelation, Maimonides offered in the *Guide* a foundation from which it was possible to arrive at a harmony between the demands of reason and the principles of revealed faith. He envisaged intellectual self-perfection as the road—and the precondition—to a closeness to God, and interpreted the laws, ritual and ethical, as steps on that road.

The *Guide,* written in Arabic, was translated into Hebrew by

Samuel ibn Tibbon in the author's lifetime, and was first published in Italy before 1480. Another translation into Hebrew, by the poet Judah al-Harizi, became the basis for a translation into Latin by August Justinianus (Paris, 1520). Ibn Tibbon's version was rendered into Latin by Johannes Buxtorf (Basel, 1629). In 1580 the work appeared in an Italian translation. The Arabic original was published by Solomon Munk (Paris, 1856–66). The importance of the *Guide* was not restricted to Judaism; the work was studied by Christian scholastics, and is often quoted by Thomas Aquinas.

I will begin the subject of this chapter with a simile. A king is in his palace, and all his subjects are partly in the city, and partly abroad. Of the former, some have their backs turned towards the king's palace, and their faces in another direction. Others are making for the palace, seeking to obtain entry to it and to have audience with the king, but have not yet seen even the face of the wall of the house. Of those that are going towards the palace, some reach it, and go round about in search of the entrance gate; others have passed through the gate, and walk about in the ante-chamber; and others have succeeded in entering into the inner part of the palace, and being in the same room with the king in the royal palace. But even the latter do not immediately on entering the palace see the king, or speak to him; for, after having entered the inner part of the palace, another effort is required before they can stand before the king—at a distance, or close by—hear his words, or speak to him.

I will now explain the simile which I have made. The people who are abroad are all those that have no religion, neither one based on speculation nor one received by tradition. Such are the outlying tribes of the Turks that wander about in the distant north, the Kushites who live in the distant south, and those in our country who are like these. I consider these irrational beings, and not as human beings; they are below mankind, but above the apes, since they have the form and shape of man, and a mental faculty above that of the apes.

Those who are in the city, but have their backs turned towards the king's palace, are men of thought and speculation who have arrived at false doctrines, which they either adopted in consequence of great errors made in their own speculations, or received from others who misled them. Because of these doctrines they recede more and more from the royal palace the more they seem to proceed. These are worse than the first class.

Those who are making for the palace, and aim to enter it, but have never yet seen it, are the mass of religious people; the multitude that observe the divine commandments, but are ignorant.

Those who arrive at the palace, but go round about it, are those who devote themselves exclusively to the study of the practical law; they believe traditionally in true principles of faith, and learn the practical worship of God, but are not trained in philosophical treatment of the principles of their faith, and do not endeavor to establish the truth of their faith by proof.

Those who undertake to investigate the principles of religion, have come into the forecourts; and there is no doubt that these can also be divided into different grades. But those who have succeeded in finding a proof for everything that can be proved, who have a true knowledge of God, so far as a true knowledge can be attained, and are near the truth, wherever an approach to the truth is possible, they have reached the goal, and are in the presence of the king in the inner parts of the palace.

My son, so long as you are engaged in studying the mathematical sciences and logic, you belong to those who go round about the palace in search of the gate. When you understand physics, you have entered the hall; and when, after completing the study of natural sciences, you master metaphysics, you have entered the innermost court, and are with the king in the same palace. You have attained the degree of the wise men, who include men of different grades of perfection. There are some who direct all their mind toward the attainment of perfection in metaphysics, devote themselves entirely to God, exclude from their thought every other thing, and employ all their intellectual faculties in the study of the universe, in order to find in it guidance towards God, and to learn in every possible way how God rules all things; they form the class of those who have entered the audience chamber. This is the rank of the prophets.

One of these [Moses] has attained so much knowledge, and has concentrated his thoughts to such an extent in the idea of God, that it could be said of him, "And he was with the Lord"

(Exod. 34:28). During that holy communion he could ask Him, answer Him, speak to Him, and be addressed by Him, enjoying beatitude in that which he had obtained to such a degree that "he did neither eat bread nor drink water" (*ibid.*); his intellectual energy was so predominant that all coarser functions of the body, especially those connected with the sense of touch, were in abeyance. Some prophets are only able to see, and of these some approach near and see, whilst others see from a distance.

We have already spoken of the various degrees of prophets; we will therefore return to the subject of this chapter, and exhort those who have attained a knowledge of God, to concentrate all their thoughts in God. This is the worship peculiar to those who have acquired a knowledge of the highest truths; and the more they reflect on Him, and think of Him, the more are they engaged in His worship.

Those, however, who think of God, and frequently mention His name, without any correct notion of Him, but merely following some imagination, or some theory received from another person, are, in my opinion, like those who remain outside the palace and distant from it. They do not mention the name of God in truth, nor do they reflect on it. That which they imagine and mention does not correspond to any reality; it is a thing invented by their imagination. The true worship of God is only possible when correct notions of Him have previously been conceived. When you have arrived by way of intellectual research at a knowledge of God and His works, then commence to devote yourselves to Him, try to come near Him and strengthen the intellect, which is the bond that links you to Him. The Torah distinctly states that the highest kind of worship to which we refer in this chapter, is only possible after the acquisition of the knowledge of God: "To love the Lord your God, and to serve Him with all your heart and with all your soul" (Deut. 11:13). As we have shown several times, man's love of God is identical with His knowledge of Him. The divine service enjoined in these words must, accordingly, be preceded by the love of God. Our sages have pointed out to us that it is a service in the heart, which I understand to mean this that man concentrates all his thoughts upon Him, and is absorbed in these thoughts as much as possible.

It has thus been shown that after having acquired the knowledge
of God, the aim should be complete devotion to God and constant exercising of intellectual thought in His love. He accom-
plishes this generally by seclusion and retirement. Every man of
virtue should therefore seek seclusion, and should only in case of
necessity associate with others.

IN THE PRESENCE OF GOD

Solomon ibn Gabirol

Solomon ibn Gabirol was born in Malaga about 1020 and died in
Valencia about 1060. He wrote (in Arabic) *Mekor Hayyim* (Fons Vitae,
Source of Life), a metaphysical and ontological system in the Neo-
platonic tradition; ethical treatises, presented elsewhere in this volume;
and religious and secular poetry. Some of his liturgic poems became a
part of the prayer book, especially of the Sephardic and oriental rites.
The most profound of them is the long hymn, *Keter Malkhut* (*The
Kingly Crown*), selections from which are here reprinted.

While most of his poems, and indeed most creations by Hebrew
poets in Spain, employed Arabic meters and stylistic forms, *The
Kingly Crown* is free of this influence; it is composed in a freely flow-
ing rhymed prose; an external unity of the sequence of stanzas is
established by a Biblical quotation that concludes each stanza; the
internal unity is provided by the poem's theme: the praise of God,
the creator of the universe. From among the attributes of God, it is
His will, manifested in the creation of the cosmic system, that the poet
describes in terms of the astronomical knowledge of his age. The
hymn concludes with a confession and a prayer from the humble man
to whom the vision of the ultimate was granted. "*The Kingly Crown*
is, by common consent, the greatest Hebrew religious poem of the
Middle Ages, and indeed one of the major works of Hebrew literature
since the completion of the Old Testament" (Bernard Lewis). Although
it is not a part of the liturgy, it has been included in the prayer book
for the Day of Atonement for private reading.

Translations of the hymn include Latin (1618), Yiddish (1674),
Spanish (1769), French (1773), and Persian (1895).

Thine are the greatness and the strength and the splendor and the
glory and the majesty.

Thine O God is the Kingdom and the rising above all things and the
    richness and the honor.
Thine are the higher and the lower creatures, and they bear witness
    that they perish and Thou dost endure.
Thine is the might whose secret our thoughts are wearied of seeking,
    for Thou art so much stronger than we.
Thine is the mystery of power, the secret and the foundation.

Thine is the name that is hidden from the wise, the strength that
    sustains the world over the void, the power to bring to light all
    that is hidden.
Thine is the mercy that rules over Thy creatures and the goodness
    preserved for those who fear Thee.
Thine are the secrets that no mind or thought can encompass, and the
    life over which decay has no rule, and the throne that is higher
    than all height, and the habitation that is hidden at the pinnacle
    of mystery.
Thine is the existence from the shadow of whose light every being was
    made to be, and we said "Under His shadow we shall live" (Lam.
    4:20).
Thou art, but the hearing of ears and the seeing of eyes cannot reach
    Thee, and how and why and where have no rule over Thee.
Thou art, but for Thine own essence, and for no other with Thyself.
Thou art, and before all time was Thou wert, and without place Thou
    didst dwell.
Thou art, and thy secret is hidden and who can reach it—"far off,
    and exceeding deep, who can find it out?" (Eccles. 7:24).

Thou livest, but not from determined time or known epoch.
Thou livest, but not with soul or breath, for Thou art soul of the soul.[3]
Thou livest, but not as the life of man that is like vanity, its end in
    moths and worms.
Thou livest, and whoever attains Thy secret will find eternal delight—
    "and eat, and live for ever" (Gen. 3:22).

Thou art the supreme light, and the eyes of the pure of soul shall see
    Thee, and clouds of sin shall hide Thee from the eyes of sinners.
Thou art the light hidden in this world and revealed in the world of
    beauty, "In the mount of the Lord it shall be seen" (Gen. 22:14).
Thou art the eternal light, and the inward eye yearns for Thee and
    is astonished—she shall see but the utmost part of them, and shall
    not see them all.[4]

Who can contain Thy might, when from the abundance of Thy glory
    Thou didst create a pure radiance, hewn from the quarry of the
    Rock,[5] and dug from the mine of Purity? [6]

And on it Thou didst set a spirit of wisdom, and Thou didst call it
   the Soul.

Thou didst fashion it from the flames of fire of the Intelligence,[7] and
   its spirit is as fire[8] burning in it.

Thou didst send it into the body to serve it and to guard it, and it is
   as a fire within, and yet it does not burn it.

From the fire of the spirit it was created, and went forth from nothingness to being, "because the Lord descended upon it in fire" (Exod.
   19:18).

Who can reach Thy wisdom, when Thou gavest the soul the power of
   knowledge which inheres in her?

So that knowledge is her glory, and therefore decay has no rule over
   her, and she endures with the endurance of her foundation; this
   is her state and her secret.

Who can requite Thy bounties, when thou gavest the soul to the body,
   to give it life, to teach and show it the path of life, to save it from
   evil?

Thou didst form man out of clay,[9] and breathe into him a soul and
   set on him a spirit of wisdom, by which he is distinguished from
   a beast, and rises to a great height.

Thou didst set him enclosed in Thy world, while Thou from outside
   dost understand his deeds and see him,

And whatever he hides from Thee—from inside and from outside
   Thou dost observe.[10]

Who can know the secret of Thine accomplishments, when Thou
   madest for the body the means for Thy work?

Thou gavest him eyes to see Thy signs,

Ears, to hear Thy wonders,

Mind, to grasp some part of Thy mystery,

Mouth, to tell Thy praise,

Tongue, to relate Thy mighty deeds to every comer,

As I do to-day, I Thy servant, the son of Thy handmaid,

I tell, according to the shortness of my tongue, one tiny part of Thy
   greatness.

O my God, if my sin is too great to bear, what wilt Thou do for Thy
   great name?

If I cannot hope for Thy mercies, who but Thou will have pity on me?

Therefore, though Thou kill me, I shall hope in Thee,[11]

And if Thou search out my sin, I shall flee from Thee to Thee, and
   hide myself from Thy wrath in Thy shadow.

I shall hold on to the skirts of Thy mercy until Thou hast pity on me.
   "I will not let Thee go, except Thou bless me" (Gen. 32:26).

Let it be Thy will, O Lord our God and God of our fathers, sovereign
     of all the worlds, to have pity on me and be near to me.
To visit me with the visitation of Thy will, to bear to me the light of
     Thy countenance, to let me find Thy grace.
And do not recompense me according to my deeds, nor make me the
     reproach of the foolish,
In the midst of my days do not take me away, and do not hide Thy
     face from me.
Cleanse me of my sins, and do not cast me from Thy countenance,
Let me live with honor, and after that with honor take me,[12]
And when Thou shalt take me out of this world, bring me in peace to
     the life of the world to come,
Summon me on high, and let me dwell among saints,
Number me among those who have a portion in eternal life
And make me worthy to shine with the light of Thy countenance.
Give me new life, and from the depths of the earth raise me up again,
And I shall say: I praise Thee, Lord, for though Thou wert angry,
     with me Thou didst soften Thine anger and pity me,[13]
Thine is the mercy, O God, in all the good which Thou hast vouch-
     safed to me and which Thou wilt vouchsafe to me until the day I
     die.

LORD WHERE SHALL I

FIND THEE?

Judah ha-Levi

Jewish prayer books of all rites contain a wealth of poetic creations by
Judah ha-Levi; they accompany the celebration of the Sabbath, the
Pilgrimage Festivals, the Days of Awe, fast days and the minor feasts.
They were chosen for inclusion because they gave profound expression
to the spiritual forces that affected Israel as a community of faith; the
presence of God, the sanctity of life, the meaning of exile and of the
return to Zion, the hope for redemption.

Not all of the several hundred pieces of Judah ha-Levi's religious
poetry were made a part of the liturgy and not all of his poetic work
was religious. We know of more than four hundred secular poems from
his pen—in praise of nature, friendship, love, beauty and wine—and
topical verse. Major libraries preserve collections of this poetry. An
edition in four volumes, based on manuscripts and early imprints, was
prepared by H. Brody (Berlin, 1901–1930); Franz Rosenzweig wrote a
theological and aesthetic commentary to ninety of the poems, which
appeared as an appendix to a translation into German.

Judah ben Samuel ha-Levi, born about 1080 in Toledo, Castile, combined Hebrew scholarship and poetry with the medical profession. "My heart is in the east, and I in the uttermost west," he wrote. His revolt against the social conditions in Spain and his longing for the Land of Israel made him leave his home, his only daughter, and his friends to start on a journey to Zion (about 1140), a goal he never reached. On the poet's philosophical work, *Kuzari,* see the preface to "The God of Abraham and the God of Aristotle."

My thought awaked me with Thy Name,
    Upon Thy boundless love to meditate;
        Whereby I came
The fullness of the wonder to perceive,
    That Thou a soul immortal shouldst create
To be embound in this, my mortal frame.
    Then did my mind, elate,
Behold Thee and believe;
    As though I stood among
    That hushed and awe-swept throng
And heard the Voice and gazed on Sinai's flame!

    I seek Thee in my dreams,
    And lo, Thy glory seems
To pass before me, as of old, the cloud
    Descended in his sight, who heard
    The music of Thy spoken word.
Then from my couch I spring, and cry aloud,
"Blest be the glory of Thy Name, O Lord!"

⤳

With all my heart, O Truth, with all my might
I love Thee; in transparency, or night,
Thy Name is with me; how then walk alone?
    He is my Love; how shall I sit alone?
He is my Brightness; what can choke my flame?
    While He holds fast my hand, shall I be lame?
Let folk despise me; they have never known
    My shame for Thy sake is my glorious crown.
O Source of Life, let my life tell thy praise,
    My song to Thee be sung in all my days!

⤳

Let my sweet song be pleasing unto Thee—
    The incense of my praise—

O my Beloved that are flown from me,
   Far from mine errant ways!
But I have held the garment of His love,
Seeing the wonder and the might thereof.
The glory of Thy name is my full store—
My portion for the toil wherein I strove:
Increase the sorrow:—I shall love but more!
   Wonderful is Thy love!

⤷

Lord, where shall I find Thee?
High and hidden is Thy place;
And where shall I not find Thee?
The world is full of Thy glory.

Found in the innermost being,
He set up the ends of the earth:
The refuge for the near,
The trust for those far off.
Thou dwellest amid the Cherubim,
Thou abidest in the clouds;
Thou art praised by Thine hosts
Yet art raised above their praise.
The whirling worlds cannot contain Thee;
How then the chambers of a temple?

And though Thou be uplifted over them
Upon a throne high and exalted,
Yet art Thou near to them,
Of their very spirit and their flesh.
Their own mouth testifieth for them
That Thou alone art their Creator.
Who shall not fear Thee,
Since the yoke of Thy kingdom is their yoke?
Or who shall not call to Thee,
Since Thou givest them their food?

I have sought Thy nearness,
With all my heart have I called Thee,
And going out to meet Thee
I found Thee coming toward me,
Even as, in the wonder of Thy might,
In the sanctuary I have beheld Thee.
Who shall say he hath not seen Thee?—
Lo, the heavens and their hosts

Declare the fear of Thee,
Though their voice be not heard.

Doth then, in very truth,
God dwell with man?
What can he think—every one that thinketh,
Whose foundation is in the dust—
Since Thou art holy, dwelling
Amid their praises and their glory?
Angels adore Thy wonder,
Standing in the everlasting height;
Over their heads is Thy throne,
And Thou upholdest them all!

II. The Love for God

Pascal's "The entire religion of the Jews consisted only of the love for God" points indeed to a core issue in Jewish thought from the Biblical "Thou shalt love the Lord thy God" to Franz Rosenzweig's interpretation of revelation as becoming conscious of divine love which is responded to by human love. Approaches and emphases vary from thinker to thinker. While Maimonides (twelfth century) considered knowledge an essential pre-condition to the love of God, Hasdai Crescas (fourteenth–fifteenth century) saw in love itself the way to God, who is pure love; his disciple, Joseph Albo (fifteenth century), spoke of the love of God as the highest possible love and emphasized God's love for man, though reason was not able to explain it.

Here follow four texts on the subject: one by Maimonides; another by Bahya ibn Pakuda, the eleventh-century moralist; a third from the *Zohar*, chief document of Kabbalah, and, in conclusion, a discussion by Moses Hayyim Luzzatto, eighteenth-century mystic and moralist (see "The House of Study in Padua," and "Humility"). Compare also "The Universality of Love."

Moses Maimonides

Let no man say, "I will observe the precepts of the Torah and occupy myself with its wisdom, so that I may receive all the blessings described in the Torah, or merit the life in the world to come; I will abstain from transgressions against which the Torah warns, so that I may be saved from the curses described therein, or that I may not be cut off from life in the world to come." It is not right to worship the Lord after this fashion, for whoever does so, worships Him out of fear. This is not the standard set by the prophets and sages. Only those serve God in this way, who

are ignorant men, women or children whom one trains to serve
out of fear, until their knowledge increases when they will worship out of love.

Whoever serves God out of love, occupies himself with the
study of the Torah and the fulfilment of commandments and
walks in the paths of wisdom, impelled by no external motive
whatsoever, moved neither by fear of evil nor by the desire to
inherit the good; such a man does the true thing because it is true
and, ultimately, happiness comes to him as a result of his conduct.
This standard is indeed a very high one; not every sage attained
to it. It was the standard of Abraham our father, whom God
called His lover, because he worshiped only out of love. It is the
standard which God, through Moses, bids us achieve, as it is said,
"And thou shalt love the Lord, thy God" (Deut. 6:5). When a
person loves God with the proper love, he will momentarily observe all the commandments out of love.

What is the proper love of God? It is to love the Lord with a
great and very strong love, so that one's soul shall be tied to the
love of the Lord, and one should be continually enraptured by
it, like a love-sick individual, whose mind is at no time free from
his passion for a particular woman, the thought of her filling his
heart at all times, when sitting down or rising up, even when he
is eating or drinking. Still more intense should be the love of God
in the hearts of those who love Him. And this love should continually possess them, even as He commanded us, "with all thy
heart and with all thy soul" (Deut. 6:5). This, Solomon expressed
allegorically, saying, "for I am sick with love" (Cant. 2:5). The
entire Song of Songs is indeed an allegory on this subject.

The ancient sages said: "Peradventure you will say, 'I will
study Torah, in order that I may become rich, that I may be
called rabbi, that I may receive a reward in the world to come.'
It is therefore said, 'To love the Lord,' meaning: Whatever you
do, do it out of love only." [1] [. . .] So too, the greatest sages
were wont to exhort particularly those among their disciples who
were understanding and intelligent, "Be not like servants who
minister to their master upon the condition of receiving a reward." But it is proper to be like servants who serve their master

not for the sake of receiving aught.[2] Only because he is the master, it is right to serve him; that is, serve him out of love.

Whoever engages in the study of the Torah, in order that he may receive a reward or avoid calamities is not studying the Torah for its own sake. Whoever occupies himself with the Torah, neither out of fear nor for the sake of reward, but solely out of love for the Lord of the whole earth who enjoined us to do so, is occupied with the Torah for its own sake. The sages however said, "One should always engage in the study of the Torah, even if not for its own sake; for he who begins thus will end by studying it for its own sake." [3] Hence, when instructing the young, women or the ignorant generally, we teach them to serve God out of fear or for the sake of reward, till their knowledge increases and they have attained a large measure of wisdom. Then we reveal to them this secret, little by little, and train them by easy stages till they have comprehended it, and serve God out of love.

It is known and certain that the love of God does not become tied up in a man's heart till he is continuously and thoroughly possessed by it and gives up everything else in the world for it; as God commanded us, "with all thy heart and with all thy soul" (Deut. 6:5). One only loves God by the measure of knowledge that one knows Him. According to that knowledge will be that love; if the former be little or much, so will the latter be little or much. A person ought therefore to dedicate himself to the understanding and comprehension of those sciences and studies which will inform him concerning his Master, as far as it lies in human power to understand.

Bahya ibn Pakuda

Once the light of reason rises in the soul . . . she distinguishes truth from falsehood; the true face of her Creator and Guide is revealed to her. Once she understands the greatness of His power and the might of His awe, she bows to Him in fear and trembling. In this position she remains until the Creator calms her fear and dread. Then she drinks from the cup of divine love; she will be alone with God and dedicate herself to Him, love Him, trust Him, long for His will. If He deals kindly with her, she will be grateful; if He brings suffering upon her, she will suffer while her trust will grow even stronger.

Of one of the pious men they tell that he used to arise in the middle of the night and pray: "My God, thou hast made me hunger, and naked forsaken me, and set me in the darkmost of night, and taught me thy power and height. Though thou burn me in fire I shall but continue to love thee and to joy in thee, as Job said: 'Though He cut me down, to Him I shall aspire' (Job 13:15)."

The *Zohar*

"Thou shalt love the Lord thy God" (Deut. 6:5). This means that man should bind himself to Him with very strong love, and that all service performed by man to God should be with love, since there is no service like the love of the Holy One, blessed be he. Rabbi Abba said: These words are the epitome of the whole Law, since the Ten Commandments are summed up here. Nothing is so beloved of God as that a man should love Him in the fitting manner. How is this? As it is written, "with all thy heart," which includes two hearts, one good and one evil; "with all thy soul," one good and one evil; and "with all thy might." What lesson can be learnt from the word "all" here?

Rabbi Eleazar said: The word "might" refers to money, and "all" means both money which comes to a man from inheritance and money which a man earns himself. Rabbi Abba said: To return to the words "and thou shalt love": one who loves God is crowned with loving-kindness on all sides and does loving-kindness throughout, sparing neither his person nor his money. We know this from Abraham, who in his love for his Master spared neither his heart nor his life nor his money. He paid no heed to his own desires because of his love for his Master; he spared not his wife, and was ready to sacrifice his son because of his love for his Master; and he sacrificed his money also by standing at the cross-roads and providing food for all comers. Therefore he was crowned with the crown of loving-kindness. Whoever is attached in love to his Master is deemed worthy of the same, and what is more, all worlds are blessed for his sake.

Happy those to whom the love of their Master cleaves; there is no limit to their portion in the other world. Rabbi Isaac said: Many are the abodes of the righteous in the other world, one above another, and highest of all that of those to whom was attached the love of their Master, for their abode is linked with the palace that surpasses all, the Holy One, blessed be he, being crowned in this one. This Palace is called Love, and it is established for the sake of love. So it is too with the Holy Name, the forms of the letters of which are linked together, so that the whole is called "love"; wherefore he who loves his Master is linked to that Love. Hence it is written, "And thou shalt love the Lord thy God."

Moses Hayyim Luzzatto

To love God is to long passionately for His near presence, and to follow in the wake of His holiness, as we follow after anything which we passionately desire. To mention His name, or to discern His wonderful deeds, or to study His Torah, or His divine nature, is then as real a source of pleasure as the intense love of a husband for the wife of his youth, or of a father for an only son. Such is the love which renders communion a delight.

Such love must spring from no ulterior motive. A man must love the Creator, blessed be he, not because He bestows welfare, wealth and success upon him, but because to love God is as natural and as imperative to him, as for a son to love his father. In the words of Scripture, "Is not He thy father, that hath created thee?" (Deut. 32:6). And the test of this love is hardship and adversity. Commenting upon the commandment, "Thou shalt love the Lord thy God with all thy soul and with all thy might" (*ibid*. 6:5), our sages added, " 'With all thy soul' means, even at the cost of thy life, and 'with all thy might' means, even at the cost of thy possessions." [4]

Those who possess true knowledge do not think of themselves at all; what they pray for is that the glory of God be extolled, and that they may be able to afford Him joy. The greater
the hindrances and, therefore, the greater the effort required to
remove those hindrances, the more happy they are to prove the
firmness of their faith.

The element of joy is one of the great essentials in the worship of God. "Serve the Lord with gladness," exhorted David,
"come before His presence with singing" (Ps. 100:2). Elsewhere,
"Let the righteous be glad: let them exalt before God: yea, let
them rejoice with gladness (*ibid.* 68:4). "The Divine Presence,"
said our sages, "rests only upon one who finds joy in the performance of a commandment." [5] In commenting upon the verse,
"Serve the Lord with gladness," Rabbi Aibu said, "Whenever
thou art about to pray, let thy heart rejoice that thou art about to
pray to a God who is without a peer." [6] Here, indeed, is cause
for true rejoicing, that we are privileged to serve the Lord who is
incomparable, and to occupy ourselves with His Torah and his
commandments, which are means to the attainment of perfection
and eternal glory. In the words of Solomon, "Draw me to Thee,
we will run after Thee; the King hath brought me into His
chambers; we will be glad and rejoice in Thee" (Cant. 1:4). The
farther a man is permitted to penetrate into the innermost re-
cesses of the knowledge of God's greatness, the greater will be his
joy, and the more will his heart exult within him.

WHY IS MY LOVED ONE WROTH

Moses ibn Ezra

Moses ibn Ezra (born in Granada, *ca.* 1060, died in Castile, 1139) is
one of the most productive of the classical Hebrew poets in Spain.
His sacred poetry (much of which was incorporated into the liturgy)
sings of the glory of creation, dwells upon the transitoriness of life and
man's sinful state, prays for forgiveness and divine mercy, and for
Israel's return to the Holy Land. Ibn Ezra was among the first to
cultivate secular themes; using the style and forms of Arabic poetry,

he wrote of nature, friendship, wine, and composed elegies occasioned
by an unfortunate love for his niece. His outlook on life was gloomy:
"The years of man are dreams and death is the interpreter."

> Why is my loved One wroth—
> That He should be disdainful of me,
> While my heart, in its yearning for Him,
> Is shaken like a reed?
> He hath forgotten the time
> When, joyously, I followed Him into the wilderness;
> Why do I cry this day,
> And He answer not?
>
> But though He slay me
> Yet will I trust in Him;[7]
> And if He hide His face,
> I will bethink me of His tenderness, and turn thereto.
> The loving-kindness of the Lord will not fail His servant
> For pure gold changes not, nor dims.[8]

THE UNIVERSALITY OF LOVE

Judah Abrabanel (Leone Ebreo)

Love as the all-pervading force in life temporal and eternal was one
of the most pondered themes among Italian humanist writers. One of
the first writings in this field was Marsilio Ficino's commentary on
Plato's *Symposium* (1475). The motif of universal love penetrated
Hebrew works of the period, such as *Heshek Shelomoh* (The Delight
of Solomon), a commentary on the Song of Songs by Johanan Alem-
anno, teacher of Pico della Mirandola in Hebrew and Kabbalah.

Dialoghi d'Amore (The Dialogues of Love) is considered to be the
most important document exemplifying this trend of thought. Written
in 1501–1502, it presents three dialogues between Philo, the lover, and
Sophia, wisdom, his beloved. The discussion of the nature of love
(first dialogue) leads to the contemplation of the universality of love
(second dialogue) and culminates in the appreciation of the cosmic
significance of divine love. The author of the *Dialoghi*, Judah Abrabanel (Leone Ebreo), was born in Lisbon about 1460. He was a victim
of the expulsion of the Jews from Spain and Portugal, and together
with his famous father Isaac Abrabanel (statesman, Biblical scholar)
he settled in Italy. Medicine was his profession; as philosopher he
followed the Neoplatonic trend. His work (which, in certain respects,

is reminiscent of Giordano Bruno's philosophical system) was published in 1535 in Rome and enjoyed considerable popularity; it was
translated into French, Spanish, Latin, and Hebrew. Spinoza had a copy
of the Spanish edition in his library.

Philo: You have heard from me ere now, O Sophia, that
the whole Universe is one individual (i.e., like a single person),
each one of these bodies and spirits, eternal or corruptible, being
a member or part of this great individual. And all and every
one of its parts was created by God with a purpose common to
the whole as well as with a purpose peculiar to each part. It follows that whole and parts alike are perfect and happy in proportion as they rightly and completely discharge the functions for
which they were designed by the Supreme Artificer. The purpose
of the whole is the perfection in unity, as planned by the Divine
Architect, of the entire Universe; but the purpose of each part is,
not merely the perfection of that part in itself, but also the right
promotion by that perfection of the perfection of the whole,
which is the universal end and the first purpose of the Godhead.

For this general end, rather than for its own, each part was
created, ordained and consecrated; so much so that failing in a
portion of that service, whereof the activities appertain to the
perfection of the Universe, would involve it in a graver fault and
in greater unhappiness than if it failed in its own activity. So too
it is made happier by the general, than by its own [weal], even as
in a human individual the perfection of a part, e.g., the eye or
hand, consists not merely nor even chiefly in the beauty of the
eye or the hand, nor again in the ability of the eye to see much
or of the hand to ply many crafts: but first and principally it consists in the eye's seeing and the hand's doing what is requisite for
the weal of the whole person, and their worth and excellence are
measured by their true service to the whole person, for their own
beauty is their own activity. Wherefore the part often offers and
exposes itself to immediate danger, as nature bids, for the protection of the whole person: e.g., an arm will encounter a sword to
guard the head.

As then this law is constantly observed throughout the Universe, the intelligence finds more happiness in turning the heavenly spheres (such activity, though alien and corporeal, being

necessary to the existence of the whole) than by its inward essential contemplation, which is its own activity. This is what Aristotle means by saying the intelligences move for the sake of a higher and more excellent cause, namely God: that they are realizing His plan of the Universe. Thus by loving and turning their spheres they bind the Universe in unity, and so properly win the divine love and grace, and even to union with God, that love and union being alike what holds the Universe together and their ultimate end and desired happiness.

Sophia: I am well pleased with this solution. And I suppose it is for the same reason that the spiritual intelligence of man unites with a body as frail as the human: to execute the divine plan for the coherence and unity of the whole Universe.

Philo: You have said well, and so it is in truth. For as our souls are spiritual intelligences, no benefit can accrue to them from association with the frail and corruptible body, but they would be far better off in their intimate and pure activity of intellect: but they coalesce with our bodies merely for love and service of the Supreme Creator of the World, taking intellectual life and knowledge and the light of God down from the upper world of eternity to the lower world of decay, that even this lowest part of the world may not be without divine grace and eternal life, and that this great animal may have every one of its parts as vital and intelligent as is the whole.

And as in this way our souls realize the unity of the whole Universe according to the divine plan, which was the general and chief end of the creation of things, they rightly enjoy the divine love, and after separation from the body achieve the union with God, which is their supreme happiness. But failing in its office, the soul is deprived of this divine love and union: and therein lies its supreme and eternal punishment: for, having the faculty to mount on high to Paradise by rightly governing its body, it is retained by its iniquity in the lowest hell, banned eternally from union with God and its own felicity, unless indeed the Divine Compassion were so great as to offer it an opportunity of atonement.

Sophia: God guard us from such aberration and make us upright in the execution of His holy will and divine plan!

Philo: Amen! But you already know, O Sophia, that it cannot be accomplished without love.

Sophia: Indeed love is not only common to all things in the world, but even supremely necessary, since none can be blessed without love.

Philo: Without love not only can there be no felicity; but the world would not exist nor would anything be found therein, if there were no love.

Sophia: Why all this?

Philo: Because the world and all in it can exist only insofar as it is wholly one, bound up with all it contains as an individual with his members. On the other hand, any division would involve its total destruction, and, as nothing unites the Universe with its different components save love alone, it follows that love itself is the condition of the existence of the world and all in it.

Sophia: Tell me how love animates the world and out of so many things forms a single unity.

Philo: From what has already been said you can easily understand that. God Most High creates and governs the world by love, and binds it together in unity: for as God is one with the most perfect simplicity of unity, that which derives from Him must needs be one with entire unity. For one derives from one, and from pure unity perfect union. Moreover, the spiritual world is united with the material by means of love: nor would the separate intelligences or angels of God ever unite with, or inform, or become animating souls of, the heavenly bodies, unless they loved them. Nor would intelligent souls unite with human bodies to make them rational, if love did not constrain them thereto. Nor [finally] would the soul of this world unite with this sphere of birth and decay, if it were not for love. Again, inferiors unite with superiors, the corporeal world with the spiritual, the corruptible with the eternal, and the whole Universe with its Creator, through the love it bears Him and its desire to unite with Him and be blessed in His divinity.

Sophia: It is even so. For love is a vivifying spirit penetrating all the world and a bond uniting the whole Universe.

Philo: Seeing that you feel thus about love, there is no need to tell you further of its universality, which we have spent all to-day in expounding.

SAINTLINESS

Moses Hayyim Luzzatto

Hasid is the Hebrew term here translated by "saint." Both this term and that designating saintliness, *Hasidut,* have different shades of meaning and emphasis, the variations depending on whether reference is to the period of the Second Commonwealth, the period of Judah the Pious and Eleazar Rokeah, or the great movement founded by the Baal Shem Tov. Underlying all the uses is the Biblical *Hesed,* "loving concern," a term applied both to God and to man. *Mesillat Yesharim* (Path of the Upright), Luzzatto's work on Jewish ethics, first published in Amsterdam in 1740, holds the sanctification of God to be the only proper motivation of human action and that man's duty is to bear the yoke with one's fellow-man. "Saintliness," he postulates, "is latent in the character of every normal person," yet this trait must be carefully cultivated. He counsels solitude, renunciation of material concerns, dedicated study of sacred writings, and concentration upon the divine. (See also "The Love for God.")

Luzzatto the moralist and the mystic (see the preface to "The House of Study in Padua") was also a poet. In his lyric and dramatic verse, he, well acquainted with Italian literature, employs purely human motifs: the beauty of nature, love, friendship. Heir of classical Judaism and its tensions, he is at the same time the forerunner of modern Hebrew secular poetry.

In all his works the saint's motive must be the furtherance of the well-being of his generation and securing for it divine favor and protection. Those who belong to the same generation as the righteous man, enjoy the fruit of his actions. It is, indeed, the will of God that Israel's saints should win atonement for those who are spiritually their inferiors. The Holy One, blessed be he, desires not the destruction of the wicked, and it is the task of the saint to strive to win for them divine grace and atonement. This should be his purpose in serving God, and this petition he should utter in his prayers. He should pray in behalf of the men of his

generation that God grant forgiveness to all those who need forgiveness, and cause to repent all those who are in need of repentance. The true shepherds of Israel in whom the Holy One,
blessed be he, takes delight are those who are ready to sacrifice
themselves for the flock; who by every possible means earnestly
strive to secure for it peace and well-being; who always stand in
the breach and who, by means of prayer, seek to avert the evil
decrees against it and to open for it the gates of blessing.

III. The Faith of Israel

THE DUTIES OF THE HEART

Bahya ibn Pakuda

The aim of the Arabic-written *Guide to the Duties of the Heart* was the reconstruction of the Jewish faith from within. The author, Bahya ibn Pakuda (Spain), who wrote his book between 1080 and 1090, realized that no Jewish work explored "the hidden wisdom" which (as distinct from "the visible wisdom" and the discussion of "the duties of the limbs") concerns itself with "the duties of the heart" and which constitutes the firm foundation of religion. Such duties (which are not bound to particular seasons or situations as are rituals and ceremonies) are belief in the one and incorporeal Creator, readiness to worship Him, ethical conduct, and purity of thought. Bahya is a rationalist, but he does not spend his intellectual energies on reconciling philosophy and revelation. In addition to Saadia, Bahya was also influenced by a Neoplatonically interpreted Aristotelianism and by Islamic mysticism (the "Faithful Brethren"). But Bahya is not a mystic; he is firmly rooted in the world of men—a world, however, that demands humility, conquest of passions, and a complete trust in divine mercy.

The work—one of the most popular in pre-modern Judaism—was translated into Hebrew by Judah ibn Tibbon in 1161 (*Torat Hovot ha-Levavot*), and was first printed in Naples in 1489. Another early translation into Hebrew was by Joseph Kimhi. Many imprints followed, also translations into Spanish (1569), Portuguese (1670), German (1836), Italian (1847), and other languages. The original Arabic text was edited by A. S. Yahuda in 1912.

The noblest of the gifts which God bestowed on His human creatures, next to having created them with mature faculties of perception and comprehension, is wisdom. This constitutes the life of their spirit, the lamp of their intellect.

All departments of science, according to their respective topics, are gates which the Creator has opened to rational beings, through which they may attain to a comprehension of the Torah and of the world. This knowledge affords instruction concerning the secrets of the physical world and the uses and benefits to be derived from it. They also furnish information concerning industries and arts conducive to physical and material well-being.

But essential to the understanding of Torah is the sublime knowledge of theology, which we are under an obligation to acquire. To acquire it, however, for the sake of worldly advantages is forbidden. The text, "To love the Lord, thy God, to listen to His voice, and to cleave to Him" (Deut. 30:20), has been thus expounded by our teachers: "Let not a man say, 'I shall read Scripture, in order that they may call me scholar, I shall study Mishnah that they may call me rabbi, I shall study Mishnah, that I may be a senior, entitled to a seat at the college.' Learn out of love and honor will follow." [1]

The avenues which the Creator has opened for the knowledge of His Torah are three. The first is a sound intellect; the second, the Book of His Law revealed to Moses, His prophet; the third, the traditions which we have received from our ancient sages, who received them from the prophets. These avenues have already been discussed at adequate length by our great teacher, Saadia. [2]

The science of the Torah, moreover, falls into two parts: The first aims at the knowledge of practical duties and is the science of external conduct. The second deals with the duties of the heart, namely, its sentiments and thoughts, and is the science of the inward life.

Of the duties of the heart, I shall mention a few that occur to me to serve as examples of those not cited. Among affirmative duties of the heart are: to believe that the world had a Creator, that He created it *ex nihilo,* and that there is none like unto Him; to accept His oneness; to worship Him with our hearts; to meditate on the wonders exhibited in His creatures, that these may serve us as evidences of Him; that we put our trust in Him; that we humble ourselves before Him, and revere Him; that we tremble and be abashed when we consider that He observes our visible and our hidden activities; that we yearn for His mercy; that we devote our works to the glory of His name; that we love

Him and love those that love Him, and thus draw nigh to Him; that we reject His adversaries—and similar duties, not apprehended by the senses.

Negative duties of the heart are the converse of those just mentioned. Also included among them are: that we shall not covet, avenge, nor bear a grudge; that our minds shall not dwell on transgressions, nor hanker after them, nor resolve to commit them; that we shall abstain from transgressions of a similar character—all which are purely mental and observed by none but the Creator; as it is written, "I, the Lord, search the heart; I try the reins" (Jer. 17:10); "The lamp of God is the soul of man, searching all the inward parts" (Prov. 20:27).

On closer study, I found that the class of the duties of the heart is in force continuously, throughout our lives, without intermission, and that we have no excuse for neglecting them; this applies to such duties, for example, as to confess the oneness of God with all our heart, to render Him service inwardly, to revere Him and to love Him, to yearn to fulfill the precepts obligatory upon us, to trust in Him and surrender ourselves to Him, to remove hatred and jealousy from our hearts, to abstain from the superfluities of this world which disturb and hinder us in the service of God. For all these are obligatory at all seasons, in all places, every hour, every moment, and under all circumstances, as long as we have life and reason.

After I had become convinced of the obligatory character of the duties of the heart and that we are bound to observe them; after I had noticed that these duties had been neglected and that no book had been composed specially treating of them and had further realized in what condition our contemporaries were as a result of their inability to comprehend, much less fulfil, these duties and occupy themselves with them, I was moved by the grace of God to inquire into the science of inward duties.

It became clear to me that all works done for God's sake must have as their roots purity of heart and singleness of mind. Where the motive is tainted, good deeds, however numerous and even though practised continuously, are not accepted; as Scripture says, "Yea, when ye make many prayers, I will not hear. Wash you, make you clean, put away the evil of your doings from before mine eyes" (Isa. 1:15–16). Further, "But the word is very nigh unto thee, in thy mouth and in thy heart, that thou mayest do it" (Deut. 30:14).

Again it is said, "But let him that glorieth glory in this, that he understandeth and knoweth Me, that I am the Lord, doing kindness, justice and righteousness" (Jer. 9:23). The meaning is that a man who glories should glory in comprehending God's ways, recognizing His beneficence, reflecting on His creation, realizing His might and wisdom, as manifested in His works.

All the texts here adduced are proofs of the obligatory character of the duties of the heart and the discipline of the soul. You should realize however that the aim and value of the duties of the heart consist in their securing the equal cooperation of body and soul in the service of God, so that the testimony of heart, tongue and the other bodily organs shall be alike, and that they shall support and confirm, not contradict or differ from, each other. This harmony it is which is called in Scripture wholeheartedness, or uprightness, in such texts as the following, "Thou shalt be whole-hearted with the Lord thy God" (Deut. 18:13). "He that walketh uprightly, and worketh righteousness and speaketh truth in his heart" (Ps. 15:2).

THE SERVANT OF GOD

Judah ha-Levi

Judah ha-Levi (see the preface to "Lord Where Shall I Find Thee") wrote his *Kuzari*, from which the chapter that follows is taken, against the historical and intellectual background of his time. In the eleventh century Israel, in exile, found herself betwixt Christianity and Islam, engaged in the crucial struggle for power. Intellectually, Judaism had to defend itself against the proud claims of Aristotelian philosophy and Karaite (anti-Rabbinic) criticism. Ha-Levi's Arabic-written work is entitled: *Book of Arguments and Proofs in Defense of the Despised Faith*. The title of the Hebrew translation, *Sefer ha-Kuzari*, refers to the pagan king of the Chazars searching for a new religion, whom the author presents in a dialogue with a Jewish sage (the Master) on the nature of Israel. Judah ha-Levi employs this setting for the propagation of his theory of Judaism as the road to an intuitive, prophetic knowledge of God, as opposed to the speculative, philosophical knowledge of the "First Cause."

The passage below is the master's answer to the king's request for a description of "a servant of God according to your conception." The discussion of the master's answer is followed by the rabbinic arguments against the Bible-centered and anti-talmudic Karaites.

The *Kuzari*, written during the last decade of the poet's life, was translated into Hebrew by Judah ibn Tibbon and was first printed in Fano in 1506, then in Venice in 1547. The Hebrew text with a Latin translation by Johannes Buxtorf appeared in Basel in 1660; a Spanish translation, in 1663. A critical edition of the Arabic text was published by H. Hirschfeld (Leipzig, 1887).

The Master: According to our view a servant of God is not one who detaches himself from the world, lest he be a burden to it, and it to him; or hates life, which is one of God's bounties granted to him. On the contrary, he loves the world and a long life, because it affords him opportunties of deserving the world to come. [. . .] He feels no loneliness in solitude and seclusion, since they form his associates. He is rather ill at ease in a crowd, because he misses the Divine Presence which enables him to dispense with eating and drinking. Such persons might perhaps be happier in complete solitude; they might even welcome death, because it leads to the step beyond which there is none higher.

Philosophers and scholars also love solitude to refine their thoughts, and to reap the fruits of truth from their researches, in order that all remaining doubts be dispelled by truth. They only desire the society of disciples who stimulate their research and retentiveness, just as he who is bent upon making money would only surround himself with persons with whom he could do lucrative business. Such a degree is that of Socrates and those who are like him.

There is no one nowadays who feels tempted to strive for such a degree, but when the Divine Presence was still in the Holy Land among the people capable of prophecy, some few persons lived an ascetic life in deserts and associated with people of the same frame of mind. They did not seclude themselves completely, but they endeavoured to find support in the knowledge of the Torah and in holy and pure actions which brought them near to that high rank. These were the disciples of prophets. He however, who in our time, place, and people, "whilst no open vision exists" (1 Sam. 3:1) the desire for study being small, and persons with a natural talent for it absent, would like to retire into ascetic solitude, only courts distress and sickness for soul and body. The misery of sickness is visibly upon him, but one might regard it as the consequence of humility and contrition. He considers himself in prison as it were, and despairs of life from disgust of his prison and pain, but not because he enjoys his seclusion. How could it be otherwise? He has no intercourse with the divine light, and cannot associate himself with it as did the prophets. He lacks the necessary learning to be absorbed in it and to enjoy it, as the philosophers did, all the rest of his life. [. . .]

The Kuzari: Give me a description of the doings of one of your pious men at the present time.

The Master: A pious man is, so to speak, the guardian of his country, who gives to its inhabitants provisions and all they need. He is so just that he wrongs no one, nor does he grant anyone more than his due. Then, when he requires them, he finds them obedient to his call. He orders, they execute; he forbids, they abstain.

The Kuzari: I asked thee concerning a pious man, not a prince.

The Master: The pious man is nothing but a prince who is obeyed by his senses, and by his mental as well as his physical faculties, which he governs corporeally. He is fit to rule, because if he were the prince of a country he would be as just as he is to his body and soul. He subdues his passions, keeping them in bonds, but giving them their share in order to satisfy them as regards food, drink, cleanliness, etc. He further subdues the desire for power, but allows them as much expansion as avails them for the discussion of scientific or mundane views, as well as to warn the evil-minded. He allows the senses their share according as he requires them for the use of hands, feet, and tongue, as necessity or desire arise. The same is the case with hearing, seeing, and the kindred sensations which succeed them; imagination, conception, thought, memory, and will power, which commands all these; but is, in its turn, subservient to the will of intellect. He does not allow any of these limbs or faculties to go beyond their special task, or encroach upon another.

If he, then, has satisfied each of them (giving to the vital organs the necessary amount of rest and sleep, and to the physical ones waking, movements, and worldly occupation), he calls upon his community as a respected prince calls his disciplined army, to assist him in reaching the higher or divine degree which is to be found above the degree of the intellect. He arranges his community in the same manner as Moses arranged his people round Mount Sinai. He orders his will power to receive every command issued by him obediently, and to carry it out forthwith. He makes faculties and limbs do his bidding without contradiction, forbids them evil inclinations of mind and fancy, forbids them to listen to, or believe in them, until he has taken counsel with the intellect. [. . .] He directs the organs of thought and imagination, relieving them of all worldly ideas mentioned above, charges his imagination to produce, with the assistance of memory, the most splendid pictures possible, in order to resemble the divine things sought after. Such pictures are the scenes of Sinai, Abraham and Isaac on Moriah, the Tabernacle of Moses, the Temple service, the presence of God in the Temple, and the like.

He, then, orders his memory to retain all these, and not to forget them; he warns his fancy and its sinful prompters not to confuse the truth or to trouble it by doubts; he warns his irascibility and greed not to influence or lead astray, nor to take hold of his will, nor subdue it to wrath and lust. As soon as harmony is restored, his will power stimulates all his organs to obey it with alertness, pleasure, and joy. [. . .]

The moment [of prayer] forms the heart and fruit of his time, whilst the other hours represent the way which leads to it. He looks forward to its approach, because while it lasts he resembles the spiritual beings, and is removed from merely animal existence. The three times of daily prayer are the fruit of his day and night, and the Sabbath is the fruit of the week, because it has been appointed to establish the connection with the Divine Spirit and to serve God in joy, not in sadness, as has been explained before. All this stands in the same relation to the soul as food to the human body. The blessing of one prayer lasts till the time of the next, just as the strength derived from the morning meal lasts till supper. The further his soul is removed from the time of prayer, the more it is darkened by coming in contact with worldly matters. [. . .] During prayer he purges his soul from all that has passed over it, and prepares it for the future.

According to this arrangement there elapses not a single week in which both his soul and body do not receive preparation. Darkening elements having increased during the week, they cannot be cleansed except by consecrating one day to service and to the physical rest. The body repairs on the Sabbath the waste suffered during the six days, and prepares itself for the work to come, whilst the soul remembers its own loss through the body's companionship. He cures himself, so to speak, from a past illness, and provides himself with a remedy to ward off any future sickness. He, then, provides himself with a monthly cure, which is "the season of atonement for all that happened during this period," [3] i.e., the duration of the month.

He further attends the Three Festivals and the great Fast Day,[4] on which some of his sins are atoned for, and on which he endeavors to make up for what he may have missed on the days of those weekly and monthly cycles. His soul frees itself from the whisperings of imagination, wrath, and lust, and neither in thought or deed gives them any attention. [. . .] The fast of this day is such as brings one near to the angels, because it is spent in humility and contrition, standing, kneeling, praising and singing. All his physical faculties are denied their natural requirements, being entirely abandoned to religious service, as if the animal element had disappeared. The fast of a pious man is such that eye, ear, and tongue share in it, that he regards nothing except that which brings him near to God. This also refers to his innermost faculties, such as mind and imagination. To this he adds pious works.

THE FAITH OF ABRAHAM

Moses Maimonides

Monotheism was known to earliest humanity, Maimonides believed (see "The Oneness of God"); polytheism, "the worship of stars and images," was a descent from an original knowledge of God. "As time passed the Name of God was forgotten by mankind," and recognized only by a few solitary individuals, such as the Biblical Enosh, Methuselah, Noah, Shem, and Eber. It was Abraham who found his way back from idolatry to monotheism. He is pictured as inquiring into the nature of the universe and finally postulating One God who "guides the celestial sphere and creates everything." Abraham realized "that the whole world was in error" and became the propagator of the truth at which he had arrived through reason and without the benefit of a teacher. Maimonides thus presents the patriarch as a philosopher turned theologian, and the Hebrews as a missionary people sent out to spread the knowledge of God. The excerpt below is from the *Mishneh Torah*. See also "The Proselyte."

Abraham was forty years old when he recognized his Creator. Having attained this knowledge, he began to refute the inhabitants of Ur of the Chaldees, arguing with them and saying to them, "The course you are following is not the way of truth." He broke the images and commenced to instruct the people that it was not right to serve any one but the God of the universe, to Whom alone it was proper to bow down, offer up sacrifices and make libations, so that all human creatures might, in the future, know Him; and that it was proper to destroy and shatter all the images, so that the people might not err like these who thought that there was no god but these images. When he had prevailed over them with his arguments, the king [of the country] sought to slay him. He was miraculously saved, and emigrated to Haran.

He then began to proclaim to the whole world with great power and to instruct the people that the entire universe had but one Creator and that Him it was right to worship. He went from city to city and from kingdom to kingdom, calling and gathering together the inhabitants till he arrived in the land of

Canaan. There too, he proclaimed his message, as it is said, "And he called there on the name of the Lord, God of the universe" (Gen. 21:33): When the people flocked to him and questioned him regarding his assertions, he would instruct each one according to his capacity till he had brought him to the way of truth, and thus thousands and tens of thousands joined him. These were the persons referred to as "men of the house of Abraham."

He implanted in their hearts this great doctrine, composed books on it, and taught it to Isaac, his son. Isaac, from his seat of learning, gave instructions and exhortations. He imparted the doctrine to Jacob and ordained him to teach it. He, too, at his seat of learning, taught and morally strengthened all who joined him. The patriarch Jacob instructed all his sons, set apart Levi, appointed him head and placed him in a house of study to teach the way of God and keep the charge of Abraham. He charged his sons to appoint from the tribe of Levi, one instructor after another, in uninterrupted succession, so that the learning might never be forgotten. And so it went on with ever increasing vigor among Jacob's children and their adherents till they became a people that knew God.

When Israel had stayed a long while in Egypt, they relapsed, learnt the practices of their neighbors and, like them, worshipped idols, with the exception of the tribe of Levi, which steadfastly kept the charge of the fathers. This tribe of Levi never practised idolatry. The root planted by Abraham would, in a very short time, have been uprooted, and Jacob's descendants would have relapsed into the error and perversities universally prevalent. But because of God's love for us and because He kept the oath made to our father Abraham, He appointed Moses to be our teacher and the teacher of all the prophets, and charged him with his mission. After Moses had begun to exercise his prophetic functions and Israel had been chosen by the Lord as His heritage, he crowned them with commandments and made known to them the way to worship Him.

Devotion

Moses Maimonides

Kavvanah (here translated as "devotion"), a term already employed
in talmudic literature, denotes direction of the mind, concentration,
attention (to the meaning of a religious law, especially of prayer),
devotion. Negatively, it means exclusion of extraneous, distracting
thoughts. The talmudic dictum, "A fulfilment of a commandment requires *Kavvanah*" (Berakhot 13a), was elaborated on by the various
branches of post-Biblical literature. Cultivation of *Kavvanah* was the
mark of the pious person. The Kabbalists went a few steps further by
probing into the hidden, mystic meanings underlying the sacred words
of prayer and enjoining concentration upon these meanings; an effect
upon "the upper worlds" was to result from such exercise; the Hasidim
adopted this system. Maimonides states the normative position of
Kavvanah; the quotation is from his *Mishneh Torah.*

Prayer without devotion is no prayer at all. He who has
prayed without devotion ought to pray once more. He whose
thoughts are wandering or occupied with other matters should
not pray before he has collected his thoughts. If he has returned
from a journey tired or troubled let him pray only after he has
collected his thoughts.

What then is devotion? One must free his heart from all
other thoughts and regard himself as standing in the presence
of God. Therefore, before engaging in prayer, a man ought to
go aside for a little in order to bring himself into a devotional attitude, and then he should pray quietly and with feeling, not like
one who carries a weight and goes away. Then after prayer the
worshipper ought to sit quiet for a little and then depart. The
early pious men [*Hasidim*] waited an hour before prayer and an
hour after, and engaged in prayer for a whole hour.

THE SEVEN BENEDICTIONS

AT THE MARRIAGE SERVICE

Prayer Book

In the traditional Jewish marriage service, the seven benedictions are recited by the celebrant following the ring ceremony, in which the bride becomes consecrated to the groom, and the reading of the marriage contract (*Ketubah*); upon the conclusion of the benedictions the cup of wine is presented to the bridegroom and the bride, and a glass is broken by the bridegroom in memory of the destruction of the Temple. Customarily, the service ends with the priestly blessing pronounced over the couple.

Blessed art thou, O Lord our God, king of the universe,
who createst the fruit of the vine.

Blessed are thou, O Lord our God, king of the universe,
who hast created all things to His glory.

Blessed are thou, O Lord our God, king of the universe,
Creator of man.

Blessed art thou, O Lord our God, king of the universe,
who hast made man in His image,
after His likeness,
and hast prepared unto him, out of his very self, a perpetual fabric of
    life.
Blessed art thou, O Lord,
Creator of man.

May Zion who was barren be exceeding glad and exult,
when her children are gathered within her in joy.
Blessed art thou, O Lord,
who makest Zion joyful through her children.

O make these loved companions greatly to rejoice,
even as of old thou didst gladden thy creature in the garden of Eden.
Blessed art thou, O Lord,
who makest bridegroom and bride to rejoice.

Blessed art thou, O Lord our God, king of the universe,
who hath created joy and gladness, bridegroom and bride,

mirth and exultation, pleasure and delight,
love, brotherhood, peace and fellowship.
Soon may there be heard in the cities of Judah, and in
    the streets of Jerusalem,
the voice of joy and gladness,
the voice of the bridegroom and the voice of the bride,
the jubilant voice of bridegrooms from their canopies,
and of youths from their feasts of song.
Blessed are thou, O Lord,
who makest the bridegroom to rejoice with the bride.

IV. Man

MAN—THE CENTER

OF THE UNIVERSE

Saadia Gaon

In the tenth century educated men in the Islamic East became fully aware of the philosophical heritage of classical Greece; Platonic and Aristotelian writings were now available in Arabic or Syriac translations. Both Moslem and Jewish thinkers were confronted with the need of reconciling faith and reason. For Islam, this reconciliation was affected by the free-thinking *Mutazilites;* for Judaism, by the writings of Saadia (892–942), the Gaon of Sura, Babylonia. Saadia's major work, *The Book of Doctrines and Beliefs* (933), written in Arabic and translated into Hebrew by Judah ibn Tibbon under the title *Sefer ha-Emunot ve-ha-Deot,* undertook to demonstrate that the teachings of Judaism conform to the principles of reason. However, revelation is necessary; it guides man before he can make full and unerring use of reason. Saadia departs from the philosophers only in his interpretation of Creation (which implies the concept of man's uniqueness). Ibn Tibbon's version was first printed in Constantinople in 1562 and frequently republished. The Arabic original was edited by S. Landauer in 1880.

I commence my discussion of this point with the following prefatory observation. In spite of the great multiplicity of created things, we need have no difficulty in deciding which of them is the most essential part of Creation, because this is a point which the science of nature is able to elucidate for us. From the teaching of science on this point we find that man is the most essential part of Creation, because it is the rule and habit of nature to place the most excellent [part of anything] in the center with things of less excellence surrounding it.

To take our first illustration from something very small: The grain is in the middle of the grain-sheaf because it is the most excellent part of the stalk; for the plant grows out, and is fed, from the grain. Likewise the kernel from which the tree grows is in the middle of the fruit, no matter whether the kernel is edible as in the case of an almond tree, or whether it is a stone as in the case of the date. In the latter case the edible part of the fruit is of less importance and left at the outside as a protecting shell for the kernel. Likewise the yolk is in the middle of the egg because the young of birds and the chickens develop from it. Likewise, the heart of man is in the middle of his chest because it is the seat of the soul and of the natural warmths. Likewise the pupil is in the middle of the eye because it is the chief organ of sight. We notice that the same observation applies to a great number of things besides.

Then we found that the earth occupied the center of the universe, entirely surrounded by the celestial spheres. This made it clear to us that the earth was the most essential part in the created universe. Then we examined everything which the earth contains, and observed that earth and water are both inanimate things; the beast we found to be lacking in reason; there remained nothing superior but man. This makes it certain for us that he is undoubtedly the ultimate object of Creation. We searched the Scriptures and found therein the divine proclamation, "I, even I, have made the earth, and created man upon it" (Isa. 45:12). Moreover, the opening chapter of the Torah first goes through all categories of creatures and at the end of them says, "Let us make man" (Gen. 1:26), just like an architect who builds a palace, furnishes it, puts everything in order, and then invites the owner to occupy it.

After these preliminary remarks I come to my subject proper.

Our Lord has informed us through His prophets that He endowed man with superiority over all His creatures. Thus He said, "And have dominion over the fish of the sea, and over the fowl of the air. . . ." (Gen. 1:38). This is also the theme of Psalm 8 from beginning to end. God further informed us that He gave man the ability to obey Him, placing it as it were in his hands, endowed him with power and free will, and commanded him to choose that which is good, as is said, "See, I have set before thee this day life and good . . .", and concludes, "Therefore choose life" (Deut. 3:15, 19).

Afterwards we studied well the question wherein man's superiority consisted, and we found that he was raised to superiority by virtue of the wisdom which God bestowed upon and taught him, as is said, "Even He that teacheth man knowledge" (Ps. 94:10). By virtue of it man preserves the memory of deeds that happened long ago, and by virtue of it he foresees many of the things that will occur in the future. By virtue of it he is able to subdue the animals so that they may till the earth for him and bring in its produce. By virtue of it he is able to draw the water from the depth of the earth to its surface; he even invents irrigating wheels that draw the water automatically. By virtue of it he is able to build lofty mansions, to make magnificent garments, and to prepare delicate dishes. By virtue of it he is able to organize armies and camps, and to exercise kingship and authority for establishing order and civilization among men. By virtue of it he is able to study the nature of the celestial spheres, the course of the planets, their dimensions, their distances from one another, as well as other matters relating to them.

If one imagines that the highest degree of excellence is given to some being other than man, let him show us such excellence or a similar one in any other being. He will not find it. It is therefore right and proper that man should have received commandments and prohibitions, and that he should be rewarded and punished, for he is the axis of the world and its foundation, as is said, "For the pillars of the earth are the Lord's . . ." (I Sam. 2:8), and furthermore, "The righteous is the foundation of the world" (Prov. 10:25).

When I reflected on these fundamental facts and what follows from them, I became convinced that our belief in man's superiority is not a mere delusion, nor the result of our inclination to judge in favor of man; nor is it out of vanity and boastfulness that we make such a claim for ourselves, but it is something demonstrably true and perfectly correct. The reason why God in His wisdom endowed man with this excellence can only be to make him the recipient of commandments and prohibitions, as it says, "Behold, the fear of the Lord, that is wisdom; and to depart from evil is understanding" (Job 28:28).

ON CREATION

Moses Maimonides

While Maimonides insisted on the rational character of the revealed laws, he opposed the philosophical (Aristotelian) concept of the eternity of the world in favor of the non-rational, Jewish doctrine of *creatio ex nihilo* (creation from nothing). He took this position, because the Judaic concept of Creation implied purpose, will, and a personal, free, God (His freedom expressing itself in His ability to do miracles), while the Aristotelian view suggested necessity, and an impersonal, mechanical law. In such a universe there was no room for freedom of will, for man choosing between good and evil. In respect to these concepts the rationalist Maimonides put himself in a scientifically weaker position in order to safeguard a definition of man fundamental in Judaism. On the other hand, he followed an anti-traditional trend by making immortality of the soul dependent on intellectual attainments.

The excerpt below is from *Moreh Nebukhim* (The Guide to the Perplexed). See preface to "Knowledge of God."

We do not reject the eternity of the universe, because certain passages in the Torah confirm the Creation; for such passages that indicate that the universe is created are no more numerous than those in which God is represented as a corporeal being. The method of allegorical interpretation is no less possible or permissible in the matter of the universe being created than in any other. We might have explained them allegorically in the same manner as we did when we denied corporeality. We should perhaps have had an easier task in showing that those passages referred to are in harmony with the theory of the eternity of the universe if we accepted the latter, than we had in explaining the anthropomorphisms in the Bible when we rejected the idea that God is corporeal.

For two reasons, however, we have not done so, and have not accepted the eternity of the universe. First, the incorporeality of God has been demonstrated by proof; those passages in the Bible, which in their literal sense contain statements that can be refuted by proof, must and can be allegorically interpreted. But the eternity of the universe has not been conclusively proved. A mere argument in favor of a certain theory is not sufficient reason for rejecting the literal meaning of a Biblical text, and explaining it allegorically, when the opposite theory can be supported by an equally good argument.

Secondly, our belief in the incorporeality of God is not contrary to any of the fundamental principles of our Torah; it is not contrary to the words of any prophet. Only ignorant people believe that it is contrary to the teaching of Scripture. We have shown that this is not the case; on the contrary, this is the real intention of the text. If, on the other hand, we were to accept the eternity of the universe as taught by Aristotle, that everything in the universe exists by necessity, that nature does not change, and that nothing deviates from its fixed behavior, we should necessarily be in opposition to the foundation of our religion, we should disbelieve automatically every miracle, and certainly reject all hopes and fears derived from Scripture, unless the miracles are also explained allegorically. The Allegorists amongst the Moslems have done this, and have thereby arrived at absurd conclusions.

If, however, we accepted the eternity of the universe and assumed, with Plato, that the heavens are likewise transitory, we should not be in opposition to the fundamental principles of our Torah; this theory would not imply the rejection of miracles, which, on the contrary, would be possible. The Scriptural text might have been interpreted accordingly, and many expressions might have been found in the Torah and in other writings that would confirm and support this theory. But there is no necessity for this expedient, unless that theory were proved. As there is no proof sufficient to convince us, this theory need not be taken into consideration [. . .]

Accepting Creation, all miracles become possible, the Torah itself becomes possible, and any difficulty in this question is removed. We might be asked, Why has God inspired a certain person and not another? Why has He revealed the Torah to one particular nation, and at one particular time? Why has He commanded this, and forbidden that? Why has He shown through a prophet certain particular miracles? What is the object of these laws, and why has He not made the commandments and the prohibitions part of our nature, if it was His object that we should live in accordance with them?

We answer to all these questions: He willed it so; or, His wisdom decreed it. Just as He created the world according to His will, at a certain time, in a certain form, and as we do not understand why His will or His wisdom decided upon these peculiar forms or that time, so we do not know why His will or wisdom determined any of the things mentioned in the preceding questions. But if we assume that the universe has the present form as the result of fixed laws, there is occasion for the above questions; and these could only be answered in a reprehensible way, implying denial and rejection of the Biblical texts, concerning which no intelligent person can doubt that they are to be taken in their literal sense.

Owing to the absence of all proof, we reject the theory of the eternity of the universe. It is for this very reason that people of worth have spent and will spend their days in speculating on this problem. For if Creation had been demonstrated by proof, even if only according to the Platonic hypothesis, all arguments of the philosophers against us would be of no avail. If, on the other hand, Aristotle had a proof for his theory, the whole teaching of the Torah would be rejected, and other manners of thinking would take its place. I have thus shown that all depends on this one point. Note it.

On free will

Moses Maimonides

Biblical laws and the call to "choose life" (Deut. 30:19) tacitly presuppose man's free will; the prophets postulate man's moral responsibility, implying his freedom. The Talmud is more explicit: "Everything is in the hand of Heaven, except the fear of Heaven" (Berakhot

33b), which is the realm of human decision and action. Determinism is rejected; divine omniscience is assumed, but no attempt is made to resolve the contradiction between freedom of will and divine foreknowledge. This became a central issue in medieval Jewish religiophilosophical thought. Saadia Gaon maintained God's full and free knowledge of all events, including those in the future, but denied that this knowledge is the cause of human action; in order to be able to exercise his responsibility toward the laws, man must be considered free. Consequently, Saadia rejected the Islamic doctrine of predestination. He included freedom of will among the three central teachings of Judaism (the others being God and immortality). The Averroist Gersonides (thirteenth–fourteenth century), who accepted natural causality as the principle regulating the affairs of the world, had no difficulty separating divine knowledge from the realm of human action. On the other hand, Hasdai Crescas (fourteenth–fifteenth century), opponent of extreme rationalism, moved in the direction of determinism. Within this centuries-long thought process, and within the given limits, Maimonides' position is possibly the soundest. His statement on the issue, reprinted below, is from his *Mishneh Torah*.

Free will is bestowed on every human being. If he desires to turn towards the good path and be just, he has the power to do so. If he wishes to turn towards the evil path and be wicked, he is at liberty to do so. And thus is it written in the Torah, "Behold, the man is become as one of us, to know good and evil" (Gen. 3:22)—which means that the human species stands alone in the world—there being no other kind like him as regards this subject of being able of his own accord, by his reason and thought to know what is good and what is evil, with none to prevent him from either doing good or evil. And since this is so [there is reason to fear] "lest he put forth his hand etc." (*ibid.*).

Let not the notion, expressed by the foolish among other peoples and most of the senseless folk among Israelites, pass through your mind that at the beginning of a person's existence, the Holy One, blessed be he, decrees that he is to be just or wicked. This is not so. Every human being may become righteous like Moses, our teacher, or wicked like Jeroboam; wise or foolish, merciful or cruel; niggardly or generous; and so with all other qualities. There is no one that coerces him or decrees what he is to do, or draws him to either of the two ways; but every person turns to the way which he desires, with the consent of his mind and of his own volition. Thus Jeremiah said, "Out of the mouth of the Most High, proceedeth not evil and good" (Lam. 3:38); that is to say, the Creator does not decree either that a man shall be good or wicked.

Accordingly it follows that it is the sinner who has inflicted harm on himself. He should, therefore, weep for, and bewail what he has done to his soul—how he has mistreated it. This is expressed in the next verse, "Wherefore doth a living man complain, or a strong man? Because of his sins" (Lam. 3:39). The prophet continues: Since liberty of action is in our hands and we have, of our free will, committed all these evils, it behoves us to return in a spirit of repentance: "Let us search and try our ways, and return to the Lord" (Lam. 3:40).

This doctrine is an important principle, the pillar of the Torah and the commandment, as it is said, "See, I set before thee this day life and good, and death and evil" (Deut. 30:15); and again it is written, "Behold, I set before you this day, a blessing and a curse" (Deut. 11:26). This means that the power is in your hands, and whatever a man desires to do among the things that human beings do, he can do, whether they are good or evil; and, because of this faculty, it is said, "O that they had such a heart as this always" (Deut. 5:26), which implies that the Creator neither forces the children of men nor decrees that they should do either good, or evil, but it is all in their own keeping.

If God had decreed that a person should be either just or wicked, or if there were some force inherent in his nature which irresistibly drew him to a particular course, or to any branch of knowledge, as to a given view or activity, as the foolish astrologers, out of their own fancy, pretend, how would He have charged us through the prophets: "Do this and do not do that, improve your ways, do not follow your wicked impulses," when, from the beginning of his existence, his destiny has already been decreed, or his innate constitution drew him to that from which he could not set himself free? What room would there be for the whole of the Torah? By what right or justice could God punish the wicked or reward the just? "Shall not the Judge of all the earth act justly?" (Gen. 18:25).

Do not, however, wonder: How can a man do whatever he

desires, and act according to his discretion? Can aught in the world be done without the Master's will and pleasure? The Scripture itself says, "Whatsoever the Lord pleased, that hath He done in heaven and on earth" (Ps. 135:6). Know then that everything takes place according to His will, notwithstanding that our acts are in our power. How so? Just as it was the will of the Creator that fire and air shall ascend, earth and water descend, and that the sphere shall revolve in a circle, and all other things in the universe shall exist in their respective ways which He desired, so it was His will that man should have freedom of will, and all his acts should be left to his discretion; that nothing should force him or draw him to aught, but that, of himself and by the exercise of his own mind which God had given him, he should do whatever it is in a man's power to do. Hence, he is judged according to his deeds. If he does well, good is done to him; and if he does ill, evil is done to him.

Perchance you will say, "Does not the Holy One, blessed be he, know everything that will be before it happens?" He either knows that a certain person will be just or wicked, or He does not know. If he knows that he will be just, it is impossible that he should not be just; and if you say that He knows that he will be just and yet it is possible for him to be wicked, then He does not know the matter clearly. As to the solution of this problem, understand that "the measure thereof is longer than the earth and wider than the sea" (Job 11:9), and many important principles of the highest sublimity are connected with it. It is essential that you know what I am about to say.

We have already explained[1] that God does not know with a knowledge which exists outside of Himself, like human beings whose knowledge and self are separate entities, but He, blessed be His Name, and His knowledge are one. This, the human intellect cannot clearly apprehend. And just as it is not in human power to apprehend or discover the truth of the Creator, as it is said, "For there shall no man see Me and live" (Exod. 33:20), so it is not in human power to apprehend or discover the Creator's knowledge. We lack the capacity to know in what manner God knows all creatures and their actions. Yet we do know beyond doubt that a human being's actions are in his own hands

and the Holy One neither draws him on, nor decrees that he
should act thus or not act thus. It is not religious tradition alone
by which this is known, but even by evidence of the words of
wisdom. Hence, it is said in the prophetic writings that a man
will be judged for all his deeds, according to his deeds, whether
they be good or evil. And this is the principle on which all the
words of prophecy depend.

THE CREATION OF MAN

Moses Nahmanides

In the chapter "Has the Messiah Come?" we shall meet Moses ben
Nahman (Nahmanides, Ramban) as the Jewish spokesman at the
Debate at Barcelona in 1263. The religious philosopher, talmudist,
mystic, physician, is best known for his Commentary to the Pentateuch,
which he wrote in his old age and which he completed in Palestine.
Nahmanides believed that "in the Torah are hidden every wonder and
every mystery, and in her treasures is sealed every beauty of wisdom,"
as he says in the Introduction; that, mystically, the entire text of the
Torah is but a series of the unknown names of God; and on another
level of reading, the Biblical stories are prefigurations of the later
history of man. No wonder that he was opposed to the rationalist
Biblical commentary of Abraham ibn Ezra and viewed with suspicion
certain "unorthodox" opinions of Maimonides, whom he otherwise
revered. Nahmanides, in turn, was criticized for having made mysticism
accessible to the masses. The Commentary, first published in Lisbon in
1489, was later included in the editions of the Hebrew Bible and its
classical expositions.

"And God said, Let us make man" (Gen. 1:26). The reason for this signal honor is that there was nothing comparable
in the preceding creations to his being. The true interpretation
of the word na'aseh ("Let us make") is that God created ex nihilo
[out of nothing] only on the first day. From then on He used the
elements [which He had created on the first day]. In the same
way as He gave the waters the power to swarm with living creatures and brought forth beasts from the earth, He now said, "Let
us . . . ," that is, I and the earth, make man. Out of the earth

shall come forth the material elements to make up the body of man, just as is the case with animal and the wild beast, and I, the Lord will give him spirit from above . . . Thus man is like the lower creatures [in his physical structure], and like the higher beings in appearance and beauty, which is evidenced by his urge for wisdom, knowledge, and the doing of good deeds.

The eminence of the human soul, its distinction and superiority, lie in the fact, as the Torah informs us, that it was God who "blew the soul of life into the nostrils" of man (Gen. 2:7). This teaches us that man's soul does not originate in the material elements of his body, as is the case with all lower living creatures, nor is it even a substance evolved from the Separate Intelligences; instead, it is of the essence of the Holy One, since he who blows into the nostrils of another bestows upon him the breath of his own soul. Man's powers of learning and understanding come thus directly from Him.

Prior to his sin man performed his duties by inherent disposition; he was like the heavens and their hosts who [in the words of the sages] "are creatures of truth, whose achievement is truth, and who do not deviate from the path set for them." Love and hatred do not enter into the performance of their functions. It was the eating of the fruit of the Tree of Knowledge that brought desire and will into the heart of man. From then on he began choosing between one mode of action and another in accordance with his disposition for good or bad. [. . .] For this reason prior to the sin all parts of the human body were to Adam and Eve as the face and hands; they entertained no thoughts of shame concerning any part of the body. But after they ate of the tree they acquired the power to choose between good and evil. The power is indeed divine; but as far as man is concerned it also contains a potential of evil, since his deeds became dependent upon his desires and passions.

Consider it in your heart that the Holy One, blessed be he, has created all lower creatures for the benefit and use of man, since we know of no purpose for the creation of all objects who have no recognition of the Creator, except this—that they serve man. Now man has been created for the prime purpose that he recognize his Creator. Should he fail to know his Creator altogether, and what is even worse, should he fail to gain a realization of the fact that certain deeds are pleasing to God and others are displeasing, then man becomes as the unknowing beast. If man shows no desire to acquire a knowledge of God, and the realization that there is a difference between good and bad, the whole purpose of the world is lost.

The intent of all the commandments is that we acquire a firm belief in God, and proclaim Him as the One who has created us all. This is, in fact, the very purpose of Creation. The Supreme Being desires of man only that he know Him and acknowledge that He is the Creator. The prayers we recite, the synagogues we build, the holy convocations we hold, are all designed to give us an opportunity to gather and give outward expression to our inner conviction that He is our Creator and that we are His creatures.

ARGUMENT FOR
THE IMMORTAL SOUL

Leone Modena

Kol Sakhal (The Voice of the Fool), a seventeenth-century book of uncertain authorship (Isaiah Sonne attributed it to the heretic Uriel da Costa), is primarily an attack on the authority of the Oral Law in Judaism. The author's position was refuted by Leone Modena (1571–1648), rabbi in Venice, a late Renaissance figure, in his *Shaagat Arye* (The Lion's Roar). Attack and refutation were published in 1852 by Isaac S. Reggio, who believed Leone Modena, the skeptic rabbi, to be the author of both. The section from which the excerpt that follows is taken precedes the polemic part and outlines the writer's personal beliefs.

Just as, from the point of view of sense perception, we have no reason to believe that man's soul was in existence before he himself came into being, so we would be inclined to say that with his death, his soul, too, must perish. No man has ever returned after his death and given us any compelling testimony to his soul's immortality. He, therefore, who would not deceive himself must admit that no decisive proof of man's spiritual immortality has ever been furnished by either a Jewish or a Gentile thinker. On the contrary, since the burden of proof is upon him who would maintain a given belief, rather than on him who denies it, it might almost be said that those who deny the belief in immortality have positive proof of the soul's disintegration.

It is not my task here to enumerate the arguments on either side. I merely wish to state my own conclusions, arrived at after a careful consideration of all these arguments.

Most frightening for every Jew is the fact that, when we read through the whole Pentateuch from the beginning of Genesis to the end of Deuteronomy, we fail to find in all the words of Moses a single indication pointing to man's spiritual immortality after his physical death, or the existence of any world beside this one. Even though Moses [. . .] on several occasions speaks about how the observance of the commandments would be duly rewarded, he contents himself with promising the people physical rewards and success in this life—children, honor, and wealth.

Not when he spoke, before the revelation of the Torah, about God's promises to the patriarchs and saints, nor at the time that the Torah was revealed through him, nor even after then, did Moses say a single word to the effect that God has promised: If you will walk in My statutes, then your soul will enjoy everlasting bliss after death. Moses speaks instead of seasonal rain, bread, natural increase, life secure in the land, the defeat of enemies, and the like. Even in the Prophets and in the Writings there are only vague hints concerning immortality; and all such supposed hints might just as well be interpreted as having reference to physical life.

Nevertheless, when we contemplate our present existence, reason inclines us (if it does not altogether compel us) to believe that the soul continues on after our physical death. There is, first, some sense of this in the fact that nature, doing nothing in vain, has implanted in the human mind a desire for eternal life that is not realized in the life of the body. Then there is the evidence from the increase of our mental powers at the very time when old age brings with it a weakening of the body; if the connection between body and mind were absolute rather than incidental, we should expect the opposite to be true: the mind becoming weaker in proportion to the body's enfeeblement.

But what I consider to be the decisive proof is derived from our basic assumption that man is *sui generis,* neither like the angels nor like the beasts, and that he has been created for the purpose of giving God pleasure by his wide range of intelligent actions. How, then, can we say that ultimately man has no advantage over the beasts, and that the same fate, the same death, will befall him as them? How can we say that the creature who, by dint of his intellect, builds cities and moves mountains, changes the course of rivers, knows the paths of the high heavens, and can recognize his God—that this creature should come in the end to perish entirely like a horse, or a dog, or a fly?

Moreover, if this were so, then man's consciousness would be a sorry drawback. Animals are not troubled by anything about life or death other than by those things which they actually experience at a given moment. Man's consciousness, on the other hand, increases his pain by anticipating troubles yet to come, and dwelling on those already present. This is far more painful than the actual trouble: as it has rightly been said, the trouble of death is the thought of it before it comes.

Rather should it be said that the Creator Who, having joined man's soul to his body, takes pleasure in, or abhors, man's deeds, and bestows His rewards or punishments accordingly—that this Creator has made it possible for a man at his death to have his soul separated from his body, so that the soul may remain to receive the pleasure or the pain of which, in his lifetime, the man was judged deserving, in accordance with his deeds.

THE MAN AND HIS SOUL

A Midrash

The Talmud and the Midrash record popular tales about the Angel of Night and Conception, who brings the semen before God, who determines the future fate of the new being yet grants him freedom of will, and about the unborn being's journey through Paradise and Hell and all the places it is to inhabit on earth. An anonymous early medieval compiler gathered such material (some of which show Platonic and Stoic influence) and composed this dramatic story of the soul: *Midrash Yetzirat ha-Velad* (The Midrash of the Creation of the Child).

In what manner does the conformation of the child happen? In the hour when a man approaches his wife, the Holy One, blessed be he, calls out to His messenger, the one who is guardian over pregnancy, and says to him: "Know that this man tonight shall beget a child; go now and watch over the seed."

The messenger then does as he is bid. He takes the seed, brings it before the Holy One, blessed be he, and speaks to Him thus: "Lord of the universe, I have done as you told me, but what is to become of this seed? Make what disposition you choose."

Then the Holy One, blessed be he, determines at once whether it shall be strong or weak, tall or short, male or female, foolish or wise, rich or poor. But whether it is to be just or wicked He does not determine, for as we say: "Heaven ordains all, save the fear of heaven." [2]

At once the Holy One, blessed be he, beckons His messenger, him who holds sway over souls, and says to him: "Deliver that soul before me. For in this manner have all creatures been formed since the beginning and so shall it be unto the end."

At once the soul comes before the Holy One, blessed be he, and bows down before Him. At this hour He speaks to it thus: "Enter into that seed." On the instant the soul opens its mouth and declares: "Lord of the universe, the world in which I have resided from the day You made me is sufficient unto me;

give me leave, if this be Your pleasure, to remain without and not enter into that mortal seed, for I am holy and pure."

And the Holy One, blessed be he, speaks to the soul: "The world into which I would have you enter is better than the world in which you find yourself now. It was for this seed that you were meant on the day I made you."

At once He bids the soul enter that seed, though against its will. And the messenger returns and bids the soul enter into the womb of the mother. Then he summons thither two messengers to watch over the creature lest it fall. And over its head a light is kindled, as the Scripture has it: "When His candle shone upon my head" (Job 29:3), and it looks about and beholds the world from beginning to end.

And on the morrow the messenger takes this creature and leads it into the Garden of Eden and shows it the just, those who are dwelling in glory, and says to the creature: "Do you know whence this soul came?" And the creature makes answer and says: "No." Then the messenger speaks to the creature thus: "Him whom you behold in such glory and so exalted was formed like you in his mother's womb; and so was this one, and this one; and they all obeyed the laws and ordinances of the Holy One, blessed be he. If you do as they have done, after death—for they too have died—you will be exalted in glory, as they are. However, if you do not, your destiny will be to dwell in a place which I shall show you presently."

And in the evening he takes the creature to the place of the damned and shows it the sinners, those whom the minions of hell confound and strike with fiery rods until they cry: Woe is us!—but no one takes pity on them. And once more the messenger speaks to the creature: "My son, do you know who these are that the flames burn?" And the creature answers: "No." Whereupon the messenger says: "Know that these too were formed from mortal seed in the wombs of their mothers, but they failed to obey and bear witness to the Holy One, blessed be he; it is for this that they suffer so. Know, my child, that you are destined to leave your abode and die. Therefore, do not choose the path of the sinner but the path of the just: and thus you shall live eternally."

And he journeys with the creature from morning until night and shows it all the places where it will tread, and the place in which it will dwell, and the place in which it will be buried at last. And after this he shows it the world of the good and the ill.

Toward evening he returns the creature to the womb of its mother. But the Holy One, blessed be he, shuts it up with doors and bars, as it is written: "Or who shut up the sea with doors, when it brake forth, as it had issued out of the womb?" (Job 38:8) and it is written: "And I have put My words in thy mouth, and I have covered thee in the shadow of Mine hand" (Isa. 51:16). So the child lies in its mother's womb for nine months; for the first three months it dwells in the lower part, for the second three months in the middle part, for the last three months in the upper part. It partakes of all that its mother eats and drinks; its waste, however, it does not pass, for else its mother would die.

When the time has come for the creature to issue from the womb, that selfsame messenger visits it and says: "Come forth, for it is time now to enter the world." But the creature replies: "Did I not say once before to Him who spoke to me, Lord of the universe, that the world in which I have dwelt all this time is sufficient unto me?" The messenger replies: "The world which I would have you enter is more beautiful than that other one;" and he adds: "Perforce you were fashioned in the womb of your mother; perforce you are born and step forth into the world." The creature cries as it hears these words. And why does it cry? Because it must leave the world it has dwelt in. The moment it issues forth the messenger strikes it under the nose, and extinguishes the light that shone over its head and bids it step forth, unwilling; and the creature forgets all it has ever seen. And as it steps forth it cries. Why? Because at that hour seven worlds are led past it.

The first world resembles that of a king: every one inquires into the child's pleasure; everyone desires to see and to kiss it, for this is the first year of his life.

The second world resembles that of a pig that is always completely surrounded by filth—and so is the child in his second year.

The third world resembles that of a kid gamboling in the pasture: so does the child frolic until his fifth year.

The fourth world resembles that of a horse proudly prancing along the road: so does the child bear himself proudly, flaunting his youth, until he has reached his eighteenth year.

The fifth world resembles that of a donkey on whose shoulders a pack-saddle is laid: in like manner burdens are placed upon him; he is given a wife, he begets sons and daughters, and has to provide for his children and servants.

The sixth world resembles that of a dog that must provide for itself: it snatches its food where it can, snatches from this one and pilfers from that one, and is not ashamed.

The seventh world resembles that of a scarecrow: for now he is utterly changed, even his servants curse him and wish him dead, and his children mock him to his face.

At last the time has come for his death. The messenger of the Lord appears before him and says: "Do you recognize me?" And he replies: "Yes." Then he adds: "What brings you to me today?" And the messenger says: "I have come to take you away from this world."

Then he cries, his voice resounding from one end of the world to the other, but not a creature can hear him. And he says to the messenger: "Did you not lead me out of two worlds and set me down in this world in which I dwell now?"

And the messenger says to him: "Have I not told you long since that perforce you were fashioned and born, and so you are destined to die, and at last will give account and reckoning before the King over kings of kings, the Holy One, blessed be he?"

THE BRIDGE OF TIME

Yedayah ha-Bedersi

In his *Behinat Olam* (The Examination of the World), of which a quotation appears below, Yedayah ha-Bedersi, thirteenth-fourteenth-century Provencal poet, physician, and philosopher, meditates about both the lofty state and the predicaments of the sage, about the transitoriness of worldly goods and the permanence of wisdom and goodness, and the triumph of truth. First published in Mantua, between 1476 and 1480, the work was republished about seventy times, and translated into Latin (1650), French (1629), and other languages.

The world is a tempestuous sea of immense depth and breadth, and time is a frail bridge constructed over it, the beginning of which is fastened with the cords of chaos that preceded existence, while the end thereof is to behold eternal bliss, and to be enlightened with the light of the King's countenance. The width of the bridge is a cubit and it lacks borders. And thou, son of man, against thy will art thou living, and art continually travelling over it, since the day thou hast become a man.

HEALING

Jacob ben Asher

It is an ancient Judaic view that the physician's art is not an act of interference with the divine will but a legitimate exercise of human knowledge and skill, even a duty. Among the formulations of this concept is the one quoted below, taken from *Arbaa Turim*, authoritative code of Jewish law compiled by Jacob ben Asher (1269–1343) of Germany and Spain. *Arbaa Turim* became the basis for the extensive work of Halakhah, *Bet Yosef*, and the definitive code, *Shulhan Arukh*, both by Joseph Caro (Safed, sixteenth century).

The school of Rabbi Ishmael derived from Exod. 21:19 ("and the offender shall cause the victim to be thoroughly healed,") that permission is granted the physician to heal. The physician may not say "Why borrow trouble? I may err and appear like one who killed a person unwittingly." He shall indeed be exceedingly careful in exercising his art even as a judge must be careful in deciding criminal cases. In like manner, the physician may not say: "God smites, and shall I heal?" This is not the way of men with regard to healing, as we find King Asa in his sickness consulting not God, but physicians (II Chron. 16:12). Hence Scripture came to teach us that the physician is permitted to heal. Indeed, healing is a duty; it is saving life. He who is zealous in the work of healing is praiseworthy; and he who refuses to heal is a shedder of blood.

THE END OF MAN

Prayer Book

The Jewish attitude to life is reflected in the attitude to death. Both come from God, and, therefore, both are affirmed as good. As life is lived in the consciousness of the Divine Presence, so the Jew hopes to die in full consciousness of the divine. He prays in life to express his communion with God, and so he prays when death approaches and dies with the affirmation of God on his lips. His body is returned to dust, but death and destruction are transcended in the glorification of God and the vision of a perfect world. The content of the *Kaddish* is this glorification and this vision rather than an expression of mourning. Even the phrase, "words of solace," does not refer to the mourners, but to Zion. But the reference to the quickening of the dead and to life eternal caused the *Kaddish*, originally intended as a closing prayer at study sessions, to be transferred to the burial liturgy. The liturgy that is here reprinted is taken from the traditional prayer book of the Ashkenazic ritual; there are, of course, other customs and variant liturgies.

Prayer to be said by a sick person

A prayer of the afflicted when he fainteth and poureth out his complaint before the Lord. Hear my prayer, O Lord, and let my cry come unto Thee. Hide not Thy face from me in the day of my distress: incline Thine ear unto me; in the day when I call answer me speedily.

O Lord, healer of all flesh, have mercy upon me, and support me in Thy grace upon my bed of sickness, for I am weak. Send me and all who are sick among Thy children relief and cure. Assuage my pain, and renew my youth as the eagle's. Vouchsafe wisdom unto the physician that he may cure my wound, so that my health may spring forth speedily.

Hear my prayer, prolong my life, let me complete my years in happiness, that I may be enabled to serve Thee and keep Thy commandments with a perfect heart. Give me understanding to know that this bitter trial hath come upon me for my welfare, so that I may not despise Thy chastening nor weary of thy reproof.

O God of forgiveness, who art gracious and merciful, slow to anger and abounding in loving-kindness, I confess unto Thee with a broken and contrite heart that I have sinned, and have done that which is evil in Thy sight. Behold, I repent me of my evil way, and return unto Thee with perfect repentance.

Help me, O God of my salvation, that I may not again turn unto folly, but walk before Thee in truth and uprightness. Rejoice the soul of Thy servant, for unto Thee, O Lord, do I lift up my soul. Heal me, O Lord, and I shall be healed, save me, and I shall be saved, for Thou art my praise. Amen.

Prayer on a death bed

I acknowledge unto Thee, O Lord my God and God of my fathers, that both my cure and my death are in Thy hands. May it be Thy will to send me a perfect healing. Yet if my death be fully determined by Thee, I will in love accept it at Thy hand.

May my death be an atonement for the sins, iniquities and transgressions of which I have been guilty against Thee. Vouchsafe unto me of the abounding happiness that is treasured up for the righteous. Make known to me the path of life; in Thy presence is fullness of joy; at Thy right hand are pleasures for evermore.

Thou who art the father of the fatherless and judge of the widow, protect my beloved kindred with whose soul my own is knit. Into Thy hand I commend my spirit; Thou hast redeemed me, O Lord God of truth. Amen.

When the end is approaching:

The Lord reigneth; the Lord hath reigned; the Lord shall reign for ever and ever.

Blessed be His name, whose glorious kingdom is for ever and ever.

The Lord he is God.

Hear, O Israel: the Lord our God, the Lord is one.

The Burial Service

The Rock, His work is perfect, for all His ways are judgment: a God of faithfulness and without iniquity, just and right is He. The Rock, perfect in every work, who can say unto Him, What workest Thou? He ruleth below and above; He killeth and maketh alive: He bringeth down to the grave, and bringeth up again. The Rock, perfect in every deed, who can say unto Him, What doest Thou? O Thou who speakest and doest, of Thy grace deal kindly with us, and for the sake of him who was bound like a lamb [Isaac], O hearken and do. Just in all Thy ways art Thou, O perfect Rock, slow to anger and full of compassion.

Spare and have pity upon parents and children, for Thine, Lord, is forgiveness and compassion. Just art Thou, O Lord, in causing death and in making alive, in whose hand is the charge of all spirits; far be it from Thee to blot out our remembrance: O let Thine eyes mercifully regard us, for Thine, O Lord, is compassion and forgiveness. If a man live a year or a thousand years, what profiteth it him? He shall be as though he had not been.

Blessed be the true Judge, who causes death and maketh alive. Blessed be he, for His judgment is true, and His eye discerneth all things, and He awardeth unto man his reckoning and his sentence, and all must render acknowledgment unto Him. We know, O Lord, that Thy judgment is righteous: Thou art justified when Thou speakest, and pure when Thou judgest, and it is not for us to murmur at Thy method of judging; just art Thou, O Lord, and righteous are Thy judgments.

O true and righteous Judge! Blessed be the true Judge, all whose judgments are righteous and true. The soul of every living thing is in Thy hand; Thy right hand is full of righteousness. Have mercy upon the remnant of the flock of Thy hand, and say unto the angel, Stay thy hand. Thou art great in counsel and mighty in deed; Thine eyes are open upon all the ways of the children of men, to give unto every one according to his ways, and according to the fruit of his doings. To declare that the Lord is upright; He is my Rock, and there is no unrighteousness in Him.

The Lord gave, and the Lord hath taken away; blessed be the name of the Lord. And He, being merciful, forgiveth iniquity and destroyeth not: yea, many a time He turneth his anger away, and doth not stir up all his wrath.

(*Psalm 16 is read*).

The coffin is borne to the burial ground. Those who have not visited the burial ground for thirty days, say the following:
Blessed be the Lord our God, King of the universe, who formed you in judgment, who nourished and sustained you in judgment, who brought death on you in judgment, who knoweth the number of you all in judgment, and will hereafter restore you to life in judgment. Blessed art Thou, O Lord, who quickenest the dead.

Thou, O Lord, art mighty for ever, Thou quickenest the dead, Thou art mighty to save.

Thou sustainest the living with loving-kindness, quickenest the dead with great mercy, supportest the falling, healest the sick, loosest the bound, and keepest Thy faith to them that sleep in the dust. Who is like unto Thee, Lord of mighty acts, and who resembleth Thee, O King, who killest and quickenest, and causest salvation to spring forth?

Yea, faithful art Thou to quicken the dead.

When the coffin is lowered into the grave, the following is said:
May he come to his place in peace.
Or, may she come to her place in peace.

On quitting the burial ground it is customary to pluck some grass, and to say one of the following sentences:
And they of the city shall flourish like the grass of the earth.
He remembereth that we are dust.

All those who have been present at the burial wash their hands, and say:

He will destroy death for ever; and the Lord God will wipe away tears from off all faces; and the rebuke of His people shall He take away from off all the earth: for the Lord hath spoken it (Isa. 25:8).

They then return from the burial ground and recite Psalm 91. Children after the burial of a parent recite the Kaddish.

The Kaddish

Exalted and sanctified be His great name
in the world that is to be created anew
where He will quicken the dead, and raise them up unto life eternal;
will rebuild the city of Jerusalem and establish His temple in the
    midst thereof;
and will uproot worship of idols from the earth and restore the
    worship of God.
O may the Holy One, blessed be he, reign in his sovereignty and glory
in the days of your lifetime
and in the life of the whole house of Israel
speedily and soon,
Let us say, Amen.
May His great name be blessed for ever and to all eternity.
Blessed and praised, honored, adored and extolled, glorified and
    lauded supremely,
be the name of the Holy One, blessed be he.
He is high above all blessings and hymns, praises and words of solace
that may be uttered throughout the world.
Let us say, Amen.
May there be abundant peace from heaven,
and life for us and for all Israel.
Let us say, Amen.
May he who maketh peace in His hights
bring peace to us and to all Israel.
Let us say, Amen.

Prayer in the House of Mourning, after the ordinary Daily Service and the reading of Psalm 49:

O Lord and King, who art full of compassion, in whose hand is the soul of every living thing and the breath of all flesh who

causest death and makest alive, who bringest down to the grave
and bringest up again, receive, we beseech Thee, in Thy great
loving-kindness the soul of ———— who hath been gathered unto
his [her] people. Have mercy upon him [her]; pardon all his [her]
transgressions, for there is not a just man upon earth, who doeth
good and sinneth not. Remember unto him [her] the righteousness which he [she] wrought, and let his [her] reward be with him
[her], and his [her] recompense before him [her].

O shelter his [her] soul in the shadow of Thy wings. Make
known to him [her] the path of life: in Thy presence is fulness of
joy; at Thy right hand are pleasures for evermore. Vouchsafe
unto him [her] of the abounding happiness that is treasured up
for the righteous, as it is written, "Oh how great is Thy goodness,
which Thou hast laid up for them that fear Thee, which Thou
hast wrought for them that trust in Thee in the sight of the sons
of men" (Psalm 31:20).

O Lord, who healest the broken-hearted and bindest up their
wounds, grant Thy consolation unto the mourners: put into their
hearts the fear and love of Thee, that they may serve Thee with
a perfect heart, and let their latter end be peace. Amen.

"As one whom his mother comforteth, so will I comfort you,
and in Jerusalem shall ye be comforted. Thy sun shall no more
go down, neither shall thy moon withdraw itself; for the Lord
shall be thine everlasting light, and the days of thy mourning
shall be ended" (Isa. 66:13, 60:20).

He will destroy death for ever; and the Lord God will wipe
away tears from off all faces; and the rebuke of His people shall
He take away from off all the earth: for the Lord hath spoken it
(Isa. 25:8).

V. Knowledge

THE STUDY OF TORAH

Moses Maimonides

In the following passages, quoted from the *Mishneh Torah,* Maimonides summarizes the attitude of classical Judaism to learning, its emphasis on the centrality of the knowledge of Torah as the key to religious faith and ethical behavior. His sources are mainly the talmudic writings; his aim, to keep this spirit alive.

When should a father commence his son's instruction in Torah? As soon as the child begins to talk, the father should teach him the text, "Moses commanded us a law" (Deut. 33:4), and [the first verse of] the *Shema* ("Hear O Israel, the Lord our God, the Lord is One," Deut. 6:4). Later on, according to the child's capacity, the father should teach him a few verses at a time, till he be six or seven years old, when he should take him to a teacher of young children.

If it is the custom of the country for a teacher of children to receive remuneration, the father is to pay the fee, and it is his duty to have his son taught, even if he has to pay for the instruction, till the child has gone through the whole of the Written Law [the Scriptures]. Where it is the custom to charge a fee for teaching the Written Law, it is permissible to take payment for such instruction. It is forbidden however to teach the Oral Law [the Tradition] for payment. [. . .] If a person cannot find one willing to teach him without remuneration, he should engage a paid teacher, as it is said, "Buy the truth" (Prov. 23:23). It should not however be assumed that it is permissible to take pay for teaching. For the verse continues, "And sell it not," the inference being, that even where a man had been obliged to pay for instruction [in the Oral Law], he is nevertheless forbidden to charge, in his turn, for teaching it.

Every man in Israel is obliged to study Torah, whether he be poor or rich, in sound health or ailing, in the vigor of youth or very old and of weakened vitality. Even a man so poor that he is maintained by charity or goes begging from door to door, as also a man with a wife and children to support, are obliged to set aside a definite period during the day and at night for the study of the Torah.

Among the great sages of Israel, some were hewers of wood, some, drawers of water, while others were blind. Nevertheless, they devoted themselves by day and by night to the study of the Torah. Moreover, they are included among the transmitters of the tradition in the direct line from Moses our master.

Until what period in life is one obliged to study Torah? Even until the day of one's death, as it is said, "And lest they [the precepts] depart from thy heart all the days of thy life" (Deut. 4:9). Whenever one ceases to study, one forgets.

The time allotted to study should be divided into three parts. A third should be devoted to the Written Law; a third to the Oral Law; and the last third a person should spend thinking and reflecting so that he may understand the end of a thing from its beginning, and deduct one matter from another and compare one matter to another, and reason out by the hermeneutical rules by which the Torah is interpreted till one knows which are the principal rules and how to deduce therefrom what is forbidden and what is permitted and other like matters which he has learnt from oral tradition. This is termed Talmud.

A woman who studies Torah has a reward coming to her, but not in the same measure as a man because she was not commanded to do so [. . .].

With three crowns was Israel crowned: the crown of the Torah, the crown of the priesthood and the crown of kingship. The crown of the priesthood was bestowed upon Aaron, as it is said, "And it shall be unto him and unto his seed after him, the covenant of an everlasting priesthood" (Num. 25:13). The crown of kingship was conferred upon David, as it is said, "His seed shall endure forever, and his throne as the sun before Me" (Ps. 89:37). The crown of the Torah, behold, there it lies ready within the grasp of all Israel, as it is said, "Moses commanded us a Law, an inheritance of the congregation of Jacob" (Deut. 33:4). Whoever desires it can win it. Do not suppose that the other two crowns are greater than the crown of the Torah, for it is said, "By me, kings reign and princes decree justice; by me, princes rule" (Prov. 8:15–16). Hence the inference, that the crown of the Torah is greater than the other two crowns.

The sages said, "A bastard who is a scholar takes precedence of an ignorant High Priest." [1]

Of all precepts, none is equal in importance to the study of the Torah. Nay, study of the Torah is equal to them all, for study leads to practice. Hence, study always takes precedence of practice.

At the judgment hereafter, a man will first be called to account in regard to his fulfillment of the duty of study, and afterwards concerning his other activities. Hence, the sages said, "A person should always occupy himself with the Torah, whether for its own sake or for other reasons. For study of the Torah, even when pursued from interested motives, will lead to study for its own sake." [2]

He whose heart prompts him to fulfill this duty properly, and to be crowned with the crown of the Torah, must not allow his mind to be diverted to other matters. He must not aim at acquiring Torah as well as riches and honor at the same time. "This is the way for the study of the Torah: A morsel of bread with salt thou shalt eat, and water by measure thou shalt drink; thou shalt sleep upon the ground and live a life of hardship, the while thou toilest in the Torah." [3] "It is not incumbent upon thee to complete the task; but neither art thou free to neglect it." [4]

Possibly you may say: When I shall have accumulated money, I shall resume my studies; when I shall have provided for my needs and have leisure from my affairs, I shall resume my studies. Should such a thought enter your mind, you will never win the crown of the Torah. "Rather make the study of the Torah your fixed occupation" [5] and let your secular affairs en-

gage you casually, and do not say: "When I shall have leisure, I
shall study; perhaps you may never have leisure." [6]

In the Torah it is written, "It is not in heaven . . . neither
is it beyond the sea" (Deut. 30:12-13). "It is not in heaven," this
means that the Torah is not to be found with the arrogant; "nor
beyond the sea," that is, it is not found among those who cross
the ocean.[7] Hence, our sages said, "Not he who engages himself
overmuch in business is wise." [8] They have also exhorted us, "Engage little in business and occupy thyself with the Torah." [9]

The words of the Torah have been compared to water, as
it is said, "O every one that thirsteth, come ye for water"
(Is. 55:1); this teaches us that just as water does not accumulate
on a slope but flows away, while in a depression it stays, so the
words of the Torah are not to be found in the arrogant or
haughty but only in him who is humble and lowly in spirit, who
sits in the dust at the feet of the wise and banishes from his heart
lusts and temporal delights; works a little daily, just enough to
provide for his needs, if he would otherwise have nothing to eat,
and devotes the rest of the day and night to the study of the
Torah.[10]

One however who makes up his mind to study Torah and
not work but live on charity, profanes the name of God, brings
the Torah into contempt, extinguishes the light of religion,
brings evil upon himself and deprives himself of life in the world
to come, for it is forbidden to derive any temporal advantage
from the words of the Torah. The sages said, "Whoever derives
a profit for himself from the words of the Torah takes his own
life away from the world." [11] They have further charged us,
"Make not of them a crown wherewith to aggrandize thyself, nor
a spade wherewith to dig." [12] They likewise exhorted us, "Love
work, hate lordship." [13] "All study of the Torah, not conjoined
with work, must, in the end, be futile, and become a cause of
sin." [14] The end of such a person will be that he will rob people
for his living.

It indicates a high degree of excellence in a man to maintain
himself by the labor of his hands. And this was the normal practice of the early pious men [Hasidim]. Thus, one secures all
honor and happiness here and in the world to come, as it is said,

"When thou eatest of the labor of thine hands, happy shalt thou be, and it shall be well with thee" (Ps. 128:2). Happy shalt thou be in this world, and it shall be well with these in the world to come, which is altogether good.[15]

The words of the Torah do not abide with one who studies listlessly, nor with those who learn amidst luxury, and high living, but only with one who mortifies himself for the sake of the Torah, enduring physical discomfort, and not permitting sleep to his eyes nor slumber to his eyelids. "This is the Law, when a man dieth in a tent" (Num. 19:14). The sages explained the text metaphorically thus: "The Torah only abides with him who sacrifices his life in the tents of the wise." [16]

While it is a duty to study by day and by night, most of one's knowledge is acquired at night. Accordingly, when one aspires to win the crown of the Torah, he should be especially heedful of all his nights and not waste a single one of them in sleep, eating, drinking, idle talk and so forth, but devote all of them to study of the Torah and words of wisdom. Whoever occupies himself with the study of the Torah at night—a mark of spiritual grace distinguishes him by day, as it is said, 'By day the Lord will command His loving-kindness, and in the night His song shall be with me, even a prayer unto the God of my life' " (Ps. 42:9).[17]

In praise of learning, education,

AND THE GOOD LIFE

Judah ibn Tibbon

Judah ibn Tibbon is best known for his translations of philosophical and philological works from the Arabic into Hebrew. Born about 1120, Judah was forced to leave his native Granada and he settled in Lunel, Provence, where he practiced medicine. Among the works which his translations made accessible to the Hebrew reader were Saadia Gaon's *Doctrines and Beliefs,* Bahya ibn Pakuda's *Duties of the Heart,* Solomon ibn Gabirol's *Introduction to the Improvement of the Qualities of the Soul,* Judah ha-Levi's *Kuzari,* and grammatical treatises by Jonah ibn Janah. In his Preface to the translation of the *Duties of the Heart,* he discussed the problem of literalness versus readability, the crux of translators to this day. He died in 1190.

His son, Samuel ibn Tibbon (*ca.* 1150–1230), to whom the admonitions that follow are addressed, was also a physician. He continued the family's tradition of translating and is best known for his Hebrew rendition of Maimonides' *Guide to the Perplexed.*

Judah's "ethical will," a testimony to his broad culture, love of books, and humanism, has been preserved in manuscript in the Bodleian Library and was published in London and in Berlin, both in 1852.

Thou knowest, my son, how I swaddled thee and brought thee up, how I led thee in the paths of wisdom and virtue. I fed and clothed thee; I spent myself in educating and protecting thee, I sacrificed my sleep to make thee wise beyond thy fellows, and to raise thee to the highest degree of science and morals. These twelve years I have denied myself the usual pleasures and relaxations of men for thy sake, and I still toil for thine inheritance.

I have assisted thee by providing an extensive library for thy use and have thus relieved thee of the necessity of borrowing books. Most students must wander about to seek books, often without finding them. But thou, thanks be to God, lendest and borrowest not. Of many books, indeed, thou ownest two or three copies. I have besides procured for thee books on all sciences. Seeing that thy Creator had graced thee with a wise and understanding heart, I journeyed to the ends of the earth and fetched for thee a teacher in secular sciences. I neither heeded the expense nor the danger of the ways. Untold evil might have befallen me and thee on those travels, had not the Lord been with us!

But thou, my son, didst deceive my hopes! Thou didst not choose to employ thine abilities, hiding thyself from all the books, not caring to know them or even their titles. Hadst thou seen thine own books in the hand of others, thou wouldst not have recognized them; hadst thou needed one of them, thou wouldst not have known whether it was with thee or not, without asking me; thou didst not even consult the catalogue of the library.

All this thou hast done. Thus far thou hast relied on me to rouse thee from the sleep of indolence, thinking that I would live with thee for ever! Thou didst not bear in mind that death must divide us, and that there are daily vicissitudes in life. But who will be as tender to thee as I have been, who will take my place—to teach thee out of love and goodwill? Even if thou couldst find such a one, lo! thou seest how the greatest scholars, coming from the corners of the earth, seek to profit by my society and instruction, how eager they are to see me and my books. [. . .] May thy God endow thee with a new heart and spirit, and instill into thee a desire to retrieve the past, and to follow the true path henceforward!

Thou art still young, and improvement is possible, if Heaven but grant thee a helping gift of desire and resolution, for ability is of no avail without inclination. If the Lord please to bring me back to thee, I will take upon me all thy wants. For whom indeed do I toil but for thee and thy children? May the Lord let me see their faces again in joy!

Therefore, my son! stay not thy hand when I have left thee, but devote thyself to the study of the Torah and to the science of medicine. But chiefly occupy thyself with the Torah, for thou hast a wise and understanding heart, and all that is needful on thy part is ambition and application. I know that thou wilt repent of the past, as many have repented before thee of their youthful indolence. [. . .] Devote thyself to science and religion; habituate thyself to moral living, for "habit is master over all things." As the Arabian philosopher holds, there are two sciences, ethics and physics. Strive to excel in both!

Contend not with men, and meddle not "with strife not thine own" (Prov. 26:17). Enter into no dispute with the obstinate, not even on matters of Torah. On thy side, too, refrain from subterfuges in argument to maintain thy case even when thou art convinced that thou art in the right. Submit to the majority and do not reject their decision. Risk not thy life by taking the road and leaving thy city in times of disquiet and danger.

Show respect to thyself, thy household, and thy children, by providing decent clothing, as far as thy means allow; for it is unbecoming for any one, when not at work, to go shabbily dressed. Spare from thy belly and put it on thy back.

And now, my son! if the Creator has mightily displayed His love to thee and me, so that Jew and Gentile have thus far honored thee for my sake, endeavor henceforth so to add to thine honor that they may respect thee for thine own self. This thou canst effect by good morals and by courteous behavior; by steady devotion to thy studies and thy profession, as thou wast wont to do before thy marriage.

My son! Let thy countenance shine upon the sons of men: tend their sick, and may thine advice cure them. Though thou takest fees from the rich, heal the poor gratuitously; the Lord will requite thee. Thereby shalt thou find favor and good understanding in the sight of God and man. Thus wilt thou win the respect of high and low among Jews and non-Jews, and thy good name will go forth far and wide. Thou wilt rejoice thy friends and make thy foes envious.

My son! Examine regularly once a week thy drugs and medicinal herbs, and do not employ an ingredient whose properties are unknown to thee. I have often impressed this on thee in vain when we were together.

My son! If thou writest aught, read it through a second time, for no man can avoid slips. Let not any consideration of hurry prevent thee from revising a short epistle. Be punctilious in regard to grammatical accuracy, in conjugations and genders, for the constant use of the vernacular sometimes leads to error in this matter. A man's mistakes in writing bring him into disrepute; they are remembered against him all his days. Endeavor to cultivate conciseness and elegance, do not attempt to write verse unless thou canst do it perfectly. Avoid heaviness, which spoils a composition, making it disagreeable alike to reader and audience.

See to it that thy penmanship and handwriting are as beautiful as thy style. Keep thy pen in fine working order, use ink of good color. Make thy script as perfect as possible, unless forced to write without proper materials, or in a pressing emergency. The beauty of a composition depends on the writing, and the beauty of the writing, on pen, paper and ink; and all these excellencies are an index to the author's worth. [. . .]

[In the past] when thou didst write thy letters or compose

thine odes to send abroad, thou wast unwilling to show a word
to me and didst prevent me from seeing. When I said to thee,
"Show me!" thou wouldst answer: "Why dost thou want to see?"
as if thinking that my help was unnecessary. And this was from
thy folly, in that thou wast wise in thine own eyes.

If, my son, thou desirest to undo the past, the Creator will
grant His pardon, and I shall forgive all without reserve or reluc-
tance. Reject not my word in all that I have written for thee in
this, my testament, and wherein thou hast not honored me here-
tofore, honor me for the rest of my days, and after my death! All
the honor I ask of thee is to attain a higher degree in the pursuit
of wisdom, to excel in right conduct and exemplary character,
to behave in friendly spirit to all and to gain a good name, that
greatest of crowns, to deserve applause for thy dealing and association with thy fellows, to cleave to the fear of God and the
performance of His commandments—thus wilt thou honor me
in life and in death!

My son! I command thee to honor thy wife to thine utmost
capacity. She is intelligent and modest, a daughter of a distinguished and educated family. She is a good housewife and mother,
and no spendthrift. Her tastes are simple, whether in food or
dress. Remember her assiduous attendance on thee in thine illness, though she had been brought up in elegance and luxury.
Remember how she afterwards reared thy son without man or
woman to help her.

If thou wouldst acquire my love, honor her with all thy
might; do not exercise too strict an authority over her; our sages
have expressly warned men against this. If thou givest orders or
reprovest let thy words be gentle. Enough is it if thy displeasure
is visible in thy look, let it not be vented in actual rage.

My son! Devote thy mind to thy children as I did to thee;
be tender to them as I was tender; instruct them as I instructed
thee; keep them as I kept thee, try to teach them Torah as I
have tried, and as I did unto thee do thou unto them! Be not
indifferent to any slight ailment in them, or in thyself (may God
deliver thee and them from all sickness and plague), but if thou
dost notice any suspicion of disease in thee or in one of thy
limbs, do forthwith what is necessary in the case. As Hippocrates

has said: "Time is short, and experiment is dangerous." Therefore be prompt, but apply a sure remedy, avoiding doubtful treatment.

Examine thy Hebrew books at every new moon, the Arabic
volumes once in two months, and the bound codices once every
quarter. Arrange thy library in fair order, so as to avoid wearying
thyself in searching for the book thou needest. Always know the
case and chest where the book should be. A good plan would be
to set in each compartment a written list of the books therein
contained. If, then, thou art looking for a book, thou canst see
from the list the exact shelf it occupies without disarranging
all the books in the search for one. Examine the loose leaves in
the volumes and bundles, and preserve them. These fragments
contain very important matters which I have collected and
copied out. Do not destroy any writing or letter of all that I have
left. And cast thine eye frequently over the catalogue so as to
remember what books are in thy library.

Never refuse to lend books to anyone who has not means
to purchase books for himself, but only act thus to those who
can be trusted to return the volumes. Cover the bookcase with
rugs of fine quality; and preserve them from damp and mice, and
from all manner of injury, for thy books are thy good treasure.
If thou lendest a volume make a note of it before it leaves thy
house, and when it is returned, draw thy pen over the entry.
Every Passover and Feast of Booths call in all books out on
loan.

Make it a fixed rule in thy home to read the Scriptures and
to peruse grammatical works on Sabbaths and festivals, also to
read Proverbs and the Ben Mishle.[18] Also I beg of thee, look at
the chapter concerning Jonadab son of Rechab[19] every Sabbath,
to instill in thee diligence to fulfill my commands. [. . .]

May He who gives prudence to the simple, and to young
men knowledge and discretion, bestow on thee a willing heart
and a listening ear! Then shall our soul be glad in the Lord
and rejoice in His salvation!

THE GIFT OF THE LAW

Obadiah ben Abraham

The passage that follows is part of a treatise attributed to Rabbi Obadiah, grandson of Moses Maimonides. In it Obadiah offers an introduction to the perfect spiritual life which is to lead to a union with
God. Maimonides considered reason to be a bond between God and
man (Guide III, 51); but in contradistinction to the grandfather's in-
tellectualism, the grandson, using a similar phrase, gives it a mystical
turn. The treatise is contained in the Judaeo-Arabic manuscript, Oriental 666, of the Bodleian Library.

Know, my son, that reason forms the bond between God and
thyself. The food which nourishes it is the science of the unal-
terable things; without these it is unable to subsist or to maintain
itself. Just as the body cannot subsist except by the healthy food
that suits it, so reason is only maintained by the true sciences,
whose permanency guarantees its own. But [for] him who studies
the sciences whose meaning he is ignorant of, [the object of his
study] so to speak lacks consistency and serves no useful purpose
either in this world or in the next [. . .]. As for us, God has
made us a gift of the Law, perfect in itself and giving perfection,
that Law which we now possess. It lends us mastery over our
moral qualities as well as intellectual vigor, for sound reason is
the perfect Law and the divine Law is sound reason.

PROPOSED JEWISH ACADEMY

IN MANTUA

David Provenzal

In the Renaissance period Jews in Italy found it possible to study—
mainly medicine—at the universities of that country. In Sicily the Jewish communities were authorized in 1466 to establish a *studium gene-*

rale (university) for the training of medical men and jurists. Little more is known about this project. There are records of Jewish teachers at Italian schools of higher learning; in 1529 Jacob Mantino (Giacobbe Giudeo) was appointed Lecturer in Medicine at the University of Bologna and, a few years later, Professor of Practical Medicine at the "Sapienza" in Rome.

Some staunch traditionalists opposed such "modernist" tendencies. Other community leaders realized the futility and unreality of opposition and wished to counteract Jewish assimilation to secular society by establishing an academy in which the curriculum would combine the study of sciences with Hebrew training. Such was the proposal of 1566, here reprinted. The graduates were expected to complete their studies at a regular university.

Authors of the proposal were Rabbi David Provenzal of Mantua and his son Abraham, a physician. David Provenzal was a talmudist with considerable knowledge of Latin and philosophy. His curious collection of some two thousand Latin and Greek words, which he tried to trace back to a supposedly original Hebrew, has not been preserved. Provenzal's friend was the literary historian Azariah de Rossi.

The Hebrew text was originally a Mantua broadside; it was published in *Ha-Lebanon* V, 1868.

Now these are the rules that we intend to observe with the aid of God who will help us as He helps anyone whose purpose is lofty. The following requirements, though they be many, will be fulfilled in every sense of the word, without fail. Man has a will whereby he can accomplish anything he wishes if he but have God's help, and so with His aid do we intend to proceed at all times.

Young students who come from out of town to board in my house will be provided with a bed, table, chair, and lamp, and will be completely free from providing for their bodily needs. At the table they will always speak of both religious and secular matters so that there will be imparted to them intellectual and social qualities to be employed in all their conduct, and thus "they will behold God while eating and drinking" (Exod. 24:11). Those who come to register in my home shall not be transients but shall come for a period of five years until they show good progress in their studies, or they must at least stay three years, for one must labor at least that length of time to maintain his grasp on knowledge.

In studying the Bible we will read the best of the old and the new commentators both for the purpose of explaining the basis for the commandments, judgments, and laws, and for the purpose of understanding the science of the Torah which many call divine philosophy. We will also add new interpretations which have not yet been published, in accordance with the point of view that investigation is always worth while, for there is no study that does not result in something new. With God's help we will pursue the same method a part of the time with the Prophets and the Writings as well as with those Midrashim that are useful and valuable for furthering knowledge.

We will fix periods for the study of Hebrew grammar in order to get into its spirit and to know its rules. For many fundamental questions are dependent upon this: both the true meaning of the Biblical verses as well as the understanding of the secrets hidden in them like apples of gold in frames of silver. We will also study the Masorah.[20]

While studying grammar they can also learn to speak idiomatically and write correctly—whether they say little or much —as for instance when dealing with a matter of law. When studying poetry they will be taught the methods of the best of the poets.

At special hours the students will learn Latin, which is almost indispensable now in our country, for no day passes by that we do not require this knowledge in our relations with the officials. We have a precedent for this since even the members of the household of Judah the Prince were allowed to trim their hair like the pagans because they had frequent contact with the Roman government. The students shall also write themes in Hebrew and in good Italian and Latin with the niceties and elegances of style that are characteristic of each language and the knowledge of which redounds to one's fame and reputation.

Those who are versed in Latin can read the scientific books dealing with logic, philosophy, and medicine and thus get acquainted with them step by step, so that any one who wishes to become a physician need not waste his days and years in a university in sinful neglect of Jewish studies. On the contrary, through his own reading he should inform himself gradually of all that he need know, and then if he should study in a university for a brief period he can, with God's help, get his degree. After this he may enter practice with competent Jewish and Christian physicians. But even those who do not as yet know any Latin may read those scientific books which have already been translated into Hebrew, and thus save time, for the basic thing in knowledge is not language but content, for everything depends on what the mind really grasps.

Furthermore, by the aid of competent men the students will be made proficient in the different types of Christian scripts. And likewise in the science of arithmetic and calculation they will do many problems. And they will get many-sided instruction in the various forms of arithmetic, geometry, and fractions. They will also be taught and made familiar with the usual studies such as arithmetic and geometry, which have already been mentioned, as well as with geography and astrology. All these disciplines will be taught by us to the limits of our capacity, and no student will have to go anywhere else to study, for we will carry them as far as we can. For more advanced instruction we will find a competent scholar to work with us.

At fixed periods the students will engage in debates in our presence both in matters of Jewish law and in the sciences, in order to sharpen their minds. Each young man will learn more or less in accordance with his individual capacity—the main thing is that they be religious in spirit. Also they will gradually be taught to speak in public and to preach before congregations.

If God will grant us the merit of having a great many pupils, we will secure more instructors who will look after them properly, to give each student his just due. "May the graciousness of the Lord our God be upon us and mayest Thou establish the work of our hands" (Ps. 90:17). Amen. May it be Thy will.

THE INNER LIFE

OF THE JEWS IN POLAND

Nathan Hannover

This somewhat idealized portrayal of Jewish life in seventeenth-century Poland is the concluding chapter of *Yeven Metzulah* (The Deep Mire), a chronicle of the Chmielnicki massacres in 1648, 1649, and 1652. The author, Nathan Hannover of Ostrog, Volhynia, was an eyewitness to the Cossack uprisings of 1648 which brought ruin to the Jewish communities of the region. Hannover managed to flee Ostrog; he sojourned in Germany, Holland, Venice (where he published his chronicle), Livorno, Jassy and Focsani (Rumania), and finally, in Ungarisch-Brod (Moravia), where he met a martyr's death in 1683. Mystically inclined (he published a collection of Kabbalistic prayers, Prague, 1662), he believed the tragic events in Eastern Europe to be the required preparation for the advent of the Messiah. A spirit of warm humaneness permeates his description of the economic and religious life of Polish Jews, their high regard for scholarship, education, community cohesion, and social welfare.

And now I will begin to describe the practices of the Jews in the Kingdom of Poland, which were founded on principles of righteousness and steadfastness.

It is said in the Sayings of the Fathers: "Simeon the Just used to say: 'Upon three things the world is based: Upon the Torah, upon divine service, and upon the practice of charity.' " [21] Rabban Simeon, the son of Gamaliel said: "By three things is the world preserved: by truth, by judgment and by peace." [22] All the six pillars upon which the world rests were in existence in the Kingdom of Poland.

The Pillar of the Torah: Throughout the dispersions of Israel there was nowhere so much learning as in the Kingdom of Poland. Each community maintained academies, and the head of each academy was given an ample salary so that he could maintain his school without worry, and that the study of the Torah might be his sole occupation. The head of the academy did not leave his house the whole year except to go from the house of study to the synagogue. Thus he was engaged in the study of the Torah day and night. Each community maintained young men and provided for them a weekly allowance of money that they might study with the head of the academy. And for each young man they also maintained two boys to study under his guidance, so that he would orally discuss the Talmud, the commentaries of Rashi and the Tosafot,[23] which he had learned, and thus he would gain experience in the subtlety of talmudic argumentation. The boys were provided with food from the community benevolent fund or from the public kitchen. If the community consisted of fifty householders it supported not less than thirty young men and boys. One young man and two boys would be assigned to one householder. And the young man ate at his table as one of his sons. Although the young man received a stipend from the community, the householder provided him with all the food and drink that he needed. Some of the more charitable householders also allowed the boys to eat at their table, thus three persons would be provided with food and drink by one householder the entire year.

There was scarcely a house in all the Kingdom of Poland where its members did not occupy themselves with the study of the Torah. Either the head of the family was himself a scholar, or else his son, or his son-in-law, or one of the young men eating at his table. At times, all of these were to be found in one house. Thus there were many scholars in every community. A community of fifty householders had twenty scholars who achieved the title *Morenu*[24] or *Haver*.[25] The head of the academy was above all these, and the scholars accepted his authority and would go to his academy to attend his discourses.

The program of study in the Kingdom of Poland was as follows: The term of study consisted of the period which required the young men and the boys to study with the head of the academy. In the summer it extended from the first day of the month of Iyar [*ca*. May] till the fifteenth day of the month of Ab [*ca*. August], and in the winter, from the first day of the month of Heshvan [*ca*. November], till the fifteenth day of the month of Shevat [*ca*. February]. After the fifteenth of Shevat or the fifteenth of Ab, the young men and the boys were free to study wherever they preferred. From the first day of Iyar till the Feast of Weeks, and in the winter from the first day of Heshvan till Hanukkah, all the students of the academy studied Talmud, the commentaries of Rashi and Tosafot, with great diligence. Each day they studied one page of the Talmud with the commentaries.

All the scholars and the young students of the community as well as all those who showed inclination to study the Torah assembled in the academy. The head of the academy alone occupied a chair and the scholars and the other students stood about him. Before the head of the academy appeared they would engage in a discussion, and when he arrived each one would ask him that which he found difficult in the Law and he would offer his explanation to each of them.

They were all silent, as the head of the academy delivered his lecture and presented the new results of his study. After discussing his new interpretations the head of the academy would discuss a *chilluk*,[26] which proceeded in the following manner: He would cite a contradiction from the Talmud, or Rashi, or Tosafot, he would question deletions and pose contradictory statements and provide solutions which would also prove perplexing; and then he would propose solutions until the Law was completely clarified.

In the summer they would not leave the academy before noon. From the Feast of Weeks till the New Year, and from Hanukkah till Passover, the head of the academy would not engage in so many discussions. He would study with the scholars the Codes such as the *Arbaah Turim*[27] and their commentaries. With young men he would study Rav Alfas[28] and other works. In any case, they also studied Talmud, Rashi, and Tosafot, till the first day of Ab or the fifteenth day of Shevat. From then on until Passover or the New Year they studied the codes and similar works only. Some weeks prior to the fifteenth day of Ab or the fifteenth day of Shevat, the head of the academy would honor each student to lead in the discussion in his stead. The honor was given both to the scholars and the students. They would present the discussion, and the head of the academy would listen and then join in the disputation. This was done to exercise their intellect. The same tractate [of the Talmud] was studied throughout the Kingdom of Poland in the proper sequence of the Six Orders.

Each head of an academy had one inspector who daily went from school to school to look after the boys, both rich and poor, that they should study. He would warn them that they should study and not loiter in the streets. On Thursdays all the boys had to be examined by the superintendent on what they had learned during the week. [. . .] Likewise on Sabbath Eve all the boys went in a group to the head of the academy to be questioned on what they had learned during the week, as in the aforementioned procedure. In this manner there was fear upon the boys and they studied with regularity. Also during the three days preceding the Feast of Weeks and during Hanukkah, the young men and the boys were obliged to review what they had studied during that term, and for this the community leaders gave specified gifts of money. Such was the practice till the fifteenth of Ab or the fifteenth of Shevat. After that the head of the academy, together with all his students, the young men and the boys, journeyed to the fair. In the summer they travelled to the fair of Zaslaw and to the fair of Jaroslaw; in the winter to the fairs of Lwow and Lublin. There the young men and boys were free to study in any academy they preferred. Thus at each of the fairs hundreds of academy heads, thousands of young men, and tens of thousands of boys, and Jewish merchants, and Gentiles like the sand on the shore of the sea, would gather. For people would come to the fair from one end of the world to the other. Whoever had a son or daughter of marriageable age went to the fair and there arranged a match. For there was ample opportunity for everyone to find his like and his mate. Thus hundreds and sometimes thousands of such matches would be arranged at each fair. And Jews, both men and women, walked about the fair, dressed in their best garments. For they were held in esteem in the eyes of the rulers and in the eyes of the Gentiles, and the children of Israel were many like the sand of the sea, but now, because of our sins, they have become few. May the Lord have mercy upon them.

In each community great honor was accorded to the head of

the academy. His words were heard by rich and poor alike. None questioned his authority. Without him no one raised his hand or foot, and as he commanded so it came to be. [. . .] Everyone loved the head of the academy, and he that had a good portion such as fatted fowl, or capons or good fish, would honor the head of the academy, with half or all, and with other gifts of silver and gold without measure. In the Synagogue, too, most of those who bought honors would accord them to the head of the academy. It was obligatory to call him to the Torah reading third, on the Sabbath and the first days of the Festivals. And if the head of the academy happened to be a Kohen or a Levite, he would be given preference despite the fact that there may have been others entitled to the honor of Kohen or Levi, or the concluding portion of the reading. No one left the Synagogue on the Sabbath or the Festival until the head of the academy walked out first and his pupils after him; then the whole congregation accompanied him to his home. On the Festivals the entire congregation followed him to his house to greet him. For this reason all the scholars were envious and studied with diligence, so that they too, might advance to this state, and become an academy head in some community; out of doing good with an ulterior motive, there came the doing good for its own sake, and the land was filled with knowledge.

The Pillar of Divine Service: At this time prayer has replaced sacrificial service, as it is written: "So we will render for bullocks, the offering of our lips" (Hosea 14:3). At the head was the fellowship of those who rose before dawn, called "they that watch for the morning," to pray and to mourn over the destruction of the Temple. With the coming of dawn the members of the "Society of Readers of Psalms" would rise to recite Psalms for about an hour before prayers. Each week they would complete the recitation of the entire Book of Psalms. And far be it, that any man should oversleep the time of prayer in the morning and not go to the Synagogue, except for unusual circumstances. When a man went to the Synagogue, he would not depart thence to his business until he had heard some words of the Torah expounded by a scholar or a passage from the commentary of Rashi on the Torah, the Prophets, the Writings, the Mishnah or some laws of

ritual, whatever his heart desired to learn; for in all Synagogues
there were many groups of scholars who taught others in the
Synagogue immediately after evening and morning prayers.

The Pillar of Charity: There was no measure for the dispen-
sation of charity in the Kingdom of Poland, especially as regards
hospitality. If a scholar or preacher visited a community, even
one which had a system of issuing communal tickets to be offered hospitality by a householder, he did not have to humiliate
himself to obtain a ticket, but went to some community leader
and stayed wherever he pleased. The community beadle then
came and took his credentials to collect funds to show it to the
Synagogue official or the community leader for the month, and
they gave an appropriate gift which was delivered by the beadle
in dignified manner. He was then the guest of the householder
for as many days as he desired. Similarly all other transients who
received tickets, would be the guests of a householder, whose turn
it was by lot, for as many days as he wished. The guest was given
food and drink, morning, noon and evening. If they wished to
depart they would be given provisions for the road, and they
would be conveyed by horse and carriage from one community
to another. If young men or boys or older men or unmarried
girls, came from distant places, they would be forthwith furnished
with garments. Those who wanted to work at a trade would be
apprenticed to a tradesman, and those who wanted to be servants
in a house would be assigned to serve in a house.

Those who wanted to study would be provided with a
teacher, and afterwards, when he became an important young
man, a rich man would take him to his house and give him his
daughter in marriage as well as several thousand gold pieces for
a dowry, and he would clothe him in the finest. After the wedding
he would send him away from his home to study in great academies. When he returned home after two or three years, his
father-in-law would maintain a study group for him in his home
and he would spend much money among the householders who
were prominent scholars that they should attend his study group
for a number of years, until he also will become a head of an
academy in some community. Even if the lad was not yet an
important student at that time but had a desire to study, en-

abling him to become a scholar after he had studied, there would at times come a rich man who had a young daughter, and give him food and drink and clothes, and all his needs, as he would to his own son, and he would hire a teacher for him until he was ready with his studies, then he would give him his daughter in marriage. There is no greater benevolence than this.

Similarly there were very praiseworthy regulations for poor unmarried girls in every province. No poor girl reached the age of eighteen without being married, and many pious women devoted themselves to this worthy deed. May the Lord recompense them and have compassion upon the remnant of Israel.

The Pillar of Justice was in the Kingdom of Poland as it was in Jerusalem before the destruction of the Temple, when courts were set up in every city, and if one refused to be judged by the court of his city he went to the nearest court, and if he refused to be judged by the nearest court, he went before the great court. For in every province there was a great court. Thus in the capital city of Ostrog there was the great court for Volhynia and the Ukraine, and in the capital city of Lwow there was the great court for Little Russia. There were thus many communities each of which had a great court for its own province.

If two important communities had a dispute between them, they would let themselves be judged by the heads of the Council of the Four Lands[29] (may their Rock and Redeemer preserve them) who would be in session twice a year. One leader would be chosen from each important community, added to these, were six great scholars from the land of Poland, and these were known as the Council of the Four Lands. They would be in session during every fair in Lublin between Purim and Passover, and during every fair at Jaroslaw in the month of Ab [ca. August] or Elul [ca. September]. The leaders of the Four Lands had the authority to judge all Israel in the Kingdom of Poland, to establish safeguards, to institute ordinances, and to punish. Each difficult matter was brought before them and they judged it. And the leaders of the Four Lands selected judges from the provinces to relieve their burden, and these were called judges of the provinces. They attended to cases involving money matters; fines, titles, and other difficult laws were brought before them. [. . .]

The Pillar of Truth: Every community appointed men in charge of weights and measures, and of other business dealings, so that everything would be conducted according to truth and trustworthiness.

The Pillar of Peace, for it is said: "The Lord will give strength unto His people; the Lord will bless His people with peace" (Ps. 29:11). There was in Poland so much interest in learning that no three people sat down to a meal without discussing Torah, for throughout the repast everyone indulged in talks of Torah and puzzling passages in the Midrashim, in order to fulfill the words: "Thy law is in my inmost parts" (Ps. 40:9). And the Holy One blessed be he, recompensed them so that even "when they were in the land of their enemies, He did not despise them and did not break his covenant with them" (Lev. 26:44). And wherever their feet trod the ground among our brothers of the House of Israel they were treated with great generosity, above all, our brethren who were in distress and in captivity among the Tartars. For the Tartars led them to Constantinople, a city that was a mother in Israel, and to the famed city of Salonica, and to other communities in Turkey and Egypt, and in Barbary and other provinces of Jewish dispersion where they were ransomed for much money, as mentioned above. To this day they have not ceased to ransom prisoners that are brought to them each day.

Those who escaped the sword of the enemy in every land where their feet trod, such as Moravia, Austria, Bohemia, Germany, Italy, were treated with kindness and were given food and drink and lodging and garments and many gifts, each according to his importance, and they also favored them with other things. Especially in Germany did they do more than they could. May their justice appear before God to shield them and all Israel wherever they are congregated, so that Israel may dwell in peace and tranquility in their habitations. May their merit be counted for us and for our children, that the Lord should hearken to our cries and gather our dispersed from the four corners of the earth, and send us our Redeemer speedily in our day. Amen, Selah.

THE HOUSE OF STUDY

IN PADUA

An Eighteenth-Century Document

Moses Hayyim Luzzatto (1707–1746) is best known for his ethical work *Mesillat Yesharim* (Path of the Upright), passages of which appear elsewhere in this volume ("The Love for God," "How to Attain Saintliness," "Humility"). In his time, however, he was noted for his mysticism and his strongly accentuated Messianic thought. Following the tragic turn in the Sabbatianic movement of the seventeenth century a mystic was easily suspected of heretic leanings, and leading rabbis saw in Luzzatto's mystical writings a threat to middle-of-the-road Judaism. They forbade him further study of Kabbalah, and, when he disregarded the prohibition, excommunicated him in 1735. Luzzatto left his native Padua, lived for a while in Amsterdam, then moved on to Palestine. Shortly after his arrival, he and his family died during a plague in 1746.

The study group which young Luzzatto founded in Padua, the regulations of which are here presented, was actually a community of mystics. One among them drew up these rules, and the text indicates that the members of the group had more in mind than the study of the *Zohar*. Uninterrupted study and saintly conduct of life aimed at "the restoration of the Divine Presence and . . . of all Israel."

With the help of God may we begin and prosper, Amen.

These are the words of the covenant, the laws and ordinances and teachings, which the holy associates hereunto subscribing have taken upon themselves for the unification of the Holy One and the Divine Presence all acting as one, because "Jephthah in his generation is even as Samuel in his generation" [30]—to perform this service of God, which shall be reckoned to the account of all. The following are the obligations which they have accepted:

First, to prosecute in this House of Study a continuous uninterrupted study of the holy book of *Zohar*, each man his portion, one after another, daily, from the morning until the Evening

Prayer, except for the Sabbaths, Festivals, Purim, the Ninth of Ab,[31] the eve of the Ninth of Ab, and except for the Friday afternoons, according to the condition which we have stipulated before God:

1. That this study shall not be reckoned a vow. That is to say, an omission shall not, God forbid, become a stumbling block to the comrades and be considered a default of a vow. But it shall be imposed upon them with all the power and stringency that mouth can utter and heart can feel.

2. That the study shall never be interrupted, and when one man takes the place of his comrade, he is to begin before his comrade has finished, so that the study shall never be interrupted.

3. If a comrade shall be absent on a journey, be it near or far, the remaining comrades shall complete his study, and it shall be reckoned to his account, as if he had studied with them.

4. This study shall not be performed for the purpose of receiving any reward, of whatever nature, not even, God forbid, in thought. But it is to be performed only for the purpose of the "restoration" of the Divine Presence, the "restoration" of all Israel, the people of the Lord, that they may bring joy to their Creator; this study shall entail no reward but the merit of doing more such deeds for the purpose of the unification of the Holy One and the Divine Presence and the "restoration" of all Israel.

5. If (God forbid!) it should happen that the study is interrupted in any manner, either through duress or error or forgetfulness, may such interruption produce no evil impression whatsoever, either on earth or on high. The object of the comrades in prosecuting this study is solely perfection, and not any iniquity whatsoever.

6. The general teachings of our teacher and master, Rabbi Moses Hayyim, which he teaches in the House of Study at noontime daily, may be reckoned as part of this study.

7. Each of the comrades may upon occasion honor one who does not belong to the holy brotherhood by allowing him to study in his place and at his hour; and it shall be considered as if it was one of the holy members doing the reading.

8. The comrades have also undertaken to combine day and night in this study.

9. This study may not be undertaken for the individual perfection of any one of the comrades, nor even in atonement for a sin; its sole meaning is the "restoration" of the Divine Presence, and the "restoration" of all Israel.

10. No one of the comrades shall be assigned any fixed hours for this study, but each shall study as his heart dictates, whenever he is able.

Those who have concluded this sure covenant subscribe hereunto: [signed] Israel Hezekiah Trevis, Isaac Marini, Yekutiel of Vilna, Jacob Israel Forte, Solomon Dina, Michael Terni, Jacob Hayyim Castel Franco.

The following regulations are subjoined to the above, that the new comrades may serve God in truth and with a whole heart. The comrades have taken the following upon themselves:

1. They will perform their service before God in truth, with humility and perfect love, with no expectation of reward for themselves, but only for the sake of the "restoration" of the Divine Presence, and the "restoration" of all Israel. Any reward due them for their fulfillment of the commandments and their good deeds they offer up as a gift to all Israel, to show their love of the holy Presence, and to bring joy to their Creator.

2. The comrades have all united to serve their Creator as one man with a simple and a pure service; when any comrade fulfills any commandment, it shall be considered as fulfilled by all the comrades for the sake of the perfection of the holy Presence. But any sin or fault committed by any single comrade shall not be reckoned to the community at large. For the community has been formed to share perfection, not iniquity.

3. The comrades have taken upon themselves to love one another, and to treat one another kind-heartedly and with brotherly love, and to accept remonstrances from one another with great love, without anger or hate, but in a loving spirit, and in a peaceful manner, so that they may be accepted before the Lord.

4. The comrades have undertaken to keep all the words of the Holy Book [the *Zohar*], which they have learned, a sealed secret, and to reveal nothing except with the permission of the master.

5. They shall all endeavor to come to the study of the *Zohar* every day at whatever hour they find it possible.

6. They are all under obligation to be present, unless detained by an accident, at the holy House of Study every Sabbath after the Afternoon Prayer for instruction by their master, may his light shine.

7. They shall make themselves resolute to perform their service before the Lord, and to pay heed neither to the jesting nor to the laughter of others.

8. The newly consecrated comrades have undertaken to leave the room without objections, in the event that the holy comrades who subscribed to the original regulations find it necessary to transact any business the nature of which cannot be revealed to others in the House of Study.

9. If any person wishes to join their company afterwards, all conditions hitherto obtaining among them shall apply to him as well.

10. The comrades shall guard their mouths and tongues from evil speech, and transact their affairs and fill their needs with all respect and reverence for the holy Presence. Far be it from them to treat lightly any stringent law or usage in Israel. But they will add observance to observance in their wish to remain pure before the Lord God of Israel.

The following are the signatures wherewith they subscribe to these regulations: [signed] Isaiah ben Joseph, Isaiah ben Abraham, Mordecai ben Rephael, Solomon ben Samuel, Moses ben Michael, Abraham ben Jacob, Isaac Hayyim ben Jacob Isaac Katz, Simeon ben Jacob Vita, Mordecai ben Benzion.

These are the statutes of this holy House of Study:

The comrades have taken it upon themselves to speak nothing but what concerns the Torah at the holy table of study of their master, Rabbi Moses Hayyim. Nor shall they linger in conversation in other houses of study, when the hour of study approaches, but they shall seat themselves at the table with reverence and awe. And Rabbi Israel, son of Rabbi Michael, one of the comrades who has been chosen for this special duty, is to raise his voice and announce: "Give glory to the Lord God of Israel!"

Immediately the holy comrades are to bow their heads, and no further word is to escape their lips. They are required to break off their conversation and to remain silent in great awe. If the comrades engage in unnecessary talk, even if it is not the hour of study and they are not at the study table, Rabbi Yekutiel has the right to motion to Rabbi Israel, and Rabbi Israel shall say, "Give glory to the Lord God of Israel!" Then everyone is immediately required to fall silent. If quarrels should break out among the comrades (God forbid) even outside the House of Study, Rabbi Israel can bring any comrade to silence by saying to him, "Give glory to the Lord God of Israel!"—and the comrade must become silent. The other statutes dealing with silence are indeed written in the book of the covenant to which the comrades have subscribed with their own hands.

In their pursuit of saintly living the comrades have taken it upon themselves not to utter any idle word whatsoever anywhere in the whole House of Study. And they have further taken the following upon themselves:

Whenever any comrade shall come into this House of Study, his head should be bowed and he should give greeting with the words, "Let the glory of the Lord endure forever!" Then those sitting in the House of Study will reply, "Blessed be the name of the Lord from this time forth and forever!"

Whenever any comrade leaves the House of Study, he must go backwards, saying, "Praised be the Lord out of Zion!"

When the master Rabbi Moses Hayyim shall enter the House of Study, he shall say, "May the Lord our God be with us!" Then those sitting in the House of Study shall reply, "May the Lord give strength unto his people!"

When the master Rabbi Moses Hayyim shall seat himself at his table, he shall say, "The Lord is high above all nations," and the comrades shall reply, "Who is like unto the Lord our God, that dwelleth so high, that looketh down so low upon the heavens and the earth?" Then Rabbi Israel shall say, "Give glory to the Lord God of Israel!" and the comrades shall immediately bow their heads and fall silent, prepared to study before the holy Presence in fear and trembling and awe. Then Rabbi Yekutiel shall say to all the holy comrades, "Apply your minds!"

The comrades have also taken it upon themselves not to raise their voices in the holy House of Study in the course of their studies, even where they may, except for talmudic dissertation. They have also taken it upon themselves to do nothing in the House of Study without the permission of their master, Rabbi Moses Hayyim, may his light shine.

Furthermore, all the holy comrades, both of the first company and of the second, have agreed to guard themselves closely against speaking any falsehoods, and to make it their endeavor to allow only truth to pass their lips, forever. Consequently, when one comrade shall say to another, "Speak the truth!"—it shall be considered the most binding oath possible.

The comrades have further taken it upon themselves that one of the comrades shall daily recite, first the Ten Commandments and then the Six Hundred and Thirteen Precepts, and then Psalm 119 from verse 9, "Wherewithal shall a young man keep his way pure," until the end of the section.

They have further taken it upon themselves to read all through the Bible, and some comrades all through the Mishnah, every month.

They have further taken it upon themselves to tithe their days before the Lord in fasting. Every tenth day shall be holy, and one of the comrades shall fast on that day. The comrades are all to fast in rotation.

Further they have taken it upon themselves to perform absolution of all reproaches and absolution of all ill will every month.

The comrades have further added to the regulation concerning the daily study of the holy *Zohar* the provision that they shall study all day until the sixth hour of the night, with the exception of the nights from the close of the Day of Atonement until after the Feast of Booths, and the nights of the fourteenth and the fifteenth of Adar,[32] and also the nights from the day of preparation for the Passover festival until after the festival, and the nights from the day of preparation for the Feast of Weeks until after the festival. Nor are they to study during the nights preceding and following the fast days of the Seventeenth of Tammuz, the Ninth of Ab, and the Day of Atonement. But if the requirements of the hour dictate the necessity of study, the decision is to lie in the hands of the master, Rabbi Moses Hayyim. [. . .]

The Lord has helped them to this point; may he nevermore forsake them, until the Messiah shall come whose coming is proper, unto whom "shall the gathering of the people be" (Gen. 49:10), as it is written, "For then will I turn to the people a pure language, that they may all call upon the name of the Lord, to serve Him with one consent" (Zeph. 3:9); "and the Lord shall be King over all the earth; in that day shall the Lord be One, and His name one" (Zech. 14:9).

VI. The Ways of Good Life

A POET'S ETHICAL COUNSEL

Solomon ibn Gabirol

Solomon ibn Gabirol (see the preface to "The Kingly Crown") wrote two popular works on morals. The one, *Improvement of Moral Qualities,* written in 1045 and translated from the original Arabic into Hebrew by Judah ibn Tibbon (*Tikkun Middot ha-Nefesh*) in 1167, relates human behavior to the five senses and four humors of medieval psychology and avoids references both to metaphysics and to Jewish law. The Hebrew version appeared first in Constantinople about 1550 (as an appendix to Bahya's *Duties of the Heart*), and in Riva di Trento in 1562. The original Arabic text was published by Stephen S. Wise, 1901.

The other work, *Choice of Pearls,* is extant in a Hebrew version (*Mivhar ha-Peninim*); of the Arabic original only two pages survive. The little book is a collection of wise, pithy sayings and ethical aphorisms, culled mainly from Arabic writings. It appeared first in Soncino in 1484, then in Cremona in 1558. A Latin translation was published in 1591, 1612, and 1630; a Yiddish rendition, in 1739.

From *Improvement of Moral Qualities*

The divine Socrates said: "From whom doth disappointment never part? He who seeks a rank for which his ability is too feeble." Again he said, "He who sets himself up as wise will be set down by others for a fool." I hold that bad manners are attributable to superciliousness.

Socrates said, "Aversion is always felt for him who has an evil nature, so that men flee away from him." Aristotle says, "As the beauty of form is a light for the body, so is beauty of charac-

96

ter a light for the soul." Again he said in his testament to Alexander his pupil, "It does not show much nobility of purpose on
the part of a king to lord it over men; [the less so] for one man
over a fellow-man." [. . .]

It is told of Ardeshir, the king, that he gave a book to a man
accustomed to stand at his side, and said unto him, "When thou
seest me become violently angry give it to me," and in the book
[was written], "Restrain thyself, for thou art not God; thou art
but a body, one part of which is on the point of consuming the
other, and in a short while it will turn into the worm and dust
and nothingness."

The greatest riches are contentment and patience. One of
the sages has said, "He who desires of this world only that which
is sufficient for him, will be content with the very least thereof."
Another sage was wont to admonish his son, "He who cannot
bear with one word, will be compelled to listen to many. He
who esteems his rank but slightly, enhances men's estimation of
his dignity." In holding the view that it may be right [at times]
to repudiate this quality, I mean thereby that a man should
not abuse himself before the wicked. With reference to such a case
it is said, "A righteous man, falling down before the wicked, is as
a troubled fountain and a corrupt stream" (Prov. 25:26). It was
said concerning this, "He who deserves [the greatest] compassion
is the wise man lost among fools." In the ethical sayings of
Lokman [we find], "when the noble man forsakes the world, he
becomes humble: the ignoble in forsaking the world becomes
haughty." In the book of al-Kuti [it is said], "Be humble without
cringing, and manly without being arrogant. Know thou that
arrogance is a wilderness and haughtiness a taking refuge therein,
and, altogether, a going astray."

A wise man was asked, "What is intelligence?" and he answered, "Modesty." Again he was asked, "What is modesty?"
and he replied, "Intelligence." This quality, although like unto
meekness and agreeing therewith, is of a nobler rank than the
latter, for it is kindred to intelligence. To every man of understanding the nobility of intellect is patent, for it is the dividing

line between man and beast, in that it masters man's natural impulses and subdues passion. With the help of intelligence man realizes the benefit of knowledge and gets to understand the true nature of things; he comes to acknowledge the oneness of God, to worship his Master, and to bear a striking resemblance to the character of the angels. Since this precious quality is of so noble a kind, it follows that modesty which resembles it is almost equally so. The proof of its being thus related is, that thou wilt never see a modest man lacking intelligence, or an intelligent man devoid of modesty. This being so, man must direct all his efforts to the attainment of this wonderful and highly considered quality. [. . .]

It was said that, "Pudency and faith are interdependent, and either cannot be complete without the other." A poet said, "Keep guard over thy modesty: truly pudency marks the countenance of a nobleman." It is said that "Impudence and a lack of pudency are offshoots of unbelief." He who wishes to acquire pudency should associate with those who are modest with respect to him. An Arab was wont to say, "Pay no regard to any man unless he show thee that he cannot do without thee, even when thou needest him most, so that, if thou sin, he will forgive and act as though he were the sinner; and, if thou wrong him, he will demean himself as though he had been the offender." Another said, "Finally, one learns from the words of prophecy, 'If thou art not pudent, do whatsoe'er thou wilt.'" In the course of a characterization of modesty, the poet said, "Upon him reposes the mantel of piety: and, in truth, a light streams from between his eyes."

Al-fadil says: "By reason of belief and piety, men dwell together for a time. Afterward they are kept together by reason of modesty, pudency, and blamelessness." Aristotle said in his discourse, "As a result of modesty [one's] helpers are multiplied." He was accustomed to say, "In chaste children modesty clearly rules over their countenance." [. . .] A philosopher said, "Modesty asserts itself in the midst of wrath." Again it was said, "The enmity of the modest man is less harmful to thee than the friendship of the fool."

With reference to valor and patience in facing danger, the poet spake: "There came a day in the heat of which some people warmed themselves, but though there was no fire, they acted as if in the fire's midst. But we had patience until the day was done. Likewise, a case of misfortune can be brought to a close only through patience."

Among the things which have been said in order to encourage the use of valor is: "Crave death, and life will be granted thee." The Arabs were accustomed to call the man of valor "safe." Among the things which have been said on the emboldening of the spirit in combat is the word of the poet: "I went to the rear to preserve my life [in battle], but I found that I could not preserve my life unless I went forward."

From *Choice of Pearls*

Love

If to his complete love for thee one adds good advice, do thou add to thy pure love for him the self-imposed duty of listening to him.

When the roots [of love] are deeply set in the heart, the branches manifest themselves upon the tongue; and true love can only manifest itself to thee from a perfect heart.

The sage was asked, "What is love?" He replied, "The mutual attraction of hearts and their close association."

The eye of a needle is not narrow for two friends, but the world is not wide enough for two enemies.

Wouldst thou know who is thy friend and who thine enemy, note what is in thine heart.

Who cast his troubles upon thee but withheld from thee his happiness, believe not in his love.

The sage was asked, "Whom lovest thou most?" He replied, "The person whose kindnesses towards me are many; otherwise it is the person towards whom my sins are many [and he forgave me]." [. . .]

Give freely to thy friend of thy soul and wealth, to thine

acquaintance of thy kindness and fair words, to everybody affability and friendly greeting, and to thine enemy fairness. Have regard to what thou hast learnt from the divine Law, be pure to all in thine actions, and [take care of] thy reputation with all men. [. . .]

No man has loved me, without my sincerely returning his love for ever; nor can anyone be mine enemy without my praying that the Creator will set him right [towards me]. Nobody confided a secret to me which I disclosed; never have I set my hand to anything which was not honorable; nor have I consented to anything and then retracted, even if it involved the loss of all my wealth.

Silence

If I speak, I may experience regret, but should I not speak, I shall not experience regret.

If I utter a word, it becomes my master; but should I not utter it, I am its master.

I am better able to retract what I did not say than what I did say.

What use is it to me to speak a word which, if it be repeated against me, may do me injury, but if unrepeated would not be of advantage to me!

Sometimes a word may involve the loss of something considerable.

The indolence of silence is better than the indolence of loquacity; die of the disease of silence, but not of the disease of loquacity.

The best worship is silence and hope.

Through silence thou mayest experience one regret, but through loquacity two regrets.

A man's silence is preferable to inopportune speech.

In much silence, reverence develops.

Treasure thy tongue as thou treasurest thy wealth.

Lackest thou instruction, cleave to silence.

The bait by which a man is caught lies concealed beneath his tongue; a man's death is between his cheeks.

The preponderance of speech over intellect leads to deception, that of intellect over speech to blame; but it is good when one graces the other.

When one's words exceed his intellect, they overpower him; but when one's intellect exceeds his words, he overpowers them.

It is related that a man from Arabia entered a company and preserved a lengthy silence. Somebody said to him, "Rightly do they call thee one of the noble men of Arabia." He replied, "My brethren, the portion of a man from his ear belongs to himself, but the portion of a man from his tongue, belongs to others."

Perception

He is not clever who carefully considers a matter after he has stumbled in it, but he who comprehends it and gives it close consideration so as not to stumble.

The summit of intellect is the perception of the possible and impossible, and submission to what is beyond his power.

The clever man, through the words he utters, arrives at the goal of his effort.

Evidence of a man's mind is his choice; and his faith is not perfected until his mind has been perfected.

It is meet for an intelligent man to be aware of his age, guard his tongue, and attend to his business.

What a man writes is an index of his intellect, and his [selection of a] representative is an index of his discrimination.

When the righteousness of a person is being recounted to thee, ask, "What is his mind?"

The mind of a man is hidden in his writings, but through criticism it is brought to light.

SIMPLE PIETY

Judah the Pious

The *Sefer Hasidim* (Book of the Pious), from which the passages that follow are taken, gives an insight into the inner life of the Jewish community in Germany in the twelfth and thirteenth centuries. The work is not a learned system in the manner of the religio-philosophical

books of the Spanish Jews, but a loosely arranged compilation of ut-
terances on practically all aspects of Jewish life and thought. But back
of them all is a definite concept of the *Hasid,* the pious man, the ideal
type of the period. The *Hasid* (a quite different *Hasid* from that of the
Second Commonwealth and talmudic periods) is a man who has with-
drawn from the affairs of the world; leading an ascetic life, he has
achieved equanimity and inner peace; he worships God in utter simplicity of the heart and surrender; his love embraces all that God has
created; he is ready to bear humiliation and insult. This concept of
the conduct of the "Pious men of Germany" (*Haside Ashkenaz*) is
rooted in a mystic concept of God and His relationship to world and
man. I. F. Baer has pointed to the fascinating parallel between Judah
the Pious, chief spokesman of German Hasidim, and Francis of Assisi,
his Christian contemporary.

Most of the material in the *Book of the Pious* comes from Judah
the Pious (died 1217); some was written by his father, Samuel the Pious
(mid-twelfth century); and some originated with Eleazar ben Judah
Rokeah of Worms, Judah's greatest disciple. The compilation was ef-
fected at the end of the thirteenth century and appeared first at Bologna in 1538.

Be not jealous of the man who is greater than thou and
despise none who is smaller than thou.

If thou hast a guest, never speak to him about learned matters unless thou knowest he is able to partake in the conversation.

Never put to shame thy man-servant or thy maid-servant.

The man who is cruel to animals will have to answer for it
on the Day of Judgment, and the very drivers will be punished
for applying the spur too often.

Those who constantly fast are not in the good way. Scribes,
teachers, and workmen are altogether forbidden to inflict penance
upon themselves. If the Holy One, blessed be he, had any particular delight in much fasting, He would have commanded it
to Israel; but, He only asked of them that they should worship
Him in humility.

If a man should ask: "Behold, I have money; shall I buy
a Scroll of the Torah for it or shall I distribute it to the destitute
poor?" Answer him with the words of Isaiah: 'When thou seest
the naked, that thou cover him, and hide not thyself from thine
own flesh' (Isa. 58:7).

If a man sees a non-Jew committing a sin, let him protest
against it if he has the power to do so; for behold, did not the

Holy One, blessed be he, send the prophet Jonah to the people of Nineveh that they may do repentance?

The Holy One, blessed be he, executes the judgment of the oppressed, whether Jew or Christian, hence cheat not anybody.

A brief summary of

ethical rules

Yehiel ben Yekutiel

The simple, modest statement on ethical behavior that follows here was written by a thirteenth-century Roman copyist (among other manuscripts, his copy of the Palestinian Talmud is still preserved) and moralist. His book, *Bet Middot* (Constantinople, 1511), later published under the title *Sefer Maalot ha-Middot* (Cremona, 1556), is based on classical Hebrew sources and, in addition, on Christian ethical writings current at the time.

And now, my children, I shall make brief mention of the various ethical principles so that you may consider them with great care, with the help of God.

Know your Creator who created you *ex nihilo,* who brought you forth from nothingness, who has vouchsafed all good unto you in the past and does it every day. His knowledge implies cleaving unto Him, to follow in His ways, to fulfill his commandments. The service of the Creator has to be rooted in love. All your deeds should be done and your words spoken out of love for Him, not out of an ulterior motif, such as expecting reward or fearing punishment. All must stem from love, just as the Holy One, blessed be he, loves those who love Him and fulfills their desire. My children, love humility, as the Holy One, blessed be he, loves the humble, the meek and those of a broken spirit. Reject the attitude of pride and haughtiness which is a mode hated alike by God and men. Pride prepares many a stumbling-block and those who are haughty fall into snares.

My children, love modesty and thus be protected from sin. The Holy One, blessed be he, created the world in modesty, gave the Torah in modesty; he loves dearly the modest ones and gives them their due reward. Be on your guard against boisterousness and impudence which are but roads to harlotry. Also, love simplicity—God has delight in the simple ones. Whosoever walks in simplicity with God and man is protected from transgression. Reject deception, a trait that leads to lie and fraud—a denial of God who is truth.

My children, love mercy which is one of the divine attributes. The world could not stand had not God brought into it the quality of mercy. He who has mercy with the human creatures brings goodness into the world and earns heavenly mercy. Contrariwise, he who is cruel with people brings wrath even upon himself and upon the world at large and exposes himself to divine retribution.

And, my children, love peace. Wherever is peace there is awe of the divine. Even the realms above are in need of peace, and all the more the lower realms. Even the dead need peace, and all the more those alive. Thus seek peace and pursue it, as the Holy One, blessed be he, loves peace. When He started His work of creation, He occupied himself with creating an object of peace, and that was light. All good blessings and consolations in the sacred writings that the Lord gives Israel conclude on a note of peace. Contrariwise, flee strife which is a very hateful thing in the eyes of God. We find that He may overlook idolatry but will not overlook strife.

HUMILITY

Moses Hayyim Luzzatto

On Luzzatto see the preface to "How to Attain Saintliness." See also "The House of Study in Padua." *Mesillat Yesharim* (Path of the Upright), from which the following is quoted, has become one of the most popular ethico-religious writings in Judaism. It takes its place with such works as *The Book of the Pious* by Judah the Pious, *Duties of the Heart* by Bahya ibn Pakuda, and *The Lamp of Illumination* by Israel ibn al-Nakawa (see "The Sabbath Bride"). The famous talmudic academy (*Yeshivah*) at Slobodka (near Kovno), which emphasized the study of ethics, used Luzzatto's work as a basic text.

Humility means that a man should be wholly persuaded of his unworthiness to be the recipient of praise and glory. A man of this sort will surely find it impossible to consider himself superior to any others. This attitude toward himself he will have not only because he is aware of his failings, but also because he realizes the insignificance of his attainments.

That in the awareness of his shortcomings a man should be humble is self-evident. It is impossible for any man to be altogether without faults, which may be due to nature, to heredity, to accidents, or to his own doings. "For there is not a righteous man upon earth that doeth good, and sinneth not" (Eccles. 7:20). Such defects leave no room for self-esteem, despite the many excellent traits that one may otherwise possess. The defects are sufficient to eclipse the virtues. The possession of learning, for example, makes dangerously for pride and self-esteem, since it is an advantage that accrues wholly to the intellect, which is the highest faculty of the human being. Yet there is no one so learned who does not make mistakes, or who is not in need of learning from his equals, and at times even from his disciples. How, then, shall a man dare to boast of his learning?

The man of understanding will, upon reflection, realize that there is no justification for pride or vainglory, even if he was privileged to become very learned. A man of understanding, who has acquired more knowledge than the average person, has accomplished nothing more than what his nature impelled him to do, as it is the nature of the bird to fly, or of the ox to pull with all its strength. Hence, if a man is learned, he is indebted to natural gifts which he happens to possess. And any one gifted by nature with a mind like his would be just as learned. The man who possesses great knowledge, instead of yielding to pride and self-esteem, should impart that knowledge to those who are in need of it. As Rabbi Johanan ben Zakkai said, "If thou hast learned much Torah, take not any merit, for thereunto wast thou created." [1] If a man is rich, let him rejoice in his portion and help those who are poor; if he is strong, let him help those who are weak, and redeem those who are oppressed. For indeed we are like the servants of a household. Every one of us is appointed to some task and is expected to remain at his post and do the work of the household as well as possible. In the scheme of life there is no room for pride.

So must he conclude whose understanding is sound and unperverted. And insofar as he is firmly and permanently of this mind, he may be called truly humble, for his humility is based on conviction. "How great are those who are lowly in spirit," said our sages.[2] A man of upright heart does not allow himself to be misled by the fact that he possesses good traits. He is fully aware that he is nonetheless unworthy, since he is bound to have some faults. Even the commandments which he succeeded in fulfilling could scarcely have enabled him to attain perfection. What ever good a man possesses is due to the divine grace accorded to him, in despite of the inherent imperfection of his physical nature. He should be grateful to God who has thus been gracious to him, and for this very reason be humble. [. . .]

Moreover, the company of the humble is very sweet, and people find delight in him. He is not given to anger or to strife; he does everything calmly and peacefully. Happy is he who is privileged to possess this virtue; all the wisdom in the world cannot compare with humility.

AT PEACE WITH THE WORLD

Joel ben Abraham Shemariah

The following excerpts from a will of an eighteenth-century Jew of Vilna (first printed in 1799 or 1800) is one of the many expressions of what truly mattered in the secluded Jewish society of the medieval and early modern periods: life according to the commands of the Torah, observance of the sacred seasons, study and prayer, charity and an ethical attitude toward one's neighbor, and—peace with the world, which is the Lord's.

To be at peace with all the world, with Jew and Gentile, must be your foremost aim in this terrestrial life. Content with no man. In the first instance, your home must be the abode of quietude and happiness; no harsh word must be heard there, but over all must reign love, amity, modesty, and a spirit of gentleness and reverence. This spirit must not end with the home, however. In your dealings with the world you must allow neither money nor ambition to disturb you. Forego your rights, envy no man. For the main thing is peace, peace with the whole world. Show all men every possible respect, deal with them in the finest integrity and faithfulness. For Habakkuk summed up the whole Torah in the one sentence: "The righteous shall live by his faith" (Hab. 2:4).

The root of all the commandments consists of the two hundred and forty-eight affirmative and the three hundred and sixty-five negative precepts. But the branches, which include all virtuous and vicious habits, extend into countless thousands of thousands. To specify them is impossible, but the Scriptures have in several places reduced them to general categories. One of these is: "In all thy ways acknowledge Him" (Prov. 3:6). Another: "Keep thy feet in an even path" (ibid., 4:26).

When, in the course of the prayers, you come to the "Sanctification," [3] fulfill the text: "I will be hallowed among the children of Israel" (Lev. 22:32). But you must at the same moment resolve to uphold the duty to love thy neighbor as thyself. For in the "Sanctification" we use the phrase: "We will sanctify Thy name in the world, even as they sanctify it in the highest heavens." We must indeed strive to imitate the angels on high, and as they are in a state of perfect love and unison, such must also be our condition.

It was oft my way at assemblies to raise my eyes and regard those present from end to end, to see whether in sooth I loved everyone among them, whether my acceptance of the duty to love my fellow-men was genuine. With God's help I found that indeed I loved all present. Even if I noticed one who had treated me improperly, then, without a thought of hesitation, without a moment's delay, I pardoned him. Forthwith I resolved to love him. If my heart forced me to refuse my love, I addressed him with spoken words of friendship, until my heart became attuned to my words. So, whenever I met one to whom my heart did not incline, I forced myself to speak to him kindly, so as to make my heart feel affection for him.

What if he were a sinner? Even then I would not quarrel with him, for I wonder whether there exists in this age one who is able to reprove another! On the other hand, if I conceived that he would listen to advice, I drew near to him, turning towards him a cheerful countenance. If, however, I fancied that he would resent my advances, I did not intrude on him. As there is a duty to speak, so is there a duty to be silent.

THE MIDDLE COURSE

Solomon Ganzfried

The *Shulhan Arukh* by Joseph Caro (sixteenth century), a compilation of Jewish Law, came to be accepted as the definitive code in all aspects of life; scholars of the subsequent periods wrote merely commentaries and supplements to the *Shulhan Arukh*. The need for abridgments for the use of laymen and for quick reference was filled by a number of works; the most widely accepted of them has been the *Kitzur Shulhan Arukh* by the Hungarian rabbi, Solomon Ganzfried (1804–1886), first published in 1864. In this manual Ganzfried condensed the first of the four parts of the major code, which deal with practical religious life, adding to it chapters based on other sections of the code, such as laws concerning charity, mourning, marriage, and business; this he supplemented by chapters on ethical conduct, selected mainly from the *Mishneh Torah* by Maimonides. The passages that follow are an abridgment of its *Hilkhot Deot* (Laws Relating to Moral Dispositions).

People differ widely with respect to their natures. There is one of an angry disposition who is always angry, and there is another who is sedate and never becomes angry, or becomes angry once in many years; there is a one who is unduly haughty, and there is another who is unduly humble; one is voluptuary, his soul is never satiated with desire, another possesses a pure heart and has no desire even for small things which are the necessities of life; one possesses an unbounded greed who is not satisfied with all the wealth the world possesses, another one is a shiftless fellow who is satisfied with little which does not even suffice for him, and he does not seek to earn enough for his necessities; one afflicts himself with hunger, keeps on saving, and whatever he eats of his own he does so with grief, another who spends all his money freely; and the same is true with all dispositions and views; e.g., the gay and the melancholy, the villain and the noble, the cruel and the compassionate, the gentle and the hardhearted, and the like.

The good and right path to follow is the middle course to which one should become habituated. He should desire only the things which are requisite for the body, and it is impossible to live without them; neither should a man be too much occupied with his business, but only sufficient to obtain things that are required for the immediate necessities of life; neither should he be tight-fisted too much, nor should he spend his money freely, but should give alms according to his means, and lend liberally to the needful; and he should not be too jocular and gay, nor morose and melancholy, but should be happy all his days with satisfaction and with friendliness. Relating to all other ethical principles also he who adopts the middle course is called a sage.

Pride is an extremely bad vice, and a person is not to become accustomed to it even to the slightest degree, but he should train himself to be humble of spirit. And how can you train yourself to be humble and low of spirit? All your words shall be quietly uttered, your head bent down, your eyes shall look downward and your heart upwards, and every man shall be considered in your estimation as greater than you are; if he is more learned than you, then you must honor him [. . .].

Anger is likewise an extremely bad vice, and it is proper that one should keep away from it, and he should accustom himself not to get angry even at things that would justify anger. But when necessary to exercise his authority over his children and his household, he may pretend to be angry in their presence in order to chastise them, while inwardly he should retain his composure. He who becomes angry it is accounted to him as if he had worshipped idols, and all kinds of Gehenna have dominion over him. The life of those who are wont to become angry is not considered life at all. [. . .] This is the proper path and the

path of the just that they are insulted and do not insult; they
hear themselves reviled, and answer not; they do things for love's
sake and rejoice even when suffering pain.

A man should always cultivate the faculty of silence, and
should converse only on matters concerning Torah, or of the
necessities of life, and even then he should not talk too much.

A man should neither be gay and jocular nor should he be
melancholy, but he should be happy. Neither should a man possess greed for wealth, nor should he go idle; but he should have
a benevolent eye, do less business and engage himself in the study
of the Torah, and he shall be happy with that little which is his
portion.

Perhaps a man will say: "Since envy, voluptuousness and
ambition and their like take a man away from the world, I will
entirely keep away from them even to the extreme," with the
result that he would not partake of meat, nor drink wine, nor
marry a woman, nor live in a comfortable abode, and not put
on respectable clothes, but he will put on sack cloth or the like;
this also is an improper path. Our sages ordered that a man
should abstain himself only from those things which the Torah
forbade us, and he shall not vow abstinence from things which
are permitted. They forbade to torment oneself with fast days
more than is required; and concerning all these things and the
like, King Solomon said: "Be not righteous over much; neither
show thyself over wise: why wouldst thou destroy thyself?" (Eccles.
7:16).

One should not be ashamed of the people who mock him
when engaged in the service of the Lord, blessed be His Name;
nevertheless he should not answer them harshly, in order that
he may not acquire a disposition of being boldfaced, even in matters not concerning the service of God. [. . .]

It is the nature of man to follow his friends and neighbors
and town folks in his actions. Therefore one should associate
himself with the just and stay always with the sages so that one
may learn their actions, and keep away from the wicked who
talk in the dark. And if one dwell in a place where its leaders
are wicked and its inhabitants do not walk in the right path, he

should move away from there to dwell in a place where its inhabitants are just men and follow in the path of the good.

One should associate himself with the learned in order to learn their deeds, as it is written: "And unto Him thou shalt cleave" (Deut. 10:20). Is it then possible for a man to cleave to the Divine Presence? But thus did our sages explain: "Cleave unto the learned in the Torah. Therefore should a man make an endeavor to marry the daughter of a scholar, to give his daughter in marriage to a learned man, to eat and drink with the learned, do business with the learned, and to associate with them in every possible connection, for it is written "And to cleave unto Him" (Deut. 11:22).[4]

VII. The Community of Isra l

THE GOD OF ABRAHAM AND
THE GOD OF ARISTOTLE

Judah ha-Levi

Certain aspects of Judah ha-Levi (see the preface to "Lord Where Shall I Find Thee" are reminiscent of the Moslem mystic and moralist Ghazali: both men attempted to free religion from dependency on philosophy, both emphasized the autonomous aspects of faith. The rationalist philosopher, Ha-Levi theorizes, "seeks Him that he may be able to describe Him accurately"; to the believer, God is an issue of personal concern; not speculation but love motivates his quest (*Kuzari* IV, 13, 16). In the section from the *Kuzari* reprinted below (see the preface to "The Servant of God"), Judah ha-Levi applies to his theory the two Biblical terms for the deity, *Adonai*, Yahve, commonly translated as "the Lord," and *Elohim*, usually rendered as "God." However, what is the basis for religious faith? It is, says Ha-Levi, the revelation on Sinai, an event that took place in the bright light of history and has been remembered as such throughout the ages.

The Kuzari: Now I understand the difference between *Elohim* and *Adonai*, and I see how far the God of Abraham is different from that of Aristotle. Man yearns for *Adonai* as a matter of love, taste, and conviction; whilst attachment to *Elohim* is the result of speculation. A feeling of the former kind invites its votaries to give their life for His sake, and to prefer death to His absence. Speculation, however, makes veneration only a necessity as long as it entails no harm, but bears no pain for its sake. I would, therefore, excuse Aristotle for thinking lightly about the observation of the law, since he doubts whether God has any cognizance of it.

The Master: Abraham bore his burden honestly, viz., the

112

life in Ur of the Chaldees, emigration, circumcision, the removal of [his son] Ishmael, and the distress of the sacrifice of Isaac, because his share of the Divine Influence had come to him through love, but not through speculation. He observed that not the smallest detail could escape God, that he was quickly rewarded for his piety and guided on the right path to such an extent that he did everything in the order dictated by God. How could he do otherwise than deprecate his former speculation? The sages explain the verse: "And He brought him [Abraham] forth abroad" (Gen. 15:5) as meaning: "give up thy horoscopy!" [1] That is to say, He commanded him to leave off his speculative researches into the stars and other matters, and to follow faithfully the object of his inclination, as it is written: "Taste and see that the Lord is good" (Ps. 34:9). [. . .] He who follows the divine law, follows the representatives of this view. His soul finds satisfaction in their teachings, in spite of the simplicity of their speech and ruggedness of their similes. This is not the case with the instructions of philosophers, with their eloquence and fine teachings, however great the impressiveness of their arguments. The masses do not follow them, because the human soul has a presentiment of the truth.

The Kuzari: I see thee turning against the philosophers, attributing to them things of which just the opposite is known. Of a person who lives in seclusion, and acts rightly, it is said, he is a philosopher, and shares the views of philosophers. Thou deprivest them of every good action.

The Master: Nay, what I told thee is the foundation of their belief, viz., that the highest human happiness consists in speculative science and in the conception by reason and thought of all intelligible matters. [. . .] This cannot, however, be obtained except by devoting one's life to research and continual reflection, which is incompatible with worldly occupations. For this reason they renounced wealth, rank, and the pleasure of children, in order not to be distracted from study. As soon as man has become acquainted with the final object of the knowledge sought for, he need not care what he does. They do not fear God for the sake of reward, nor do they think that if they steal or murder that they will be punished. They recommend good and dissuade from evil in the most admirable manner from the point of view of propriety and praiseworthiness, and in order to resemble the Creator who arranged everything so perfectly; they have contrived laws, or rather regulations without binding force, and which may be over-ridden in times of need. The law of the Torah, however, is not so, except in its social parts, and the law itself sets down those which permit exceptions and those which do not.

The Kuzari: The light [of Israel] of which thou speakest has now gone out without hope of its being re-kindled. It has completely disappeared, and no one is able to trace it.

The Master: It is only extinguished for him who does not see us with an open eye, who infers the extinction of our light from our degradation, poverty, and dispersion, and concludes from the greatness of others, their conquests on earth and their power over us, that their light is still burning.

The Kuzari: I will not use this as an argument, as I see two antagonistic religions prevailing, although it is impossible that the truth should be on two opposite sides. It can only be on one or on neither. You have explained to me in connection with the verse: "Behold My servant shall prosper" (Isa. 52:13), that humility and meekness are evidently nearer to the Divine Influence than glory and eminence. The same is visible in these two religions. Christians do not glory in kings, heroes and rich people, but in those who followed Jesus all the time, before his faith had taken firm root among them. They wandered away, or hid themselves, or were killed wherever one of them was found, suffered disgrace and slaughter for the sake of their belief. These are the people in whom they glory, whose ministers they revere, and in whose names they build churches. In the same way did the friends of Islam bear much poverty, until they found assistance. In these, their humility and martyrdom do they glory; not in the princes who boasted of their wealth and power, but rather in those clad in rags and fed scantily on barley bread. Yet they did so in the utmost equanimity and devotion to God. Had I ever seen the Jews act in a like manner for the sake of God, I would place them above the kings of David's house. For I am well aware of what thou didst teach me concerning the words: "with him also that is of a contrite and humble spirit" (Isa. 57:15), as well as that the light of God only rests upon the souls of the humble.

The Master: Thou art right to blame us for bearing our exile without compensation. But if I think of prominent men amongst us who could escape this degradation by a word spoken lightly, become free men, and turn against their oppressors, but do not do so out of devotion to their faith: is not this the way to obtain intercession and remission of many sins. [. . .] Besides this, God has a secret and wise design concerning us, which should be compared to the wisdom hidden in the seed which falls into the ground, where it undergoes an external transformation into earth, water and dirt, without leaving a trace for him who looks down upon it. It is, however, the seed itself which transforms earth and water into its own substance, carries it from one degree to another, until it refines the elements and transfers them into something like itself, casting off husks, leaves, etc. and allowing the pure core to appear, capable of bearing the Divine Influence. The original seed produced the tree bearing fruit resembling that from which it had been produced. In the same manner the Torah of Moses transforms each one who comes after him, though he may externally reject it. The nations merely serve to introduce and pave the way for the expected Messiah, who is the fruition, and they will all become his fruit. Then, if they acknowledge him, they will become one tree. They will revere the origin which they formerly despised, as we have observed concerning the words: "Behold My servant shall prosper."

THE EVENT ON SINAI

Moses Maimonides

About 1165 the Jewish community in faraway Yemen found itself in a critical situation. The fanatical Shiite ruler of Yemen initiated a forced conversion to Islam and started on a course of persecutions; a recent Jewish convert to Islam propagandized for his new religion; another Jew inaugurated a Messianic movement, with himself as the precursor of the redeemer. The thrice-troubled community turned to Moses Maimonides for guidance. In his *Iggeret Teman* (Epistle to Yemen), written about 1172, Maimonides offered sober arguments against the apostate's contention that the Bible alluded to the rise of Muhammad; he cautioned against premature Messianism, warned against pretenders, but upheld the hope of ultimate redemption. Above all, he expressed the trust that Israel would survive suffering and persecution; the strength for such survival, he stated, comes from realization of the revelation on Sinai. The selection that follows refers to this aspect of the Epistle. The Epistle, written in Arabic, was translated into Hebrew by Samuel ibn Tibbon and others.

The sages, of blessed memory, frequently allude to persecutions in the following manner: "Once the wicked government passed the following decree of persecution," or, "they decreed so and so." After a while God would make the decree null and void by destroying the power which issued it. It was this observation that led the sages to affirm that persecutions are of short duration.

The divine assurance was given to Jacob our father, that his descendants would survive the people who degraded and discomfited them as it is written: "And thy seed shall be like the dust of the earth" (Gen. 28:14). That is to say, although his offspring will be abased like dust that is trodden under foot, they will ultimately emerge triumphant and victorious, and as the simile implies, just as the dust settles finally upon him who tramples upon it, and remains after him, so shall Israel outlive its persecutors.

The prophet Isaiah has long ago predicted that various peoples will succeed in vanquishing Israel and lording over them for some time. But that ultimately God will come to Israel's assistance and will put a stop to their woes and affliction.

We are in possession of the divine assurance that Israel is indestructible and imperishable, and will always continue to be a pre-eminent community. As it is impossible for God to cease to exist, so is Israel's destruction and disappearance from the world unthinkable, as we read, "For I the Lord change not, and ye, O sons of Jacob, will not be consumed." (Malachi 3:6). Similarly, He has avowed and assured us that it is unimaginable that He will reject us entirely even if we disobey Him, and disregard

His behests, as the prophet Jeremiah avers, "Thus saith the Lord: If heaven above can be measured, and the foundations of the earth searched out beneath, Then will I also cast off all the seed of Israel for all that they have done, saith the Lord" (Jer. 31:36). Indeed this very promise has already been given before through Moses our master who says, "And yet for all that, when they are in the land of their enemies, I will not reject them, neither will I abhor them, to destroy them utterly, and to break My covenant with them; for I am the Lord their God" (Lev. 26:44).

Put your trust in the true promises of Scripture, brethren, and be not dismayed at the series of persecutions or the enemy's ascendency over us, or the weakness of our people. These trials are designed to test and purify us so that only the saints and the pious ones of the pure and undefiled lineage of Jacob will adhere to our religion and remain within the fold, as it is written, "And among the remnant are those whom the Lord shall call" (Joel 3:5). This verse makes it clear that they are not numerous, being the descendants of those who were present on Mount Sinai, witnessed the divine revelation, entered into the covenant of God, and undertook to do and obey as is signified in their saying, "we will do, and obey" (Exod. 24:7). They obligated not only themselves but also their descendants, as it is written, "to us and to our children forever." (Deut. 29:28). We have been given adequate divine assurance that not only did all the persons who were present at the Sinaitic revelation believe in the prophecy of Moses and in his Torah, but that their descendants likewise would do so, until the end of time, as it is written, "Lo, I come unto thee in a thick cloud, that the people may hear when I speak with thee, and may also believe thee forever" (Exod. 10:9).

Consequently it is manifest that he who spurns the religion that was revealed at that theophany, is not an offspring of the folk who witnessed it. For our sages have insisted that they who entertain scruples concerning the divine message are not scions of the people that were present on Mount Sinai. May God guard us and you from doubt, and banish from our midst confusion, suspicion, which lead to it.

Now, my brethren, all Israel in the diaspora, it behooves you to hearten one another, the elders to guide the youth, and the leaders to direct the masses. Give your assent to the truth that is immutable and unchangeable, and to the following postulates of a religion that shall never fail. God is one in a unique sense of the term, and Moses is His prophet and spokesman, and the greatest and most perfect of the seers. To him was vouchsafed by God what has never been vouchsafed to any prophet before him, nor will it be in the future. The entire Torah was divinely revealed to Moses of whom it was said, "with him do I speak mouth to mouth" (Num. 12:8). It will neither be abrogated nor superseded, neither supplemented nor abridged. Never shall it be supplanted by another divine revelation containing positive and negative duties. Keep well in mind the revelation on Sinai in accordance with the divine precept to perpetuate the memory of this occasion and not to allow it to fall into oblivion. Furthermore we were enjoined to impress this event upon the minds of our children, as it is written, "Only take heed to thyself, and keep thy soul diligently, lest thou forget the things which thine eyes saw, and lest they depart from thy heart all the days of thy life; but make them known unto thy children and thy children's children" (Deut. 4:9).

It is imperative, brethren, that you make this great event on Sinai appeal to the imagination of your children. Proclaim at public gatherings its momentousness. For this event is the pivot of our religion, and the proof which demonstrates its veracity. Evaluate this phenomenon at its true importance for Scripture has pointed out its significance in the verse, "For ask now of the days past, which were before thee, since the day that God created man upon the earth, and from the one end of heaven unto the other, whether there hath been any such thing as this great thing is, or hath been heard like it?" (Deut. 4:32).

Remember, my brethren in this covenant, that this great, incomparable and unique historical event, is attested by the best of evidence. For never before or since, has a whole nation witnessed a revelation from God or beheld His splendor. The purpose of all this was to confirm us in the faith so that nothing can change it, and to reach a degree of certainty which will sustain us in these trying times of fierce persecution and absolute tyranny, as it is written, "for God is come to test you" (Exod.

20:17). Scripture means that God revealed Himself to you thus in order to give you strength to withstand all future trials. Now do not slip nor err, be steadfast in your religion, and persevere in your faith and its duties.

THE PROSELYTE

Moses Maimonides

Although Judaism, after the loss of Jerusalem, refrained from missionary zeal, it always considered itself a universal religion; periods of complete exclusivity were relatively few. Individuals who, like Abraham of old, found their way to the faith of Israel were welcomed in the community; they were included in the prayer for God's mercy. There are known examples of proselytes who shared the fate of the imperiled community and ended their life as martyrs. The text that follows is a *responsum* by Maimonides (see "Moses Maimonides") addressed to a proselyte who invited an authoritative opinion on his status.

I received the question of the wise and erudite scholar, Obadiah the proselyte. You ask as to whether you, being a proselyte, should utter the prayers: "Our God and God of our fathers; Who has separated us from the nations; Who has brought us out of Egypt," and the like.

Pronounce all prayers as they are written and do not change anything. Your prayer and blessing should be the same as that of any other Israelite, regardless of whether you pray in private or conduct the service of the community. The explanation is as follows: Abraham, our father, taught mankind the true belief and the oneness of God, repudiating idolatry; through him many of his own household and also others were guided "to keep the way of the Lord, to do righteousness and justice" (Gen. 18:19). Thus he who becomes a proselyte and confesses the oneness of God, as taught in the Torah, is a disciple of Abraham, our father. Such persons are of his household. Just as Abraham influenced his contemporaries through his word and teaching, so he leads to belief all future generations, through the testament he gave to his children and his household. In this sense Abraham is the father of his descendants who follow his ways, and of his disciples, and of all the proselytes.

You should therefore pray, "Our God and God of our fathers," for Abraham is also your father. In no respect is there a difference between us and you. And certainly you should say, "Who has given unto us the Torah," because the Torah was given to us and the proselytes alike, as it is said: "As for the congregation, there shall be one statute both for you and for the stranger who lives with you; as ye are, so shall the stranger be before the Lord. One law and one ordinance shall be both for you and for the stranger that lives with you" (Num. 15:16f.). Keep in mind that most of our ancestors who left Egypt were idol worshipers; they mingled with the Egyptian heathen and imitated their ways, until God sent Moses, our teacher, the master of all the prophets. He separated us from these nations, initiated us into the belief in God, us and all the proselytes, and gave us one Law.

Do not think little of your origin: we are descended from Abraham, Isaac, and Jacob, but your descent is from the Creator, for in the words of Isaiah, "One shall say: 'I am the Lord's'; and another shall call himself by the name of Jacob" (Isa. 44:5).

BENEDICTION WHEN

FACING MARTYRDOM

Medieval Jewish chronicles, especially those from Central Europe, are replete with reports of individuals and communities that, when faced by the choice between death and apostasy, chose martyrdom. The saints of the Maccabean period, the defenders of Masada, Rabbi Akiba and other sages of the era of the Hadrianic persecution, offered examples for the "Sanctification of the Name" (*Kiddush ha-Shem*), as such martyrdom was termed. German Jewry gave rise to a special benediction for such occasions. The appended quotation is from a *responsum* by Meir of Rothenburg, a thirteenth-century German rabbi.

> Blessed art Thou, O Lord, our God, king of the universe,
> who has sanctified us by Thy commandments
> and bade us love Thy glorious and awful Name
> Who was and is and will be,

with all our heart and all our soul,
and to sanctify Thy Name in public.
Blessed art Thou, O Lord,
who sanctifies Thy Name among the many.

Once a person has made the decision to die for the sanctification of the divine Name, then people may inflict upon him all imaginable pain yet he will remain numb. That this is indeed the case is proven by the fact that no man can touch fire without crying out at the slightest contact, even if he decides to keep back his cry; yet we know that the martyrs do not cry.

WHY CATASTROPHES COME

Solomon Alami

On March 15, 1391, anti-Jewish riots broke out in Seville and spread over Castile; Jewish quarters were sacked, synagogues ruined, lives destroyed. Conversion was a possible escape, but the greed for Jewish wealth was greater than the desire for converts. Christians who were discovered sheltering Jews were punished. By the time passions subsided, some seventy communities had been attacked and over seventy thousand Jews had perished. Spanish Jewry was broken.

An eyewitness of the persecutions, Solomon Alami, scholar and community leader, addressed in 1415, his *Iggeret Musar* (Epistle of Ethical Admonition) to one of his disciples. In the spirit of Biblical prophecy, Alami interpreted the events of 1391 as occasioned by Israel's moral and religious failings. Only honest self-criticism and radical improvement of one's inner life will lead to a better future, he counseled.

The *Iggeret Musar* (the concluding part of which is here reprinted) was first printed in 1510 in Constantinople and went through several editions. In 1946, A. M. Haberman edited the Parma manuscript of the Epistle from a photostat in the Schocken Library in Jerusalem.

"Rejoice not, O Israel! Exult not like the peoples" (Hosea 9:1). Forget not the evil decrees hurled against us since the year 4908 [1148], when the Almohades made themselves masters in Spain and persecuted our communities and seats of learning. A few years later destruction came to the eastern countries. Moses Maimonides lived at that time; both in his youth and in his old age he witnessed the hardships of his people. Because of our many sins the community of Lucena was reduced to ruins, Lucena "a city and a mother in Israel," a center of learning for many generations.

The next period brought the expulsion from England [1290], from France [1306], and from other realms. From that time on we sank deeper and deeper, and our Torah was delivered unto flames. Our wives and daughters were defiled; the others were deprived of their honor. Deep calls to deep, calls for sword, famine, and captivity. Death seems preferable to such a life. Very recently, in the year 5151 [1391], we suffered much destruction in all the provinces of Castile and in the kingdom of Catalonia. Our communities in Aragon, too, were gravely tried and had to endure famine and thirst, homelessness and the death of many children.

This we cannot forget. But if we ask ourselves why all this happened to us, then we have to accept the truth: we ourselves are at fault. God is just and righteous and it was in His power to help us. We and our own iniquities caused this evil to happen.

Our sages were jealous of each other and disrespectful. Their main attention was given to minor details, to novel explanations, clever elucidations. They did not pay much attention to the Book before them, and its counsel of justice and sanctity. There was much quarreling among the wise men. What the one proved, the other disproved; what the one forbade, the other permitted. Thus the Torah, which was one, fell apart. People did not feel obliged to follow such blind leadership, and no wonder.

Then there were those scholars who attempted to interpret the Scriptures in the Greek manner and clothe it in a Greek dress. They believed that Plato and Aristotle had brought us more light than Moses our master.

Now, if a man should not be able to "live by his faith," why should he suffer death for it and endure the yoke and the shame of dispersion among the nations? It serves no good purpose to quote Scriptures as support for philosophical opinions; the way of reason and the way of faith are too far apart and will never meet. No prophets are found among the followers of Aristotle, while many prophets, young and old, arose in Israel's ancient land. Those who read a few columns in a book of Greek philosophy will soon tear to shreds the scroll of the Torah, scoff at the laws, and dispute the validity of tradition. They will never know the thought of the Lord, never understand His counsel.

The next in line of decadence were the leaders of the communities and those favored and trusted by the kings. Their riches and high position made them forsake humility and forget the general misery. "Israel hath forgotten his Maker and builded palaces" (Hosea 8:14). They acquired costly wagons and horses, dressed in precious garments; the wives and daughters of these leaders carried themselves like princesses, and proudly displayed their jewelry.

They gave up study and industry, and cultivated idleness, vainglory, and inordinate ambition. Law and wisdom, our ancient heirloom, no longer counted for them. Everyone chased after coveted positions; envy estranged a man from his fellow and they didn't mind denouncing one another before the Court. Little did they realize that their souls were the price they paid and that they faced a bitter end. They oppressed the wretched, and the poor became the victims of their tyranny. The burden of taxation they shifted to the poorer class. In the end, the Court itself found them despicable and removed them from their power. No Jew was left who could represent the cause of the people before the king and say a good word in behalf of a fellow Jew in need. Down to the ground fell the glory of the "mighty." It is time to wake up from the slumber of foolishness.

There are still other reasons for our miseries and hardships. Our heart lacks faith and modesty; we refuse to admit our failings; our good deeds lack sincerity; our prayers are light-hearted. If you take from your face the mask of hypocrisy and if you have eyes to see you will recognize that the majority of our nation have abandoned truth.

The Sabbath is being profaned and those who try to voice admonition are quickly silenced; no one likes the moralist. The seer shall not see. "Speak to us smooth things, prophesy illusions" (Isaiah 30:10).

There are many among us who repudiate the belief in divine providence, and only few who retain the idea of reward and punishment.

There is no communal spirit among us. People quarrel over trifles. Strict honesty is no longer observed; there is over-reaching, and deceit is practiced even in dealing with the people at large: thus do we desecrate in their midst the Holy Name of our God.

Who among us is ready to give up the love of the world and to consider his end? Who will repent his treason and return to his God with a perfect heart? Who will again dedicate himself to the Covenant of Israel, and in his youth or, later, in his maturity enter the service of his God? Not one man will you find among us who will seriously reflect on the fall of our own kingdom, the decline of wisdom, the cessation of prophecy, the destruction of our Temple, and the desecration of the Name of God who is our glory. Not one will divest himself of his ornaments in mourning over the disgrace of the Torah, the mar-tyrdom of our sages—events which our eyes have seen and our ears have heard—the loss of our congregation and our homes.

Surrounded by people suffering persecution, expulsion, forced conversion, some there are who manage to hold banquets, listen to music, and imitate the Gentiles in their clothes and hairdress.

The nation in whose land we sojourn offers tithes and gen-erous contributions for the support of their scholars, and this strengthens their religion; princes and noblemen desire to dedi-cate their children to the service of the church. Our own emi-nences, on the other hand, keep their sages on bread and water; no one can maintain even this meager subsistence without suf-fering humiliation; utterly disgraceful is the way in which the secretaries in charge of charity are dealt with. Our notables are not at all eager to have their sons become scholars. The word of God is not wanted by these proud men. Seeing the low state of scholars, simple people, too, prefer to let their sons learn the humblest of crafts rather than enter into the humiliating world of learning.

If you look around you in a place of worship where a

teacher expounds the Law, you will find the rich people asleep, the others engaged in idle talk, and the women in chatter. Should the speaker reprimand them the situation would grow worse. Here we could learn much from our Christian neighbors, who listen quietly and reverently to their preacher, and who are responsive to his scolding; no one will nap while he delivers his sermon.

Much ado is made about charity; the rich talk a lot and do little; what they pledge on the Sabbath they regret on Sunday; the collectors call on them ten times before they receive the promised donation. Woe unto the poor who depend on their kind hearts. The prophet had them in mind when he said: "And He looked for justice, but behold violence; for righteousness, but behold a cry" (Isaiah 5:7).

Often I hear you, my brethren, complaining about having been snubbed. It serves you right. Rarely do you yourselves respect each other. Quite often is the wise man excluded from your circles; instead, you welcome dandies and bearers of titles. In Andalusia I knew rich Jews who never invited anyone but equally rich Jews; they played hosts to monks, imams, government officials, dance masters, court contractors, comedians, circus proprietors, doubtful characters of all colors and creeds; but no Jewish scholar was ever invited, no serious author, no teacher of the ancient nobility of Israel, Jewish issues are discredited and renounced; people forget that this leads to the rejection of the human.

The imitation of the customs of the ruling Church assumed frightful proportions, especially in Mallorca. Some Jews avoided speaking the word "Jew" in the presence of Christian servants. Presents were exchanged on Christmas, not on Purim as Scripture and ancestral usage decreed. Parties were tendered on Easter; Passover, the holiday commemorating Israel's liberation from slavery, was treated like a weekday. The Sabbath was no longer observed, at least not as a day of joyous rest. Grace after meals was interrupted in honor of any Christian acquaintance who entered the door. The daughters of rich families could no longer read Hebrew. Indeed, not much remained of these families; in my youth most of them had already joined the Church.

Others were satisfied with preserving the outer forms of
religion while disregarding its inner content. On a day of peni-
tence they got rid of their prayers but not of their vices. They
used adulatory words in the street; at home you heard only in-
cessant squabbling and quarreling. There is no understanding
between father and son; mothers are despised by their "educated"
daughters. In the prayers on the Day of Atonement, the only true
things are the listings of sins; the transgressions enumerated must
sound familiar.

Much time was needed for the pursuit of pleasure, especially
by the rich families of exuberant Seville; no time was left in
which to pay attention to the poor, to friends, to teachers, or
scholars. Festivities and banquets ate up leisure, money, and—
mercy. Luxurious living bred egoism, arrogance, a negative attitude to the Torah of our fathers, and a callousness towards
Israel's needs.

Among the scholars, teachers of the laws, authors of books,
you find vanity and contentiousness competing with scholarship
and piety. Many study in order to get a position, they teach
for the fee; pretense rates higher than quiet work; the handsome
speaker displaces the solid one, the flatterer pushes aside the
honest man. Simple teachings are made complicated by unpro-
ductive sophistry, just in order to parade something "novel."
Little men, poor of mind, write books of no use to anybody; they
carry copies to their sponsors, who give them some money; they
should be ashamed to disgrace our ancient writings.

Worse, of course, is the half-educated crowd, philosophers
in their bedrooms who, blind to true knowledge, believe that
the world stands and falls on their doings. What they read but
don't understand, they reject as of no value; what they do grasp,
they have known all along. In Portugal, I found a whole class of
semi-scholars who had put their noses into various books; yet before they had time to learn anything they already felt qualified
to judge others. They appeared as the protagonists of whatever
was being much talked about; they memorized pertinent quotations from fashionable philosophers and from writers in vogue;
they were the heralds of every newest craze. Recently, in Elvas, a

man was ready to found a society for the support of some latest rage, sure of the acclaim of the young ladies.

The right way is to listen to the teachings of the prophets and of the sages of old; to advance humility, loving-kindness, and virtue; to love Israel and its Torah, and to be forbearing with the faults of our brethren. May they learn to act out of true fear of God and not out of worldly vanity. If people could be taught to restrain their desires, to be content, and to trust in divine providence, then much of what saddens my heart would be overcome and our good would increase with the good of man. May what happened to our philosophers in Catalonia not happen to us: their strength of faith was surpassed by simple people, by women and children.

The promise of our Scriptures upholds me; so great is the power of this promise, so deep the fountain of our hope, that I do not despair of the future of Israel, which one day will recognize its failings and receive forgiveness.

THE PARABLE OF

THE PRECIOUS STONES

Solomon ibn Verga

The work *Shevet Yehudah* (The Rod of Judah) by Solomon ibn Verga and his son Joseph is a compilation of popular traditions, reports on Jewish persecutions in the Middle Ages, religious disputations between Jews and Christians, and an inquiry into the causes of anti-Jewish sentiment, especially in Spain. The elder ibn Verga lived at the time of the expulsion of the Jews from Spain, went to Portugal, became a Marrano, and fled the country in 1506; Joseph emigrated as a Marrano to Turkey, where he completed his father's work. It is dedicated to a relative, Judah ibn Verga, whose records the authors may have used.

The parable reprinted below is testimony to a spirit of religious liberalism with an admixture of philosophic skepticism. It first appeared in Italian collections of anecdotes and stories (*novelle*), e.g., in Boccaccio's *Decamerone*. Later we find it in G. E. Lessing's *Nathan the Wise* (1779), the dramatic poem on tolerance.

The book was first printed in Turkey about 1550; it later appeared in Spanish (Amsterdam, 1640), and in Latin (Amsterdam, 1651).

Once, King Don Pedro the Elder had a Jewish sage, Ephraim ben Sancho, brought before him. He asked him: "Which religion is, in your opinion, the better one, the religion of Jesus or yours?" Answered the sage: "My religion is better for me, in view of my condition: I was a slave in Egypt and God has miraculously delivered me from there; but your religion is better for you, as it was always the dominant one." Said the king: "My question refers to the religions themselves, without regard to their adherents."

The sage answered: "After three days' deliberation I shall give answer to my lord—if this is acceptable." The king agreed.

After three days the sage returned and appeared to be perturbed and in a dejected mood. The king inquired about the reason for this state of mind and the sage answered: "I have been slandered today without having done anything wrong and I come to you, our Lord, for your judgment. This is what happened. A month ago my neighbor went on a long journey; in order to comfort his two sons he left them two precious stones. Now the two brothers came to me to inquire about the value of the stones and the difference between them. I told them: 'Who would know this better than your father, the *lapidario*, who is a great authority in the field of precious stones; send to him and he will tell you the truth.' Thereupon they hit me and slandered me."

Said the king: "They have done wrong and deserve to be punished."

Replied the sage: "O our king, do notice what you yourself just said. Behold, Esau and Jacob[2] were brothers each of whom received a precious stone. Now, our lord had asked which is the better one; may he send a messenger to our Father in heaven, the great *lapidario;* he will surely explain the difference between the two."

EQUALITY

Jacob ben Abba Mari Anatoli

The quotation that follows is from *Malmad ha-Talmidim,* a collection of expositions on the Pentateuch in which the author, Jacob ben Abba Mari Anatoli (France-Italy, thirteenth century) demanded a thorough knowledge of the sacred texts and their backgrounds as a precondition for piety and religious practice. Anatoli was a physician, preacher, translator, admirer of Maimonides' philosophy, and opposed to a narrow view of Judaism; in his sermons he quotes Plato, Aristotle, Averroes and Christian contemporaries, Michael Scotus and Emperor Frederick II (who sponsored his translating activity).

With regard to [the idea of] man having been created in the image of God [it must be said that] all peoples are equal and it cannot be maintained that only the people of Israel has been granted a soul [. . .]. In truth, all men are created in the image of God and this is the will of God. Israel has been distinguished as the recipient of the revealed teachings. By its dedication to them Israel is better prepared to represent this quality. Yet a Gentile who dedicates himself to Torah is greater than a Jew who turns his back upon it.

THE HEBREWS
AMONG THE NATIONS

Simone Luzzatto

Simone (Simhah) ben Isaac Luzzatto (1583–1663), rabbi in Venice, planned a work on the beliefs and customs of Judaism; a treatise on the status of the Jews among the nations, with emphasis on the conditions in Venice, was to become an appendix to this work. The larger plan probably never materialized, but the treatise is extant: *Discorso circa il stato degli Ebrei* (1638), dedicated to the Venetian doge and the Senate. This dedication explains the apologetic nature of the treatise; however, the author displays impartiality and discusses both Jewish merits and faults with equal candor. His approach is historical and socio-economical, rather than theological. (As a theologian, Luzzatto was opposed to mysticism and to Messianic speculations, and advocated a middle course between reason and revelation).

Peoples and nations have their days numbered no less than all other sublunary things. Once they have reached the very apogee of their grandeur, their plunge into the abyss of oblivion is not far:

> *Muoiono le Città, muoiono i Regni*
> *Copre is fasti e le pompe arena e herba*

> (Cities die, Kingdoms die
> And under sand and weeds their pomp and ostentation lie).

Since things come to their end in one of two ways, either by decaying utterly, or by transforming themselves, i.e., retaining their essence while breaking into fragments and losing their simple configuration (as in the instance of shattered glass and divided waters), so, in the same wise, are nations unmade and their existence concluded. Chaldea, Persia, Greece, Rome, and all the Gentilic nations were utterly abolished; they were dissolved and transformed by new metamorphoses; only the names of some of these have come down to us; and of others, only an occasional fragment of their history, which has been preserved for us like stray timbers from some shipwreck.

The Hebrew nation did not undergo such mutation and chance, but rather was shattered and divided into an infinity of pieces, and dispersed over the orb. Yet it retained in great measure its essential identity. We cannot doubt that of itself it could not have summoned up the strength to stay the ravening appetite of time, successfully to withstand its fierce onset over a space of 1600 years; but that it depended upon the will of Divine Majesty to preserve it, for ends best known to Itself.

Though captivity and dispersion be the worst scourge that can befall a people or nation, rendering it lowly and abject, and the scorn and mockery of others, it is nonetheless a sovereign remedy for its duration and preservation, for it relieves the ruling

Princes of their envy and suspicion, and the distracted people
of pride and vanity, making them to become humble and com-
pliant. [. . .]

The diaspora not only served them [the Hebrews] well by
rendering them obedient to those more mighty than they, but it
saved them from dogmatic new fangles, which cannot easily penetrate and invade the whole of the nation, since the integrant parts
are divided and dispersed.

As for the number of Hebrews, it cannot be precisely ascer-
tained, for there is not even a trustworthy record at hand, of the
places they inhabit. As for the Ten Tribes [of Israel] who were
led into captivity by Shalmaneser before the destruction of the
First Temple,[3] no certain news of them is to be had, though by
now the world has been thoroughly investigated and discovered.

Beginning with the Eastern parts, we know that under the
king of Persia a great number of Hebrews have found asylum and
a small measure of liberty. In the Turkish state is the principal
domicile of the nation, not only because they have long been
there, but also because the vast concourse of Hebrews dismissed
from Spain found their way thither. The cause of such an influx
rested, first and foremost, on liberty to practice their religion, for
the Turk is tolerant toward alien faiths. Also, because there is
to be found there an infinite quantity of Greeks, who also practice alien rite; hence, no reflection is made on those of the
Hebrews. Beyond this, they are allowed to own houses and lands,
to lend money, and to exercise whatsoever other profession. No
obstacle is placed in the way of owning lands, since there is no
nobility. Though the Greeks own a considerable portion of lands,
most of them busy themselves with the crafts, whilst the Turks
apply themselves to the militia and government of the people;
whence it comes about that no occasion is given for hatred and
conflict.

It might be supposed that like customs of circumcision must
occasion a certain friendly correspondence. Such is not the case,
for experience has shown that peoples whose religious practices
are in part alike, in part dissimilar, are less congenial to one
another than those absolutely divided and distinct therein. In
Constantinople and Salonica, there is a greater number of them

[the Hebrews] than in other cities. It is thought that these two cities alone have some 80,000; and it is estimated that in the Turkish Empire, they count more than 1,000,000. In the Holy Land and in Jerusalem, in particular, there come annually not only a considerable number of Hebrews from all the nations of the world, but also vast sums in annual revenues which are offered there for the nourishing of the poor and the support of academies.

In Germany, under the Emperor, are also a considerable number, but many more in Poland, Russia, and Lithuania, where there are academies and universities whither thousands of youths repair to study the civil and canon law of the Jews. In those regions they are freely empowered to pronounce upon any difference or dispute, whether civil or criminal, that may arise amidst the nation.

In the dominions separated from the Roman Church, Jews do not reside for the most part. It is a certainty that the Hebrew nation inclines more toward the Roman opinion than that of others. The Jews hold that Holy Writ is in many passages impenetrable without the light of tradition, by which last they set great store, as I have already shown. Further, they believe that good works are very important in the sight of God, and they practice them diligently, though ever joining them to faith. They affirm free will and judge it to be the chief article of their belief. They affirm, similarly, that the merits of others may be a prop to those deficient in virtue; hence, the living pray for the dead. They believe the purification of the penitent to be real—not putative, as Calvin hath held. And though the word Purgatory rarely figures in their authors, they make a three-fold distinction among souls: the beatified, those condemned to finite temporal punishment, and those eternally so condemned; for they hold that God absolves guilt yet exacts the penalty. Their sermons are in Hebrew, not in the vernacular.

In the Low Countries they are treated with great charity and affection, notably in Amsterdam, Rotterdam, and Hamburg. They are lands where mercantile pursuits are so flourishing that all may find an asylum there.

In the Western lands there remains only Italy; and on the

African littoral, the kingdoms of Fez and Morocco. As for Italy,
they are universally protected and favored by princes; and their
rights and privileges are inalterably respected. These are things
under the eyes of all, and I speak no further of Italy. I believe I
may give 25,000 as their number.

In Morocco, Fez, and other nearby cities not subject to the
sway of the Turk, there are a great number, many of them having
removed thither from Castile and Portugal because of the short
distance.

A vast number of Jews are reputed to inhabit the interior
countries of Africa, but about these regions so little is known that
no number can be determined with any certainty.

Though divided, riven, and dismembered, the opinions and
dogmas of the whole of this nation are uniform, the ceremonial
rites identical, and in certain non-essential things barely dissimilar.

The foregoing is what I have been moved to report concerning this nation and those aspects thereof which appertain to the
interest of the princes and peoples who harbor it; in particular,
to the Most Serene Venetian Republic, which receives the Jew
within her state with such benignity and protects him with
wonted justice and clemency, showing by her every action how
she detests and abhors that unjust and monstrous sentiment
voiced by the impious statesman Photinus to the young and
inexperienced King Ptolemy—as Lucan[4] sings:

> Dat poenas laudata fides, cum susitinet inquit
> Quos fortuna premit, fatis accede deisque,
> Et cole felices, miseros fuge, sidera terra,
> Ut distant, et flamma mari, sic utile recto.

(We praise loyalty but it pays the price when it supports those whom
Fortune crushes. Take the side of destiny and Heaven, and court the
prosperous but shun the afflicted. Expediency is far from the right as
the stars from earth or fire from water.)

The which utterance brought about the betrayal of the greatest
captain of that century; I mean the murder of Magnus Pompey,
whose decapitation strangled and severed the neck of Roman liberty, and reared a monument of eternal infamy to him who as-

sented to that execrable utterance. The admonitory prophecy (as feigned by Virgil) and uttered by a most prudent father to a pious son who was to give birth to the grandeur and the glory of the Roman people—this I would commend to this Serene Republic, so that perhaps one day, through the benevolence of Heaven, she may be the emulator of the triumphs, too, of that republic with whose virtues she vies:

> *Tu regere Imperio populos Romane memento.*
> *Hae tibi erunt artes pacisque imponere morem*
> *Parcere subiectis et deballare superbos.*

(Remember, O Roman, with might to rule the nations. These be thy arts: to impose the ways of peace, to spare the humble, to humble the proud.)

VIII. The Sabbath

SHIELD OF OUR FATHERS

Prayer Book

The two main themes of the celebration of the Sabbath, the remembrance of Creation and the memory of Israel's exodus from Egypt, recur in many places within the Sabbath liturgy and rituals. The prayer before us, which refers to the first of the two themes, is recited at the traditional Friday Evening Service, as a summary of the "seven benedictions" of the *Amidah* (Prayer of Benedictions).

> He was a shield of our fathers with His word,
> and by His bidding He will quicken the dead.
> He is the holy God, there is none like him.
> He gives rest to His people on his holy Sabbath day,
> for it pleased Him to grant them rest.
> Him we will worship with reverence and awe,
> and daily and constantly we will praise His name
> in the fitting forms of blessings.
> He is the God of our praise, the Lord of peace,
> Who hallows the Sabbath and blesses the seventh day,
> and in holiness gives rest unto a people abounding with joy,
> in remembrance of His work of Creation.

THE SANCTITY OF THE SABBATH

The *Zohar*

The mystics saw in the Sabbath the mysterious root of all faith, the hidden ground out of which the world renews itself; it is "the door through which a man enters the world to come" (Joseph Gikatila, thirteenth century). The Sabbath, which concluded the work of Crea-

135

tion, is more than a symbol of redemption; it is a foretaste of a perfected, redeemed world. It is "the root of all types of holiness" (Elijah
de Vidas, sixteenth century). The excerpt that follows is from the
Zohar (the Book of Splendor). On the *Zohar,* see "Mystical Understanding of Jewish Concepts."

"Remember the Sabbath Day, to sanctify it" (Exod. 20:8).
Said Rabbi Isaac: It is written, "And God blessed the seventh
day" (Gen. 2:3); and yet we read of the manna, "Six days ye shall
gather it, but on the seventh day, the Sabbath, in it there shall
be none" (Exod. 16:26). If there was no food on that day what
blessing is attached to it? Yet we have been taught that all blessings from above and from below depend upon the seventh day.
Why, then, was there no manna just on this day? The explanation is that all the six days of the transcendent world derive their
blessings from it, and each supernal day sends forth nourishment
to the world below from what it received from the seventh day.
Therefore he who has attained to the grade of Faith must needs
prepare a table and a meal on the eve of the Sabbath so that his
table may be blessed all through the other six days of the week.
For, indeed, at the time of the Sabbath preparation there is also
prepared the blessing for all the six days that shall follow, for no
blessing is found at an empty table. Thus one should make ready
the table on Sabbath night with bread and other food.

Said Rabbi Hiyya: Because all things are found in the Sabbath it is mentioned three times in the story of Creation: "And
on the seventh day God ended his work"; "and he rested on the
seventh day"; "and God blessed the seventh day" (Gen. 2:2, 3).
Rav Hamnuna the ancient, when he sat at his Sabbath meals,
used to find joy in each one. Over one he would exclaim: "This
is the holy meal of the Holy Ancient One, the All-hidden." Over
another he would say: "This is the meal of the Holy One, blessed
be he." And when he came to the last one he would say: "Complete the meals of the Faith." Rabbi Simon used always to say
when the time of the Sabbath meal arrived: "Prepare ye the
meal of the supernal Faith! Make ready the meal of the King!"
Then he would sit with a glad heart. And as soon as he had
finished the third meal it was proclaimed concerning him: "Then
shalt thou delight thyself in the Lord, and I will cause thee to

ride upon the high places of the earth and feed thee with the heritage of Jacob thy father" (Isa. 58:14).

Also mark this. On all festivals and holy days a man must both rejoice himself and give joy to the poor. Should he regale himself only and not give a share to the poor, his punishment will be great. [. . .] On this day—so we have been taught—the Fathers crown themselves and all the Children imbibe power and light and joy, such as is unknown even on other festive days. On this day sinners find rest in Gehenna. On this day punishment is held back from the world. On this day the Torah crowns herself in perfect crowns. On this day joy and gladness resound throughout two hundred and fifty worlds.

Mark also this. On all the six days of the week, when the hour of the Afternoon Prayer arrives, the attribute of Justice is in the ascendant, and punishment is at hand. But not so on the Sabbath. When the time of the Sabbath Afternoon prayer arrives benign influences reign, the loving-kindness of the Holy Ancient One is manifested, all chastisements are kept in leash, and all is satisfaction and joy. In this time of satisfaction and goodwill Moses, the holy, faithful prophet, passed away from this world, in order that it should be known that he was not taken away through judgment, but that in the hour of grace of the Holy Ancient One his soul ascended, to be hidden in Him. Therefore "no man knows of his sepulchre unto this day" (Deut. 36:6). As the Holy Ancient One is the All-hidden One, whom neither those above nor those below can comprehend, so was this soul of Moses hidden in the epiphany of God's good will at the hour of the Sabbath Afternoon Prayer. This soul is the most hidden of all hidden things in the world, and judgment has no dominion over it. Blessed is the lot of Moses.

On this day the Torah crowns herself with all beauty, with all those commandments, with all those decrees and punishments for transgressions—in seventy branches of light which radiate on every hand. What it is to behold the little twigs which constantly emanate from each branch—five of which stand in the Tree itself, all the branches being comprised in it!

What it is to behold the gates which open at all sides, and through which bursts forth in splendor and beauty the streaming,

inexhaustible light! A voice is heard: "Awake, ye supernal saints!
Awake, holy people, chosen from above and from below! Awake
in joy to meet your Lord, awake in perfect joy! Prepare yourselves
in the threefold joy of the three Patriarchs! Prepare yourselves
for the Faith, the joy of joys! Happy are ye, O Israelites, holy in
this world and holy in the world to come."

THE SABBATH BRIDE

Israel ibn al-Nakawa

Already the Talmud calls the Sabbath "the bride of the Congregation
of Israel" (Genesis Rabba XI, 9). This motif lent itself to further elaborations by poets, mystics, and ethical writers. The excerpt that follows
is from *Menorat ha-Maor* (The Lamp of Illumination), by Israel ibn
al-Nakawa, an ethical writer of Toledo, Spain, who died a martyr's
death in 1391.

We learn in the Midrash that the Sabbath is like unto a
bride. Just as a bride when she comes to her groom is lovely,
bedecked and perfumed, so the Sabbath comes to Israel lovely
and perfumed, as it is written: "And on the seventh day He
ceased from work and He rested" (Exod. 31:17) and immediately
afterwards we read: "And He gave unto Moses *kekhalloto*
["when he finished," but the word may be translated as] as his
bride," to teach us that just as a bride is lovely and bedecked,
so is the Sabbath lovely and bedecked; just as a groom is dressed
in his finest garments, so is the man on the Sabbath day dressed
in his finest garments; just as a man rejoices all the days of his
wedding feast, so does man rejoice on the Sabbath; just as the
groom does no work on his wedding day, so does a man abstain
from work on the Sabbath day; and therefore the sages and the
early pious men called the Sabbath a bride.

There is a hint of this in the Sabbath prayers. In the Friday
Evening Service we say: "Thou hast sanctified the seventh day,"
referring to the marriage of the bride to the groom ["sanctification" being the Hebrew word for marriage]. In the Morning

Service we say: "Moses rejoiced in the gift [of the Sabbath] bestowed upon him" which corresponds to the groom's rejoicing with the bride. In the Additional Prayer we make mention of "the two lambs, the fine flour for a meal offering, mingled with oil and the drink thereof" referring to the meat, the bread, the wine, and the oil used in the wedding banquet. In the Afternoon Prayer we say: "Thou are one" to parallel the consummation of the marriage by which the bride and groom are united.

THE SABBATH AND THE DAYS
OF THE WEEK

Judah Loew ben Bezalel

Judah Loew (Liva) ben Bezalel ("the Maharal"), *ca.* 1525–1609, rabbi in Prague, is popularly known from the legend that describes him as the creator of the "Golem," a mysterious robot. In his writings he appears as a talmudic scholar, a mildly mystical interpreter of the true meaning of Torah (Torah as the means by which the "lower" and "upper" worlds meet in the human intellect), an opponent of philosophical studies, and as early advocate of the basic natural rights of nations. The passage that follows is from *Tiferet Yisrael,* Venice, 1599.

The statement that God rested on the seventh day of the creation means that He created and completed all. The heavens also are in action, but their activity does not bring any completion and therefore they have no rest for interruption.

One may be surprised at God being linked with the idea of rest, because "The Lord . . . fainteth not, neither is weary" (Isa. 90:78), but one must consider the following: Whoever requires time for his work must finally rest. Of course the creation of the world in time is only as it appears to the recipient, man. For it is impossible that the plants should have appeared at the same moment that the earth was created, when according to the order of the creation the earth itself was to bring them forth. The same applies to all the other creations, and therefore the time had to be extended. Thus if the time required for the creation of the

world is regarded from the human point of view, then also the
rest is meant as a human conception. It is as if it were stated that
God created everything within the time stated for the sake of the
recipient, man, because the latter would faint and grow weary
if he were to receive everything at once. Hence the rest on the
seventh day.

Why there are six days of work and a seventh day of rest
can be explained in the following manner. The world is corporeal, and every body has six different sides, through which it
becomes complete, namely above, below, and the extensions to
the four quarters of the compass. These sides bound the body,
but in every body there is one point set neither to the right nor
the left, neither to the front nor to the back, and which has no
spatial extension like the six sides, namely, the middle. The
middle is not subject to space, therefore it is not corporeal. When
God created the corporeal world, He did so in six days corresponding to the six corporeal extensions. The seventh day was the
day of rest, corresponding to the incorporeal middle.

The seventh day is holy, because holiness can be attributed
only to the incorporeal. When our sages said that on the Sabbath man acquired a special soul, they meant by it that the incorporeal soul increased in strength. Therefore that day is sanctified by the kindling of lights, because light is entirely different
from other corporeal objects.

SANCTIFICATION

Prayer Book

In the liturgy of the Synagogue, the Reader's repetition of the *Amidah*
(Prayer of Benedictions) contains the insertion of the *Kedushah* (Sanctification), a series of Biblical passages spoken by the congregation, introduced and concluded by the Reader. The Biblical verses are Isa.
6:3, Ezek. 3:12, and Ps. 146:10; the *Musaf* (Additional Prayer for Sabbath and Holidays) provides for the insertion of Deut. 6:4 ("Hear, O
Israel") and Num. 15:41 ("I am the Lord"). The introduction presents
the community's glorification of God as corresponding to, and imitat-

ing, the glorification on the part of the heavenly hosts. The liturgy concludes on the theme of the kingdom of God. The core of the *Kedushah* originated in the talmudic period; various elaborations are the work of the early Middle Ages. The version that follows is from the *Musaf* Service.

Reader

We will revere thee and sanctify thee in the mystic utterance of the holy Seraphim. They hallow thy name in the heavenly sanctuary, as it is written by the hand of thy prophet, And they called unto one another saying:

Congregation

"Holy, holy, holy, is the Lord of hosts: the whole earth is full of His glory."

Reader

His glory pervades the universe; His ministering angels ask one another, Where is the place of His glory? In response they say, Blessed—

Congregation

"Blessed be the glory of the Lord from His place."

Reader

From His place may He turn in mercy and be gracious unto a people that evening and morning, twice daily, proclaim in love the unity of His name, saying, Hear—

Congregation

"Hear, O Israel: the Lord our God, the Lord is One."

Reader

One is our God; he is our Father; he is our King; he is our Savior. He will save and redeem us a second time. In his mercy He will let us hear in the presence of all living, Behold I have now redeemed you in the latter times, as at the beginning: "To be your God.

Congregation
I am the Lord your God."

Reader
And in thy Holy Words it is written, saying,

Congregation
"The Lord shall reign for ever, thy God, O Zion, unto all generations. Hallelujah."

Reader
Unto all generations we will declare thy greatness, and to all eternity we will proclaim thy holiness. Thy praise, O our God, shall never depart from our mouth; for thou, O God, art a great and holy king.
Blessed art thou, O Lord, the holy God.

IX. The Ways of the Mystics

MYSTICAL UNDERSTANDING
OF JEWISH CONCEPTS

The *Zohar*

Jewish mysticism in thirteenth-century Spain, and especially in Castile, can be interpreted, at least in some of its aspects, as a reaction against overemphasis on rationalism in thought and against secularization of life; against Judaism becoming the sole domain of technical scholarship or of the rich and the socially prominent. Mysticism (*Kabbalah*, i.e., tradition) pointed to the deeper layers of Jewish religion, which it represented as the authentic tradition of Israel. It penetrated into the mysteries of the divine being and the miracle of Creation; it applied itself to the problem of Israel's suffering in exile; it focused the adept's attention upon the origins of the world rather than upon the process of history and the "end of days"; it taught purity of thought and the right intention in prayer, study of Torah, and repentance; possibly under the influence of the Franciscan movement, it extolled the poor, the meek, and the ascetic; and it guided to the love of the living God.

The chief work of Kabbalah is the *Zohar* (the Book of Splendor). It was written toward the end of the thirteenth century by Moses de Leon, a man who in his youth had studied Maimonides' philosophical work, then turned toward Neoplatonism and Kabbalah (G. G. Scholem). Composed in Aramaic, the *Zohar* imitated the form of the midrashic works of the early Christian centuries. For three centuries after about 1500 the *Zohar* "came to fulfill the great historical task of a sacred text supplementing the Bible and Talmud on a new level of religious consciousness" (G. G. Scholem).

The work was first published (three volumes) in Mantua, in 1558–1560; there followed many editions of the text and commentaries. Portions of the *Zohar* were translated into Latin by the Christian Kabbalist Knorr von Rosenroth (*Kabbala denudata*, 1677), who was instrumental in acquainting the philosopher Leibniz with Jewish mysticism.

Body and Soul

"Ye shall be holy for I the Lord am holy" (Lev. 19:2). When God came to create the world and reveal what was hidden in the depths and disclose light out of darkness, they were all wrapped in one another, and therefore light emerged from darkness and from the impenetrable came forth the profound. So, too, from good issues evil, and from mercy issues judgment, and all are intertwined, the good impulse and the evil impulse, right and left, Israel and other peoples, white and black—all depend on one another.

Said Rabbi Abba: Why does the section of "holiness" [in Leviticus] follow immediately upon the section dealing with sexual offences? Because we have learnt that whoever preserves himself from these offences shows that he was begotten in holiness; all the more so if he sanctifies himself with the holiness of his Master. The Companions have indicated the proper time of marital intercourse for all classes. He who desires to sanctify himself according to the will of his Master should not have intercourse save from midnight onwards, or at midnight, for at that time the Holy One, blessed be he, is in the Garden of Eden, and greater holiness is abroad, wherefore it is a time for a man to sanctify himself. This is the rule for the ordinary man. But students who know the ways of the Torah should rise at midnight to study and to join themselves with the Community of Israel to praise the holy Name and the holy King; and their time of intercourse is at that hour on the night of the Sabbath when grace abounds, that they may obtain favor from the Community of Israel and the Holy One, blessed be he, and those are called holy.

Rabbi Abba quoted here the verse: "Who is like thy people Israel, one nation in the earth?" (1 Sam. 7:23). God, he said, chose Israel and made them a unique nation in the world and called them "one nation," after His own name. He gave them many precepts to be crowned withal, including the phylacteries of the head and the arm, wherewith a man becomes one and complete. For he is only called "one" when he is complete, and not if he is defective, and therefore God is called One when He is consummated with the Patriarchs and the Community of Israel. When, therefore, the Israelite puts on his phylacteries and wraps himself in the fringed garment, he is crowned with holy crowns after the supernal pattern and is called "one," and it is fitting that One should come and attend to one. And when is a man called "one"? When he is male with female and is sanctified with a high holiness and is bent upon sanctification; then alone he is called one without blemish. Therefore a man should rejoice with his wife at that hour to bind her in affection to him, and they should both have the same intent. When they are thus united, they form one soul and one body: one soul through their affection, and one body, as we have learnt, that if a man is not married he is, as it were, divided in halves, and only when male and female are joined do they become one body. Then God rests upon "one" and lodges a holy spirit in it: and such are called "the sons of God."

The Ten Words

The Ten Words contain the essence of all the commandments, the essence of all celestial and terrestrial mysteries, the essence of the Ten Words of Creation.[1] They were engraved on tables of stone, and all the hidden things were seen by the eyes and perceived by the minds of all Israel, everything being made clear to them. At that hour all the mysteries of the Torah, all the hidden things of heaven and earth, were unfolded before them and revealed to their eyes, for they saw eye to eye the splendor of the glory of their Lord. Never before, since the Holy One created the world, had such a revelation of the Divine Glory taken place. Even the crossing of the Red Sea, where, as has been said, even a simple maid-servant saw more of the Divine than the prophet Ezekiel,[2] was not so wonderful as this.

For on this day all the earthly dross was removed from them and purged away, and their bodies became as lucent as the angels above when they are clothed in radiant garments for the accomplishment of their Master's errands; in which garments they penetrate fire without fear, as we read concerning the angel who appeared to Manoah (Jud. 13:20). And when all the fleshly impurity was removed from the Israelites their bodies became, as we have said, lucent as stars and their souls were as resplendent as the firmament, to receive the light. Such was the state of the Israelites when they beheld the glory of their Lord.

It was not thus at the Red Sea, when the filth had not as yet been removed from them. There, at Mount Sinai, even the embryos in their mothers' wombs had some perception of their Lord's glory, and everyone received according to his grade of perception. On that day the Holy One, blessed be he, rejoiced more than on any previous day since He had created the world, for Creation had no proper basis before Israel received the Torah. But when once Israel had received the Torah on Mount Sinai the world was duly and completely established, and heaven and earth received a proper foundation, and the glory of the Holy One was made known both above and below, and He was exalted over all. Blessed be the Lord for ever. Amen and Amen.

The Poor and the Lowly

Rabbi Eleazar asked Rabbi Simeon, his father: "We've been taught that there are three sins which cause famine to be visited upon the earth, and all three are to be found among the rich, because of their arrogance, and are not found among the poor. Why is it then that God lets the poor perish and preserves the rich? They will only multiply their sins against Him!"

Rabbi Simeon replied: "You have asked a good question. [. . .] Observe, now! Of all the inhabitants of the earth none are as close to the Supreme King as those who serve as His 'vessels.' And who are they? 'A broken and contrite heart' (Ps. 51:19) and 'he who is of a contrite and humble spirit' (Isa. 57:15), these are the vessels of the King. And when famine strikes the world and hunger and privation bear down upon the poor, they weep and cry before the King; and the Holy One, blessed be he, feels closer to them than to anyone else, as is written, 'For He has not despised nor loathed the affliction of the poor man, nor has He hidden His face from him, but whenever he cried to Him, He listened' (Ps. 22:25). And then the Holy One, blessed be he, takes note of that which causes famine to descend upon the earth. Woe unto the wicked, who are the cause of it all, when God is moved to scrutinize the world upon hearing the cries of the poor! God save us from ever offending them, for it is written, 'I will be certain to hear his cry' (Exod. 22:22). [. . .] Woe unto the rich when there is famine in the world, and the voice of the poor reaches to God. The poor man's offering, you see, comes closest to God, for his heart is contrite."

When the Holy One, blessed be he, visits judgment upon the world, it is for the sin of the heads of the people, the sin of subverting justice and of distorting it. Do not wonder why God allows the lowly to expire through the failure of the mighty to do justice, for the poor are God's vessels and are close to him and when famine comes they cry to Him and He listens to them and He calls before the bar of justice those who brought this suffering upon the poor, as is written, "And when he will cry to me I will listen, for I am kind" (Exod. 22:26).

"A prayer of the poor man, when he grows faint and pours out his complaint before the Lord" (Ps. 102:1): The prayer of the poor man is received by God ahead of all other prayers.

"Happy is he who is considerate of the poor" (Ps. 41:2): How great is the reward that the poor merit of the Lord for they are closest to God, as is written, "A broken and contrite heart, O God, Thou wilt not despise" (Ps. 51:19).

The poor man is closer to God than anyone else, as is written, "And when he will cry to Me, I will listen," for God abides in these broken vessels, as is written, "I dwell on high, amid holiness, but also with the contrite and humble in spirit" (Isa. 57:15). Therefore, we have been taught that he who reviles the indigent scoffs at the Divinity. And it is also written, "Do not rob the poor because he is poor, or crush the needy at the gate; for the Lord will defend their cause and despoil of life those who despoil them" (Prov. 12:22f.). Their Guardian is mighty and He holds sway over all. He requires no witnesses and no associate judge, nor does He take a bond as do other judges.

He who looks after the welfare of the poor man, God sees to his welfare and prolongs his life even when his day comes to depart this world. "The wages of a hired man shall not remain with thee overnight" (Lev. 19:13). He who withholds the poor man's hire from him, in effect deprives him and his family of their life. Just as he reduces their vitality, God reduces his days

and shortens his life in this world. Even if long life and many
good things had been decreed for that man, they are all with-
drawn from him. What is more, his soul does not rise aloft.

Happy is he who encounters a poor man, for this poor man is
a gift sent to him by God.

Material Wealth

One day a young man approached his teacher and said to
him, "Master, where is the wealth?" "It is obvious," reasoned the
teacher, "that he is not motivated in the pursuit of learning by
any lofty ideal," so he retired to his chamber. There he heard a
voice saying to him, "Do not frown upon the young man, for he
shall yet be great." The master went back to the student and said
to him, "Sit down, my son; sit, and I will give you riches." Presently, a very rich man came along and gave the student some of
his wealth, and the love of Torah waxed stronger in the young
man's heart. One day the teacher found the young man sitting
and weeping; whereupon he asked him, "Why do you weep?"
The student replied, "Will I forfeit my share of the world to
come because of this wealth? I seek only the spiritual rewards for
good deeds." Thought the master, "It is evident that his study is
now heaven-intentioned." He summoned the rich man and said
to him, "Take your wealth and distribute it to the poor and the
orphaned."

THE PRACTICE OF

MYSTICAL MEDITATION

Abraham Abulafia

Abraham Abulafia was born in Saragossa, Aragon, in 1240. One of the
major figures in medieval Jewish mysticism, he became the representative of what G. G. Scholem terms "prophetic Kabbalah," an originator
of a method leading to an intuitive, "prophetic," knowledge of God
and an ecstatic communion with Him. The method consisted in a
contemplation upon the letters of the Hebrew alphabet, which in cer-

tain mystical computations and combinations (*Tzeruf*) constitute the name of God. "The systematic practice of meditation as taught by him [Abulafia], produces a sensation closely akin to that of listening to musical harmonies. The science of combination is a music of pure thought, in which the alphabet takes the place of the musical scale" (G. G. Scholem). The Kabbalist succeeded in reconciling his mystic doctrine with the religious philosophy of Maimonides, whom he greatly revered. In the last analysis, the latter's *Guide to the Perplexed* leads to mystic knowledge. In 1280, the visionary, in response to an "inner voice," journeyed to Rome, to call Pope Nicholas III to account for the sufferings of the Jews and to propose to him a conversion to Judaism. Abulafia was condemned to the stake; the Pope's death soon thereafter gained Abulafia a stay of execution. Among his many writings is the apocalypse *Sefer ha-Ot* (The Book of the Sign), published by A. Jellinek in 1887. His chief disciple was Joseph ben Abraham Gikatila. Abulafia died in Barcelona about 1292. Our first selection deals with the practice of meditation; the second describes the mystical experience.

I

Know that the method of *Tzeruf* [the combination of letters] can be compared to music; for the ear hears sounds from various combinations, in accordance with the character of the melody and the instrument. Also, two different instruments can form a combination, and if the sounds combine, the listener's ear registers a pleasant sensation in acknowledging their difference. The strings touched by the right or left hand move, and the sound is sweet to the ear. And from the ear the sensation travels to the heart, and from the heart to the spleen,[3] and enjoyment of the different melodies produces ever new delight. It is impossible to produce it except through the combination of sounds, and the same is true of the combination of letters. It touches the first string, which is comparable to the first letters, and proceeds to the second, third, fourth and fifth, and the various sounds combine. And the secrets, which express themselves in these combinations, delight the heart which acknowledges its God and is filled with ever fresh joy.

II

Be prepared for thy God, oh Israelite! Make thyself ready to direct thy heart to God alone. Cleanse the body and choose a lonely house where none shall hear thy voice. Sit there in thy closet and do not reveal thy secret to any man. If thou canst, do it by day in the house, but it is best if thou completest it during the night. In the hour when thou preparest thyself to speak with the Creator and thou wishes Him to reveal His might to thee, then be careful to abstract all thy thought from the vanities of this world. Cover thyself with thy prayer shawl and put phylacteries on thy head and hands that thou mayest be filled with awe of the Divine Presence which is near thee. Cleanse thy clothes, and, if possible, let all thy garments be white, for all this is helpful in leading the heart towards the fear of God and the love of God. If it be night, kindle many lights, until all be bright. Then take ink, pen and a table to thy hand and remember that thou art about to serve God in joy of the gladness of heart. Now begin to combine a few or many letters, to permute and to combine them until thy heart be warm. Then be mindful of their movements and of what thou canst bring forth by moving them.

And when thou feelest that thy heart is already warm and when thou seest that by combinations of letters thou canst grasp new things which by human tradition or by thyself thou wouldst not be able to know and when thou art thus prepared to receive the influx of divine power which flows into thee, then turn all thy true thought to imagine the Name and His exalted angels in thy heart as if they were human beings sitting or standing about thee. And feel thyself like an envoy whom the king and his ministers are to send on a mission, and he is waiting to hear something about his mission from their lips, be it from the king himself, be it from his servants. Having imagined this very vividly, turn thy whole mind to understand with thy thoughts the many things which will come into thy heart through the letters imagined. Ponder them as a whole and in all their detail, like one to whom a parable or a dream is being related, or who meditates on a deep problem in a scientific book, and try thus to interpret what thou shalt hear that it may as far as possible accord with thy reason.

And all this will happen to thee after having flung away tablet and quill or after they will have dropped from thee because of the intensity of thy thought. And know, the stronger the intellectual influx within thee, the weaker will become thy outer and thy inner parts. Thy whole body will be seized by an extremely strong trembling, so that thou wilt think that surely thou art about to die, because thy soul, overjoyed with its knowledge, will leave thy body. And be thou ready at this moment consciously to choose death, and then thou shall know that thou hast come far enough to receive the influx. And then wishing to honor the glorious Name by serving it with the life of body and soul, veil thy face and be afraid to look at God. Then return to the matters of the body, rise and eat and drink a little, or refresh thyself with a pleasant odor, and restore thy spirit to its sheath until another time, and rejoice at thy lot and know that God loveth thee!

THE SEARCH FOR TRUTH

Solomon ibn Adret

Solomon ibn Adret (*ca.* 1235–1310), disciple of Jonah Gerondi and Moses Nahmanides (see "Has the Messiah Come?"), rabbi of Barcelona, and widely recognized rabbinical authority and leader of Spanish Jewry ("El Rab d'Espagña"), was compelled to take a stand on two crucial issues of his day: philosophy and mysticism. Although he greatly respected both the rationalist Maimonides and the mystic Nahmanides, he saw the Jewish community imperiled by the trends the two men represented. Philosophical enlightenment bred religious skepticism; mysticism gave rise to visionaries, blindly followed by the credulous. To counteract the first, he issued (1305) a ban against those who would study philosophy before reaching the age of twenty-five (i.e., before having undergone a thorough training in the traditional talmudic discipline). To meet the second danger, he released a long and sharply worded *responsum* (Nr. 548) against the untutored and unrestrained mystics, and especially against Abraham Abulafia (see "The Practice of Mystical Meditation"). The passage that follows appears at the end of this *responsum*.

To Israel, the heir of the religion of truth, the children of Jacob, the man of truth. [. . .] it is easier to bear the burden of exile than to believe in anything before it is thoroughly and repeatedly examined and all its dross has been purged away, even though it appears to be a sign or a miracle. The undeniable evidence for Israel's love of truth and rejection of anything which is doubtful can be seen in the relation of the people of Israel to Moses. In spite of the fact that they were crushed by slavery, yet when Moses was told to bring them tidings of their redemption, he said to the Lord: "Behold, they will not believe me, nor hearken to my voice, for they will say: 'The Lord hath not appeared unto me'" (Exod. 4:1). Moses had to bring evidence. Thus it is characteristic of our people not to be satisfied unless exhaustive examination has proven a matter to be true.

LIFE IN SAFED

Solomon Shloemel ben Hayyim Meinstrl

The Land of Israel, which never ceased to attract Jewish pilgrims and settlers, gained added importance when, in the sixteenth century, the mystic doctrines of Isaac Luria of Safed spread throughout the Jewish world. The sages of Safed planned the reinstitution of the ancient rite of ordination (*Semikhah*) and of the Sanhedrin, in preparation for the Messianic age. In the same period of time, Rabbi Judah Loew (Liva) ben Bezalel of Prague propagated the basic rights of nations, declared exile and dispersion to be unnatural, and postulated a return to the land of Israel (1599). Such is the background of the decision of a little-known writer of the report that follows to leave his native Moravia and make his home in Safed. A few years later (1621), a younger contemporary of Loew ben Bezalel, Isaiah ha-Levi Horovitz, author of *Shene Luhot ha-Berit* (The Two Tablets of the Covenant) and popularizer of Kabbalah, came to settle in Safed. Politically, Safed enjoyed an era of peaceful development under the Druse ruler Fakhr ed-Din, who, except for some brief interruptions, controlled southern Lebanon and northern Galilee from 1584 to 1635.

I have come to inform you that the God of blessing in his great loving-kindness has vouchsafed me the merit of making my dwelling in the Holy Land, here in Safed, may she be rebuilt speedily and in our days, in the Upper Galilee; and I have now been here for five years in the midst of the Land, thank God, with no business other than the study of the Torah and the service of His blessed Name. The day I became twenty-two my

Maker moved me and awakened my heart and said to me: "How long, O sluggard, wilt thou sleep in the slumber of idleness? Rise now, gird up thy loins like a warrior and pursue the knowledge of the Torah and of the commandments, and become an understanding youth."

Thereupon I arose and took courage and put away all worldly affairs from me; and I prepared myself to seek and know the God of my fathers with all my heart and with all my soul; and I sat before the Lord my God and repented with all my heart.

And when my Maker brought me to my twenty-eighth year, tidings reached me of the awesome, holy, and wonderful wisdom to be gained in the Land of the Living, where are to be found the seats of Torah and Testimony; and the light of their Torah causes the Holy Spirit to shine forth over his flock, our people, so that their actions accord with their love of the will of their Maker. At once I girded my loins to run the course; and I sent my wife away with a divorce as she did not wish to go with me. I also paid her all that was due her in accordance with her marriage contract, and also left our one daughter who was at that time thirteen years old with her. So, of all that had been mine not so much as a hair was left, not even my clothes and books, for I left them behind for her alimony and for the dowry of my daughter; but I trusted in the God of Jacob and entrusted my welfare to him. So I did depart from the land of my birth, in complete destitution.

I arrived in the holy city of Safed in the mid-days of the Feast of Booths of 5363 [autumn, 1602], arriving in peace and finding a holy congregation. For this is a great city before God with close on to three hundred great rabbis, all of them pious and men of works. Eighteen talmudic academies I found here, as well as twenty-one synagogues and a large House of Study with close on to four hundred children in the charge of four teachers, who give them free instruction. For there are wealthy folk in Constantinople who pay the hire of the teachers, and likewise send them clothes every year. And in all the synagogues, after the Morning and Evening Prayer, the entire congregation gather together and sit before their rabbis, five or six groups in every synagogue, each group engaging in study before they forsake the synagogue. One group regularly studies the works of Maimonides, another studies *En Yaakov*,[4] while the third makes the [talmudic] tractate Berakhot their set study; others regularly study a daily chapter of the Mishnah with commentary; and yet another group study the Talmud with the commentaries of Rashi and Tosafot;[5] and another group regularly studies the holy *Zohar* [the Book of Splendor]; and another group regularly studies the Scriptures.

In this way there is no one who goes forth in the morning to his trade or business without having first learned his measure of the Torah. Everybody does the same in the evening, after the Evening Prayer. Then on the Sabbath day all the people go to hear the sermons of the rabbis. And every Thursday they all gather together in one great synagogue after the Morning Prayer, where they pray to his Name; an awesome prayer for the welfare of all Israel wherever they may be, and mourn the exile of the Divine Presence and of Israel, and the destruction of the house of our God. And they bless all those who send their money to aid the poor of the Land of Israel that the Holy One, blessed be he, may prolong their days and their years and make their affairs prosper and guard them against every trouble and distress.

Before they begin to pray, the great and pious rabbi, our master Rabbi Moses Galante,[6] may his Rock and Maker guard him, ascends the pulpit and utters mighty words and rouses Israel to fear of the Name and brings them to love the Creator, by means of his sweet tongue, great wisdom, and erudition and vast sanctity. Afterward there ascend two heads of academies, great and pious scholars and men of good deeds. [. . .]

Then they begin to pray in awe and fear and great dread. Who has ever seen the like of those great and bitter prayers and outcries of all Israel that weep and as one man let tears fall over the exile and the destruction because of our many sins; how they confess their iniquities!

Then every New Moon's eve they follow the practices of the eve of the Day of Atonement until midnight, proclaiming a stoppage of work until that hour. And all Israel gather together in one great synagogue or proceed to the grave of Hosea ben Beeri the prophet, over which there is a magnificent building formed like a dome, and they enter inside; or else they proceed to the cave of the divine teacher, Abba Saul,[7] may he rest in peace; or else they assemble before the grave of Rabbi Judah bar Ilai;[8] all of which saints are buried near the city. There they pray an awesome prayer until the noon, sometimes spending the entire day there praying and preaching.

Now the Gentiles who dwell on the soil of Israel are all subject to the holiness of Israel. Even though we stand all day long in the field, wearing our prayer shawls and phylacteries and calling upon the Lord our God in a great voice at the graves of the saints, not a single Gentile would approach a congregation of Jews when they are praying, or open his mouth to mock at the prayer. But they all go their ways. On the contrary, they hold the graves of our holy masters in great reverence, as well as the synagogues; and they kindle lights at the graves of the saints and vow to supply the synagogues with oil.

The villages of En Zetim and Meron contain ruined synagogues, but because of our many sins no Jews dwell there. There are countless Torah Scrolls within the Arks in the synagogues which the Gentiles treat with much honor. The keys to the synagogues are in their hands, and they clean them and light candles before the Arks, and no one would approach to touch a Torah Scroll. Sometimes we go unto those villages to pray, and recite our prayers in those synagogues.

Apart from this, I found that the entire Holy Land is filled with the blessing of the Lord, with great plenty and a great cheapness which is beyond all estimation and imagining and telling. Now when I perceived the great plenty to be found in the Holy Land, and saw that all this bounty is being consumed by the nations of the world while Israel are dispersed and have not the merit to eat of its fruits or to be sated with its goodness, I wept greatly and I said: Would that our brethren the children of Israel knew but a tenth of all this plenty and goodness and great satiety which are now to be found in the Land of Israel! For then they would weep day and night over their exile and over this pleasant, good and spacious land which they have lost, which even in its ruins brings forth fruits and oil and wine and silk for a third of the world; so that men come in ships from the ends of the world, from Venice and Spain, and France, and Portugal, and Constan-

tinople, and load up with corn and olive oil, raisins, and cakes
of figs, and honey, and silk, and good soap, all of which are as
plentiful as the sand of the seashore. [. . .]

Poultry and eggs are very cheap, a chicken costing five or six
kreutzer, and five or six eggs can be had for a coin which is worth
about two of the smallest coins of our land. [. . .] Then there
are the fine fruits: carobs, oranges, lemons, and melons, and
watermelons which are as sweet as sugar, and cucumbers, and
pumpkins, and lettuces and all sorts of other greens which are
unknown to you, so there is no advantage in my mentioning
them. There is a quality in the fruits and greens and desserts of
the Land of Israel whose like is not to be found in your parts,
like gold compared with silver or wheaten bread with barley; so
that he who has merited of the Name, be it blessed, to make his
home in the Land of Israel, and has a little money with which to
support himself, happy is he and happy his portion; for he can
win himself life in the world to come by joining the company of
the great men of piety and good deeds who are in the Land, and
can also take pleasure before the Lord and give pleasure to his
spirit in these good and fat pastures, eating of its fruits and having his fill of its goodness. All this he can achieve here in the
Land of Israel, at a third of the expenses and costs at home, and
live the life of a king. Apart from this, there are the clear and
wholesome air and the healthgiving water which prolong a man's
days. For this reason most of the inhabitants of this country, almost all of them, live very long lives up to eighty or ninety or a
hundred or a hundred and ten years.

Now the Lord who is the true God and King of the universe
knew my heart and saw my good intention, how with all my
heart and all my soul I entreated the Lord to answer me in my
time of trouble and to deliver me. So He gave me all I desired of
Him, and He brought me in peace to the Land of Israel, on the
Feast of Booths in the year 5364 [1603], where he had appointed
for me as my helpmeet a good and God-fearing woman, the
daughter of a great and very exalted and pious scholar, whose
vast holiness and tremendous piety are known to all Israel. He
is the sage, our honored master, Rabbi Israel Sarug[9] of blessed
memory.

The Holy One, blessed be he, has given me the merit of possessing all the writings prepared by that holy and godly man and teacher of all Israel, our master Rabbi Isaac Luria of blessed memory; more than are in the possession of any of the sages of the Land of Israel. I came to them through the wife I married in the Land of Israel, who inherited them from her honored father, our master Rabbi Israel Sarug of blessed memory, who tirelessly sought them out all his life long and expended more than two hundred thalers on them until he obtained them all.

I now have them, praise God, and I delight in them every day; and the blessed Name has caused me to find favor and friendship among all the sages of Safed. My rabbi and teacher, before whom I sit and from whom I learn Torah, particularly the wisdom of the Kabbalah, is the perfect and very humble sage, our honored master Rabbi Masud, the Great Light[10] of Fez. He is famous in all Israel by reason of his great holiness and vast knowledge and erudition in the entire Torah, may the blessed Name guard and preserve him.

So now I have no other business than the business of the Torah and the service of the blessed Name. Praises and thanksgiving to God who brought me here and has given me the merit of all this until now. The woman whom your servant married did not bring me either gold or silver, but a house and its vessels and the Kabbalah writings of our master Rabbi Isaac Luria and the little clothing she had; and nothing more. For I married the daughter of a pious scholar for the sake of heaven, to obtain those holy writings, for without her I could never have obtained them at all, since they are to be found only in the hands of a few rare and singular individuals, men of lofty soul and extraordinarily pious. The Creator, taking pity on me, has permitted me to obtain them, by which means He has caused me to find favor and friendship in the eyes of all sages of Safed, may it be rebuilt and established speedily and in our days; and they do not withhold from me any of all the secrets concealed in the Torah.

Written by Solomon Shloemel, son of my noble father, Rabbi Hayyim, known as Meinsterl, of blessed memory, and written in haste here at Safed, may she be rebuilt and established

speedily and in our days, in the Upper Galilee, which is in "the
Land of Beauty," on the twenty-fourth day of Tammuz 5367
[1607].

THE LIFE OF

RABBI ISAAC LURIA

Solomon Shloemel ben Hayyim Meinsterl

The "Lurianic Kabbalah," the mystic teachings associated with the
name of Isaac Luria (1534–1572), taught comprehension of the process
of Creation as a form of divine exile, dealt with the origin of evil, and
assigned to men the task of "restoration of the primordially planned
order of things in their relation to God" (G. G. Scholem). It provided
a profound answer to the pressing problem of exile, strongly accentuated by the catastrophe of the expulsion of the Jews from Spain; it
made not merely the inner circles of mystics but the people of Israel
as a whole participants in a mystically understood Messianism. Isaac
Luria was not a writer; he left the formulation of his doctrine to his
disciples, and especially to Hayyim Vital Calabrese (1543–1620). The
saintly personality of the master (who died at the age of thirty-eight)
survived in many legends. Solomon Shloemel ben Hayyim Meinsterl,
who came to Palestine in 1602, wrote letters containing a short life of
Luria (the "Ari," abbreviated from *Adonenu* [our master] Rabbi Isaac),
which incorporates the revered traditions about the man. The letters
were first printed in *Taalumot Hokhmah,* by Samuel Ashkenazi, Basel,
1629. (See also "A Godly Life.")

During his youth, the Ari, of blessed memory, lived in Egypt
although he was born in Jerusalem. At his birth the prophet
Elijah appeared to his father—for he was very pious, as was his
mother too—and said to him: "Take heed, now, on the day of
the circumcision, not to circumcise this child until you see me
standing beside you in the synagogue."

Now when the eighth day came and they took the child to
the synagogue for the circumcision the father looked around
on all sides for Elijah but did not see him there. By some sort of
a pretext, the father delayed for about a half an hour or more

and kept the congregation standing. They wondered why he held off so long and finally they all rebuked him. He, however, paid no attention to their complaint but waited till finally Elijah did come. He said to the father: "Sit down on the chair," and the father sat down with the infant in his arms. Then Elijah came, took the child from the parent, put him on his own lap and held him with his own two arms. The man who performed the circumcision went ahead with his work and saw nothing, of course, but the father. After the child had been circumcised Elijah returned him to the father, saying: "Here is your child. Take good care of him for a great light shall shine forth from him upon all the world."

Later when he was still a lad his father died. Because of poverty he went down to Egypt to the home of his uncle who was a very rich man. Luria developed into a brilliant student noted for his keenness, powers of argumentation, and sound reasoning, so that by the time he was fifteen years of age he was superior to all the sages of Egypt in his understanding of and his ability to debate in talmudic law. His uncle then gave him his daughter to wife. After the marriage he studied alone with our honored teacher, Rabbi Bezalel Ashkenazi,[11] for seven years, and after this he studied by himself for six years. In addition to this, for two years in succession, he kept himself in seclusion in a certain house built along the Nile river and sanctified himself by an unusual piety. He was altogether alone and spoke with no one. On the eve of the Sabbath, just before it grew dark, he would return to his home, but even here, too, he would talk to no one, not even his wife, except when it was absolutely necessary, and then only in Hebrew and very briefly.

It was there on the banks of the Nile that he merited for himself the descent of the Holy Spirit. At times Elijah the prophet revealed himself to him and taught him the secrets of the Torah, and he was found so worthy that throughout the night his soul would mount on high, and hosts of ministering angels would come to guard him on the way till they had led him into the heavenly assembly, and there they would ask of him in which academy he wished to study. [. . .]

After these two years of extreme asceticism in Egypt, Elijah

appeared to him. Luria was at that time only thirty-six years of
age; and he was thirty-eight years old when, from here in Safed
he was summoned to the Academy on High, because of our many
sins. Elijah had said to him: "The time of your death is approaching. And now go up to Safed. There you will find a certain scholar whose name is Rabbi Hayyim Calabrese;[12] anoint
him in your stead; lay your hands upon him and teach all your
lore for he will take your place. The sole purpose of your coming
into the world has been to "restore" the soul of Rabbi Hayyim,
for it is a precious one. Through you he will merit wisdom,
and a great light shall shine forth from him upon all Israel. I
assure you that I will reveal myself to you whenever you need
me; I will lay bare before you the secrets of the upper and the
nether worlds, and God, too, will pour out upon you his Holy
Spirit a thousand times more than you are able to acquire here in
Egypt."

All these things did our Master Luria, of blessed memory,
reveal to our teacher Rabbi Hayyim Calabrese, and he in turn
revealed them intimately to a chosen few of his associates in the
land of Israel. But our teacher Hayyim, however, wrote in the
book which he composed that it appeared to him that Luria was
the Messiah ben Joseph[13] but the Master would not admit it to
him because of his exceeding humility. However, his disciples
could surmise it from what Luria had told them. [. . .]

Luria knew all the deeds of men and even their thoughts.
He could read faces, look into the souls of men, and recognize
souls that migrated from body to body. He could tell you about
the souls of the wicked which had entered into trees and stones
or animals and birds; he could tell you what commandments a
man had fulfilled and what sins he had committed since youth;
he knew wherein a sinful man had been punished by God and
would prescribe acts of "restoration" to remove a moral blemish,
and knew just when such a moral defect had been corrected. He
understood the chirping of birds, and through their flight he
divined strange things, as is referred to in the verse: "For a bird
of the air shall carry the voice, and that which hath wings shall
tell the matter" (Eccles. 10:20). All of this he acquired because

of the piety, asceticism, purity, and holiness that he had exercised since his youth.

IN THE PRESENCE

OF THE DIVINE

Moses Cordovero

In the sixteenth century, Safed, situated in the hills of Galilee, was the home of a group of mystics who rallied around Isaac Luria (see also "The Life of Rabbi Isaac Luria" and "Life in Safed"). In this period Safed was the home of Joseph Caro, author of the *Shulhan Arukh*, code of Jewish law, and of *Solomon Alkabetz*, who wrote the Sabbath hymn *Lekha Dodi;* here Israel Najara, outstanding Kabbalist poet, spent his youth; here Hayyim Vital Calabrese (1543-1620), Luria's outstanding disciple and author of *Etz Hayyim* (Tree of Life), was born; here, too, flourished Moses Cordovero (1522-1570), mystical theologian, and his disciples, Elijah de Vidas, author of *Reshit Hokhmah* (Beginning of Wisdom), and Abraham Galante.

Cordovero's major works include *Pardes Rimmonim* (Orchard of Pomegranates), written in 1548, which is a comprehensive exposition of mystical theology and a work comparable in scope and importance to Maimonides' *Guide to the Perplexed.* His minor treatises include *Tomer Deborah* (The Palm Tree of Deborah, an allusion to Judges 4:5), a mystic's statement on ethics. He taught the classical doctrine of *imitatio dei:* in his acts and thoughts man is to imitate divine qualities (such as mercy and compassion), represented in the ten *Sephirot*, emanations through which God, the Infinite (*En Sof*), and as such beyond human knowledge, becomes manifest. (Such *Sephirot* are "Sovereignty" and "Loving-kindness" mentioned in the texts that follow.) In "imitating" divine qualities man acts upon the *Sephirot* and contributes to their functioning; man's life is of cosmic significance. The *Tomer Deborah,* from which the passages that follow are taken, was first printed in Venice in 1589 and became very popular among Jewish moralists, both mystical and non-mystical.

Who is a God Like Unto Thee? (Micah 7:18)

This refers to the Holy One, blessed is he, as a patient King Who bears insult in a manner that is above human understanding. For behold, without doubt, there is nothing hidden from His providence. Furthermore, there is no moment when man is not nourished and does not exist by virtue of the divine power which flows down upon him. It follows that no man ever sins against God without the divine affluence pouring into him at that very moment, enabling him to exist and to move his limbs. Despite the fact that he uses it for sin, that power is not withheld from him in any way. But the Holy One, blessed is he, bears this insult and continues to empower him to move his limbs, even though he uses the power in that very moment for sin and perversity offending the Holy One, blessed be he, who, nonetheless, suffers it. Nor must you say that He cannot withhold that good, for it lies in His power in the moment it takes to say the word 'moment' to wither the sinner's hand or foot, as He did to [King] Jeroboam. And yet though it lies in His power to arrest the divine flow— and He might have said: "If you sin against Me do so under your own power, not with Mine"—He does not, on this account, withhold His goodness from man, bearing the insult, pouring out His power and bestowing of His goodness. This is to be insulted and bear the insult, beyond words. This is why the ministering angels refer to the Holy One, blessed is he, as "the patient King." And this is the meaning of the prophet's words: "Who is a God like unto Thee?" He means: "Thou, the good and merciful, art God, with the power to avenge and claim Thy debt, yet Thou art patient and bearest insult until man repents." Behold this is a virtue man should make his own, namely, to be patient and allow himself to be insulted even to this extent and yet not refuse to bestow of his goodness to the recipients.

The Disease of Pride

Now I have found a cure by which a man can be cured of the disease of pride and enter the gates of humility. It is that he accustom himself to flee honor as much as possible, for if he allows honor to be paid him he will become attuned to such matters of pride and his nature will find satisfaction in it and he will find it difficult to be cured.

I have further found a good medicine, though not as effective as the other. This is that man should train himself to do two things: first, to honor all creatures, in whom he recognizes the exalted nature of the Creator Who in wisdom created man. And so it is with all creatures, that the wisdom of the Creator is in them. He should see for himself that they are therefore exceedingly to be honored for the Creator of all, the most exalted Wise One has busied Himself with them and if man despises them he touches upon the honor of their Creator.

The second is to bring the love of his fellow-men into his heart, even loving the wicked as if they were his brothers and more so until the love of his fellow-men becomes firmly fixed in his heart. He should love even the wicked in his heart saying: "Would that these were righteous, returning in repentance, so that they were all great men, acceptable to the Omnipresent; as the faithful lover of all Israel [Moses] said: 'Would that all the people of the Lord were prophets' " (Num. 11:29).

How can he love them? By recalling in his thoughts the good qualities they possess, by covering their defects and refusing to look at their faults and looking only at their good qualities. He should say to himself: "If this loathsome beggar were very rich how much then would I rejoice in his company, as I rejoice in the company of some other. But if he were to don the splendid garments of some other there would be no difference between him and his superior; why then should his honor be less in my eyes? Behold, in God's eyes he is superior to me for he is plagued with suffering and poverty and cleansed from sin and why should I hate one whom the Holy One, blessed is he, loves?" In this way man's heart will turn towards the good and he will accustom himself to ponder on all the good qualities we have mentioned.

Loving-kindness

How shall a man train himself to acquire the quality of loving-kindness? The main way in which man can enter into the secret of loving-kindness is to love God with perfect love so as not to forsake His service for any reason whatsoever for nothing has any value at all for him compared with the Blessed One's love. Therefore, he should primarily attend to the requirements of God's service and the rest of his time may be for other needs.

This love should be firmly fixed in his heart whether he receives good at the hands of the Holy One, blessed is he, or whether he receives sufferings and rebukes. These latter, too, he should look upon as tokens of God's love. As it is written: "Faithful are the wounds of a friend" (Prov. 27:6). And it is written: "With all thy might" (Deut. 6:5) which the sages explain as, "For whichever measure He measures out to thee," in order to include all measures under "Loving-kindness." It will then be found that the secret of his life's direction will be from "Sovereignty," but even when "Sovereignty" acts in judgment it is still bound to "Loving-kindness." This was the quality of Nahum of Gamzu who used to say: "This, too, is good," [14] namely, to bind it constantly to the side of "Loving-kindness" which is called "Good." He used to say: "Also this, which appears to belong to the Left bound to 'Power,' is for nothing but good, that is bound to 'Loving-kindness.'" He concentrated on the good side of the quality and concealed its judgment. This is a great method of constantly binding oneself to "Loving-kindness."

In the *Tikkunim*[15] it is explained: "Who is a saint? He who does loving-kindness to his Creator." For in the acts of benevolence man carries out in the lower worlds after the same pattern and this is what is meant by doing loving-kindness to his Creator. It is necessary, therefore, to know the types of benevolence practised among men, all of which he should do on his Creator's behalf in the upper worlds, if he wants to acquire the quality of loving-kindness.

X. The Ways of the Hasidim

ISRAEL BEN ELIEZER,

THE BAAL SHEM TOV

Hasidic Accounts

The Hasidism that rose in Eastern Europe in the eighteenth century was a reaction against an overemphasis on talmudic learning on the one hand, and on radical mystical Messianism (which had expressed itself in the Sabbatian movement) on the other. Hasidism popularized older Kabbalist ideas; it taught the immanence of God in all existence; it cultivated religious enthusiasm and stressed simple piety and ethics; it considered prayer to be a "cleaving" to God; it produced a type of charismatic leader (the *Zaddik*), around whom the hasidic fellowship centered.

Israel ben Eliezer, the Baal Shem Tov (Master of the Holy Name, *ca.* 1700–1760), founder of Hasidism, lived in Medzibozh, Podolia, from where the new movement spread. His teachings were orally transmitted; foremost among his disciples were Dov Baer of Mezrich ("The Great Maggid") and Jacob Joseph of Polnoy, the recorder of early hasidic teachings. The Baal Shem Tov's saintly life and miraculous deeds became the subject of many legends, reverently preserved by the hasidic communities. The opposition to Hasidism on the part of the orthodox community culminated in a ban of excommunication, pronounced in 1772 by Elijah, the Gaon of Vilna, spokesman of the Mitnagdim ("the opponents"). Hasidism, however, continued to function as a vital force in Judaism.

The first part of the material that follows is taken from the legendary tradition that developed around the Baal Shem Tov, as restated by Martin Buber, the modern interpreter of Hasidism. The second part consists of quotations from *Tzavaat ha-Rivash* (The Testament of the Baal Shem).

Legends

The Tree of Knowledge

They say that once, when all souls were gathered in Adam's soul, at the hour he stood beside the Tree of Knowledge, the soul of the Baal Shem Tov went away, and did not eat of the tree.

His Father's Words

Israel's father died while he was still a child.

When he felt death drawing near, he took the boy in his arms and said: "I see that you will make my light shine out, and it is not given me to rear you to manhood. But, dear son, remember all your days that God is with you, and that because of this, you need fear nothing in all the world."

Israel treasured these words in his heart.

Themselves

The Baal Shem said:

In the prayers we say: "God of Abraham, God of Isaac, and God of Jacob," and not: "God of Abraham, Isaac, and Jacob," for Isaac and Jacob did not base their work on the searching and service of Abraham; they themselves searched for the unity of the Maker and his service.

The Torah is Perfect

Concerning the verse of the psalm: "The law of the Lord is perfect" (Ps. 19:8), the Baal Shem said:

It is still quite perfect. No one has touched it as yet, not a whit and not a jot of it. Up to this hour, it is still quite perfect.

Without the World to Come

Once the spirit of the Baal Shem was so oppressed that it seemed to him he would have no part in the coming world. Then he said to himself: "If I love God, what need have I of the world to come!"

Simplicity

Once the Baal Shem said to his disciples: Now that I have climbed so many rungs in the service of God, I let go of all of them and hold to the simple faith of making myself a vessel for God. It is, indeed, written: "The simple believeth every word" (Prov. 14:15) but it is also written: "The Lord preserveth the simple" (Ps. 116:6).

To One Who Admonished

The Baal Shem said this to a zaddik who used to preach admonishing sermons: What do you know about admonishing! You yourself have remained unacquainted with sin all the days of your life, and you have had nothing to do with the people around you—how should you know what sin is!

With the Sinners

The Baal Shem said:

I let sinners come close to me, if they are not proud. I keep the scholars and the sinless away from me if they are proud. For the sinner who knows that he is a sinner, and therefore considers himself base—God is with him, for He "dwelleth with them in the midst of their uncleannesses" (Lev. 16:16). But concerning him who prides himself on the fact that he is unburdened by sin, God says, as we know from the Talmud: "There is not enough room in the world for myself and him."

Love

The Baal Shem said to one of his disciples:

The lowest of the low you can think of, is dearer to me than your only son is to you.

The Temptation

It is told:

Sabbatai Zevi, the "false Messiah" long dead, came to the Baal Shem and begged him to redeem him. Now it is well known that the work of redemption is accomplished by binding the stuff of life to the stuff of life, by binding mind to mind, and soul to soul. In this way, then, the Baal Shem began to bind himself to that other, but slowly and cautiously, for he feared he might try to harm him. Once, when the Baal Shem lay asleep, Sabbatai Zevi came and tried to tempt him to become as he himself was. Then the Baal Shem hurled him away with such vigor that he fell to the very bottom of the nether world. When the Baal Shem spoke of him, he always said: "A holy spark was within him, but Satan caught him in the snare of pride."

The Testament

Equality

The principle of equality is of major importance. This means that every person should be equal in a man's eyes whether that person lacks knowledge or whether he knows the whole Torah. How does one attain this attitude of equality? It is attained by constant clinging to God, for out of a constant concern to cling to God, one has no time to think of other matters.

If one serves God with great attachment, he should not consider himself greater than his fellow, for he himself is simply like other beings, created to serve God. God has given his neighbor intelligence, just as He has given it to him. Moreover, how is he more important than a worm, for the worm, too, serves God with all its understanding and power? Indeed, man, himself, is even a worm and grub, as it is said: "For I am a worm and not a man" (Ps. 22:7), and if God had not given man intelligence, he would only be able to serve Him as the worm does. Therefore, if man is no more important to God than a worm, can he be more important to God than other men? A man should think of himself as a worm, and should realize that all other such small creatures are just as important to God as men are, for all of them are His creations and the only ability men possess beyond the lower animals is only that which the Creator has given them.

Prayer

When a man is on a low plane of attachment to God, it is better that he pray from the prayer book, because when he reads the written words and concentrates, he will then be able to pray with more intention. But when he has already a high plane of attachment to God, it is better to close his eyes so that sight should not interfere with his attachment to the upper world of God. The Baal Shem Tov said that the upper world was revealed to him, not because he had studied much Talmud and commentaries, but because of the prayers which he always uttered with great intensity.

Sometimes the evil inclination will mislead a man by telling him that he committed a great sin even though the transgression involved nothing more than a severe application of the law or may not have been a sin at all; in which case, the evil inclination simply wishes to sadden him and thus prevent him from worshipping God. One must be careful to detect this deceit and say to the evil inclination: "I do not pay attention to the severe law you accuse me of having transgressed, for your intention is simply to keep me from serving God. But if in truth it was a sin, then God will have more joy on my account if I pay it no heed and refuse to be saddened by my transgression. On the contrary! I shall worship Him, in joy, for it is an important principle that one should avoid sadness as much as possible during the service of God.

Do not increase detailed observances in any matter, for it is the intention of the evil inclination to cause a man to fear that he has not properly fulfilled his obligation in this particular matter in order to cause a man to grow sad, and sadness severely restrains a man from serving God properly. Even if he stumbles into sin, he should not be overly sad, for this might make him neglect his worship altogether. He should only be regretful and then return to rejoice in his Creator. Even if he knows that he has not properly fulfilled an obligation because of circumstances beyond his control, he should not be sad, but rather should he consider that God inquires into man's inner intentions, and God knows that he wishes to fulfill his obligations even perfectly, but he simply cannot.

The Sinner and Repentance

"The words of his mouth are iniquity and deceit, he has ceased to be wise, to do good" (Ps. 36:4). There are two kinds of people: One is a complete sinner who knows his Master, but rebels against Him. As for the second, the evil impulse closes his eyes and he deems himself a completely righteous man and is so regarded by others. He may even study, pray and fast in self-affliction. Yet, for nothing does he toil for he possesses no genuine attachment to God, no complete faith as is required in order to be attached to God at all times. Nor does he know the main principle of worship: the proper way to study, to pray, to fulfill a commandment for its own sake.

The difference between these two men is that for the complete sinner there is a possibility of a cure, for when he comes to the awakening or repentance, he returns to God with all his heart and will beseech the Lord to lead him in the "path dwelling with light" (Job 38:19). But for the second type of man, there is no possibility for improvement, for his eyes are barred from seeing God, His greatness and works. For, he is righteous in his own eyes, so how can he return in repentance?

COMMUNION WITH GOD AND MEN

Abraham Kalisker

The following two passages are from letters of Abraham Kalisker (died 1810), a disciple of Dov Baer of Mezritch, who, however, pursued an independent course of thought; the letters were written from Palestine, whither he had emigrated in 1777. The first passage expounds the mystical *nihil* (*ayin,* naught, nothingness), self-abasement before God, thus making room for God and fellow man; the second is in praise of fellowship; true membership in a community of faith is seen as a way to the communion with God.

I

[. . .] The final aim of Torah and *Hokhmah* [i.e., wisdom] [. . .] is to attain the perfect *ayin,* everywhere a man should render his self non-existent; the very source of wisdom is *ayin.* *Ayin* is its very root and from this root grow humility and lowliness, even as our sages said: "The Torah is fulfilled only by him

who makes himself like the desert," [1] free to poor and rich alike,
and who regards himself as no greater than his fellow man, but
feels "non-existent" before him. In this way they [man and his
fellow man] are integrated one into the other, for *ayin* combines
a thing and its opposite, and therefrom results the straight lines
which encompasses peace and blessing.

II

[. . .] Whoever is smitten by his conscience let him, for
the sake of God and for his own sake, act as follows: Let him
seek peace and fortify it [. . .] and if, Heaven forbid, his heart
urges him to separate himself from the fellowship of men, let
him hasten swiftly to his spiritually stronger brethren who truly
and intently obey the voice of God, and say to them, "My breth-
ren-in-soul, save me and let me hear the word of God, that He
may heal my broken heart." Moreover, let this man school himself to fill his heart with love for his fellows even if it should
lead to the departure of the soul. Let him persevere in this until
his soul and the soul of his brethren cleave together. And when
they have all become as one, God will dwell in their midst, and
they will receive from Him an abundance of salvation and consolation. [. . .]

THE TEACHINGS

OF MENDEL OF KOTZK

Hasidic Accounts

Mendel of Kotzk, who died in 1859, was a disciple of the hasidic master
Yaakov Yitzhak of Pshysha ("the Yehudi"), who had studied under
Yaakov Yitzhak, "the Seer" of Lublin, who in turn belonged to the
group of disciples of Dov Baer of Mezritch, a successor to the Baal
Shem, founder of Hasidism. But with Mendel of Kotzk traditional
hasidic leadership and the idea of the communion between rabbi and
congregation underwent a crisis. In contradistinction to the ideals of
love, mercy, religious group life, stressed by his predecessors, Mendel

emphasized the tragic side of life, the chaotic element in man; he called for rigid discipline of learning, individual effort toward spiritual growth, and withdrawal from the crowd. The way to truth, he argued, demands solitude, suffers no imitation, and no compromise. Mendel himself spent the last twenty years of his life in virtual isolation; his disciples had left him.

After Waking

One morning after prayer the rabbi of Kotzk said:

When I woke up today, it seemed to me that I was not alive. I opened my eyes, looked at my hands, and saw that I could use them. So I washed them. Then I looked at my feet and saw that I could walk with them. So I took a few steps. Now I said the blessing: "Blessed art thou who quickenest the dead," and knew that I was alive.

The Lord of the Castle

Rabbi Mendel once spoke to his hasidim about a certain parable in Midrash: How a man passed by a castle and, seeing it on fire and no one trying to put out the blaze, thought that this must be a castle without an owner, until the lord of the castle looked down on him and said: "I am the lord of the castle." [2] When Rabbi Mendel said the words: "I am the lord of the castle," all those around him were struck with great reverence, for they all felt: "The castle is burning, but it has a lord."

To What Purpose Was Man Created?

Rabbi Mendel of Kotzk once asked his disciple Rabbi Yaakov of Radzimin: "Yaakov, to what purpose was man created?" He answered: "So that he might perfect his soul."

"Yaakov," said the zaddik, "is that what we learned from our teacher, Rabbi Bunam? No, indeed! Man was created so that he might lift up the Heavens."

The Ladder

Rabbi Mendel of Kotzk said to his disciples:

The souls descended from the realms of Heaven to earth on a ladder. Then it was taken away. Now up there they are calling the souls home. Some do not budge from the spot, for how can one get to Heaven without a ladder? Others leap and fall, and leap again and give up. But there are those who know very well that they cannot make it, but try and try over and over again until God catches hold of them and pulls them up.

Man's Advantage

This is what Rabbi Mendel said about the words in the Scriptures: "This is the law of the burnt-offering" (Lev. 6:2):

Why does God demand sacrifice of man and not of the angels? That of the angels would be purer than that of man could ever be. But what God desires is not the deed but the preparation. The holy angels cannot prepare themselves; they can only do the deed. Preparation is the task of man who is caught in the thicket of tremendous obstacles and must free himself. This is the advantage of the works of man.

Immersion

This is what the rabbi of Kotzk said concerning Rabbi Akiba's saying that "God is the waters of immersion of Israel":[3] "The waters of immersion only purify a man if he is wholly immersed, so that not a hair is showing. That is how we should be immersed in God."

God's Dwelling

"Where is the dwelling of God?"

This was the question with which the rabbi of Kotzk surprised a number of learned men who happened to be visiting him.

They laughed at him: "What a thing to ask! Is not the whole world full of his glory!"

Then he answered his own question:

"God dwells wherever man lets him in."

Fathers and Sons

A man came to the rabbi of Kotzk and complained of his sons who refused to support him, though he was old and no longer able to earn his own livelihood. "I was always ready to do anything at all for them," he said, "and now they won't have anything to do with me."

Silently the rabbi raised his eyes to Heaven. "That's how it is," he said softly. "The father shares in the sorrow of his sons, but the sons do not share in the sorrow of their father."

No Strange God

They asked the rabbi of Kotzk: "What is new about King David's saying, 'There shall no strange God be in thee' (Ps. 81:10)? For was it not specifically stated in the decalogue: 'Thou shalt have no other gods before Me'" (Exod. 20:3).

He replied: "The meaning is this: God ought not to be a stranger to you."

Worry

A hasid told the rabbi of Kotzk about his poverty and troubles. "Don't worry," advised the rabbi. "Pray to God with all your heart, and the merciful Lord will have mercy upon you."

"But I don't know how to pray," said the other.

Pity surged up in the rabbi of Kotzk as he looked at him. "Then," he said, "you have indeed a great deal to worry about."

Holiness

It is written: "And ye shall be holy men unto Me" (Exod. 22:30).

The rabbi of Kotzk explained: "Ye shall be holy unto me, but as men, ye shall be humanly holy unto me."

Afar Off

This is how Rabbi Mendel expounded the verse from the Scriptures: "Am I a God near at hand . . . and not a God afar off" (Jer. 23:23)?

"Afar off" refers to the wicked. "Near at hand" refers to the righteous. God says: "Do I want him who is already close to me, do I want the righteous? Why, I also want him who is afar off, I want him who is wicked!"

Great Guilt

Rabbi Mendel said:

He who learns the Torah and is not troubled by it, who sins and forgives himself, who prays because he prayed yesterday—a very scoundrel is better than he!

Comparing One to Another

Someone once told Rabbi Mendel that a certain person was greater than another whom he also mentioned by name.

Rabbi Mendel replied: "If I am I because I am I, and you are you because you are you, and you are you because I am I, then I am not I, and you are not you."

What Cannot Be Imitated

The rabbi of Kotzk said:

Everything in the world can be imitated except truth. For truth that is imitated is no longer truth.

First Prize

Rabbi Yehiel Meir, who was a poor man, went in to his teacher, the rabbi of Kotzk, with a beaming face and told him he had won the first prize in a lottery. "That wasn't through any fault of mine," said the zaddik. Rabbi Yehiel went home and distributed the money among needy friends.

Different Customs

A hasid of the rabbi of Kotzk and a hasid of the rabbi of Tchernobil were discussing their ways of doing things.

The disciple of the rabbi of Tchernobil said: "We stay awake all night between Thursday and Friday, on Friday we give alms in proportion to what we have, and on the Sabbath we recite the entire Book of Psalms."

"And we," said the man from Kotzk, "stay awake every night as long as we can; we give alms whenever we run across a poor man and happen to have money in our pockets, and we do not say the psalms it took David seventy years of hard work to make, all in a row, but according to the needs of the hour."

Thou Shalt Not Steal

Rabbi Yehiel Meir of Gostynin had gone to his teacher in Kotzk for the Feast of Weeks. When he came home, his father-in-law asked him: "Well, did your people over there receive the Torah differently than anywhere else?"

"Certainly!" said his son-in-law.

"What do you mean?" asked the other.

"Well, to give you an instance," said Rabbi Yehiel. "How do you here interpret 'thou shalt not steal' " (Exod. 20:15)?

"That we shall not steal from our fellow men," answered his father-in-law. "That's perfectly clear."

"We don't need to be told that any more," said Rabbi Yehiel. "In Kotzk this is interpreted to mean: You shall not steal from yourself."

Speak unto the Children of Israel

When a disciple of the rabbi of Lentshno visited the rabbi of Kotzk, his host said to him: "Give my greetings to your teacher. I love him very much. But why does he cry to God to send the Messiah? Why does he not rather cry to Israel to turn to God? It is written: 'Wherefore criest thou unto Me? Speak unto the children of Israel' " (Exod. 14:15).

The Three Pillars

Rabbi Mendel said:

Three pillars support the world: Study, worship, and good deeds, and as the world approaches its end the two first will shrink, and only good deeds will grow. And then what is written will become truth: "Zion shall be redeemed with justice" (Isa. 1:27).

IN PREPARATION FOR
THE DAY OF ATONEMENT

A Hasidic Account

Shmelke, rabbi of Nikolsburg in Moravia (died 1778), was a disciple of
Dov Baer, the Maggid of Mezrich, chief disciple of the Baal Shem.
The piece that follows, taken from *Divre Torah,* collected hasidic
teachings (Josefow, 1852), describes a "revivalist" sermon. In addition
to the actual address, the preacher's accompanying action and the people's reaction are also given: the people are not passive listeners; they
are participants in the drama of *Teshuvah* ("turning," return to God,
repentance); the whole being is involved in the response to the Zaddik's
(hasidic leader's) words.

We all entered the old House of Prayer fearful and trembling, and the entire hall was filled an hour and a half before the
prayer. When our rabbi reached the threshold of the House of
Prayer wrapped in a prayer shawl he went up to the Ark, crying
as he went in a loud voice the verse: "For on this day shall atonement be made for you, to cleanse you; from all your sins shall
ye be clean before the Lord" (Lev. 16:30); and he quoted Rabbi
Akiba: "Happy are you, O Israel; before whom do you purify
yourselves and who is it that purifies you—if not your Father
who is in heaven." [4]

At once all the people burst into tears. When the Zaddik
reached the Ark, he began to recite various verses to awaken the
people to repentance, such as: "Against Thee, Thee only, have
I sinned, and done that which is evil in Thy sight" (Ps. 51:6);
"For I do declare mine iniquity; I am full of care because of my
sin" (Ps. 38:19); "Purge me with hyssop, and I shall be clean;
wash me, and I shall be whiter than snow" (Ps. 51:9); "And I
will sprinkle clean water upon you, and ye shall be clean; from
all your uncleannesses, and from all your idols, will I cleanse
you" (Ezek. 36:35).

Afterwards he began to expound the loftiness of the holy

and awesome Day of Atonement, on which every man can find
help and redemption to enable him to redeem his soul:

"Come, my beloved brothers, my heart's companions, let us
purify ourselves before him, for on this Day of Atonement His
compassion will certainly be moved in our favor. But you must
know, my brothers, that the reciting of, 'Hear, O Israel' is one of
the principles of repentance. Let us recite, 'Hear, O Israel,' as
though we were giving our lives for the sanctification of the
Name of God. For indeed Abraham our father offered up his
life for the sanctification of the Name of God and threw himself
into the fiery furnace, and Isaac his son offered himself at the
Binding. If we follow their footseps and do as they did and sanctify his great Name with love, and cry all together, 'Hear, O Israel,' with devotion, they will stand and intercede for us on the
holy and awesome day."

At once all the people burst into tears and cried, "Hear, O
Israel, the Lord our God, the Lord is one."

Then our master and rabbi continued and said: "After having merited the sanctification and proclamation of the unity of
his Name out of His great love for us, we have no doubt merited
the purification of our hearts for His service and for his fear.
But we must still fulfill a great principle of repentance, which
is the acceptance of the commandment, 'Thou shalt love thy
neighbor as thyself' " (Lev. 19:18).

At once all the people cried after him, "Thou shalt love thy
neighbor as thyself."

Then our rabbi continued and said: "Since we have merited
the sanctification of His Name and the unification of our souls
to love our neighbors, God will help us to find forgiveness, and
we shall merit the purification of our thoughts as the Blessed
One has commanded us in His holy Torah; the Torah itself
will intercede for us."

At once all the people began to make confession of their
iniquities. After they had finished, our rabbi took a scroll and
expounded the verse, "Behold, I was brought forth in iniquity,
and in sin did my mother conceive me" (Ps. 51:7). He said, "Who
can hear these words without his heart being torn to shreds? Even
a heart of stone would melt."

Our rabbi also expounded as follows: "The principle behind our purification is alluded to in the Mishnah, 'Heave-offering seedlings that have become unclean become clean again if re-planted, for they do not carry uncleanliness,' [5] that is to say, heave-offering seedlings that became unclean when detached from the earth lose their uncleanliness when replanted. For as long as seedlings are attached to the earth they are clean. When plucked from the earth they can become unclean. But if they are attached to their source again, their uncleanliness stops.

"So it is with us. Our souls are hewn from the pure place under the throne of glory, and when our souls come to this world they become unclean because of our iniquities. But when a man attaches his thoughts to the Name of God, the soul returns and attaches itself to its source, and is cleansed of its uncleanliness, as the Scripture says, 'But ye that cleave unto the Lord your God are alive every one of you this day' (Deut. 4:4). For when a man clings to God with all his soul, he revives his soul by cleansing it of its uncleanliness, as it is said, 'are alive every one of you this day.' It is also said, 'Light is sown for the right-eous, and gladness for the upright in heart' (Ps. 97:11); for when we have cleansed our soul like a seedling that returns to its source, there will be 'gladness for the upright in heart.' "

Our master continued and said: "But you must know that the weeping on this day will not avail if there is sadness in it, for 'the Divine Presence does not rest . . . in the midst of sad-ness . . . but in the midst of joy at keeping a commandment.' [6] Indeed, this day on which we merit the stripping of all the crookedness from the hearts, and the approach to the King over all kings, the Holy One, blessed be he, and the return of our souls to their source—this day is indeed a day of joy, when his hand is opened to receive those who return, to make atonement for us and cleanse our souls. Therefore, let all the tears we shed on this day be tears of joy, for we have merited the attachment unto the Lord, we who 'are alive every one of us this day.'

DEATH

Hasidic Teachings

A person's or a group's attitude to death is indicative of his attitude to life. In a special sense this is particularly true of Hasidism, which, more than other religious trends in Judaism, realized the preciousness of life. The following reports, pertaining to a variety of hasidic masters' thoughts on death, are culled from a wide range of sources.

The Purpose of Creation

In the hour of his death the Baal Shem said: "Now I know the purpose for which I was created."

The End of Rabbi Susya

Rabbi Susya lived to a great age. For seven years before his death, he was bedridden and in pain, in atonement, it was said, for the sins of Israel. His gravestone is inscribed: "Here lieth he who served God in love, rejoiced in pain, and turned many away from guilt."

The Divine Nothing

Just before he died, Rabbi Shneur Zalman of Ladi asked his grandson: "Dost thou see aught?"

The grandson looked at the rabbi in surprise. Thereupon the dying man said: "I see as yet only the Divine Nothing that gives life to the universe."

Learning to Die

When Rabbi Bunam was lying on his deathbed, his wife wept bitterly. Thereupon he said: "Why dost thou weep? All my life has been given me merely that I might learn to die."

Optimism and Faith

When Rabbi Elimelekh of Lizensk perceived that his end was approaching, he made himself master of an extraordinary cheerfulness. One of his disciples inquired the reason for his unusual mood. The rabbi thereupon took the hand of his faithful disciple into his own, and said: "Why should I not rejoice, seeing that I am about to leave this world below, and enter into the higher worlds of eternity? Do you not recall the words of the Psalmist (23:4): 'Yea, though I walk through the valley of the shadow of death, I will fear no evil, for Thou art with me.' Thus does the grace of God display itself."

The Time of Confession

When Rabbi Zalman Hasid was nigh unto death, his friends came to his bedside, and asked him to recite the "Confession," enjoined for the occasion. The Rabbi smiled and said: "Friends, do you really believe a death-bed confession contains much merit? No, friends! A man should 'confess' when he is seated at his dining table, and eating the good food thereon."

God's Partner

Rabbi David Leikes lived more than a hundred years. He was esteemed as an authority in the civil law of the rabbis, and his decisions were admired by all the *Dayyanim* [religious judges]. Once a very complicated case arose, when the aged rabbi was on his death-bed. His demise was expected hourly. The *Dayyanim* hoped that the ancient rabbi's mind might still be sufficiently clear to aid them, perhaps for the last time. They visited his home and stated their request. The rabbi's children protested vigorously, and argued against troubling him, lest thereby his end be hastened. Suddenly the door opened, and the dying rabbi entered. "Do you know," he said, "that we are taught by the Talmud that one who judges a case correctly becomes thereby God's partner? Yet you wish to deprive me of this opportunity."

He gave his decision in the difficult case in a manner so remarkable that it left no doubt of its correctness; he returned to his bed with the help of his children, and a moment later he died.

Why We Fear to Die

The Gerer Rabbi said: "Why does a man fear to die? Is he not returning to his Father in Heaven? The reason lies in this:

in the world to come, a man obtains a clear retrospect of all his deeds upon earth. When he perceives the senseless errors he has committed, he cannot abide himself. Therein lies his Purgatory."

When the Gerer was undergoing his last illness, the physician who attended him advised him to gain a little strength by more sleep.

The rabbi replied: "Does not the wise physician know that it is Torah and prayer, not sleep, which grants strength unto a Jew?"

XI. The Land of Israel, Exile, and Redemption

JERUSALEM

Benjamin of Tudela

Much of our knowledge of the twelfth-century Jewish communities the world over is owed to the *Itinerary* of Benjamin of Tudela, Navarre. The actual purpose of Benjamin's travels which lasted several years and ended in 1173, is unknown; perhaps it was a Jew's urge to gain a comprehensive firsthand view of his dispersed people and to make a pilgrimage to the land of Israel. From Spain, Benjamin went to Rome, from there to Otranto and Corfu and across Greece to Constantinople. He visited the Greek Archipelago, Rhodes, and Cyprus, and went to Antioch. A journey through Palestine followed; from there he went to Damascus, Bagdad, and Persia, and from there home by way of Aden, Assouan, Egypt, and Sicily. Germany and France (beyond its southern part) were not included in his tour. His descriptions (based on notes made on the spot) cover the structure of a community, its leaders, and the occupational life of its members; there are also references to religious life and lore and to the sects of the time. Only a part of his travel diary is extant.

Our selection consists of the notations on his visit to Jerusalem. As a result of the First Crusade (1099) and the establishment of the Christian Kingdom of Jerusalem, the Jewish community in Palestine was greatly diminished in size and importance. But Benjamin came to the country not only to study the sorry present; mainly, he wanted to relive the glories of Israel's past and to behold its remains.

The *Itinerary*, written in Hebrew (*Masaot Benjamin*), was first published in Constantinople in 1543, then, from a better manuscript, in Ferrara in 1556. A Latin translation (Antwerp) appeared in 1575, and in 1633, the Hebrew text with a Latin rendition. An English translation was published in London (1625), a Dutch, in Amsterdam (1666), a Yiddish, in Amsterdam (1691), and a French, in Haag (1735).

Jerusalem [. . .] is a small city, fortified by three walls. It is full of people whom the Mohammedans call Jacobites, Syrians, Greeks, Georgians and Franks, and of people of all tongues. It contains a dyeing-house, for which the Jews pay a small rent annually to the king, on condition that besides the Jews no other dyers be allowed in Jerusalem. There are about two hundred Jews who dwell under the Tower of David in one corner of the city. The lower portion of the wall of the Tower of David, to the extent of about ten cubits, is part of the ancient foundation set up by our ancestors, the remaining portion having been built by the Mohammedans. There is no structure in the whole city stronger than the Tower of David.

The city also contains two buildings, from one of which—the hospital—there issue forth four hundred knights; and therein all the sick who come thither are lodged and cared for in life and in death. The other building is called the Temple of Solomon; it is the palace built by Solomon the king of Israel. Three hundred knights are quartered there, and issue therefrom every day for military exercise, besides those who come from the land of the Franks and the other parts of Christendom, having taken upon themselves to serve there a year or two until their vow is fulfilled. In Jerusalem is the great church called the Sepulchre, and here is the burial-place of Jesus, unto which the Christians make pilgrimages.

Jerusalem has four gates—the gate of Abraham, the gate of David, the gate of Zion, and the gate of Gushpat, which is the gate of Jehoshaphat, facing our ancient Temple, now called Templum Domini. Upon the site of the sanctuary Omar ben al Khataab erected an edifice with a very large and magnificent cupola, into which the Gentiles do not bring any image or effigy, but they merely come there to pray. In front of this place is the Western Wall, which is one of the walls of the Holy of Holies.[1] This is called the Gate of Mercy, and thither come all the Jews to pray before the wall of the court of the Temple. In Jerusalem, attached to the palace which belonged to Solomon, are the stables built by him, forming a very substantial structure, composed of large stones, and the like of it is not to be seen anywhere in the world. There is also visible up to this day the pool used by the priests before offering their sacrifices, and the Jews coming thither write their names upon the wall. The gate of Jehoshaphat leads to the valley of Jehoshaphat, which is the gathering-place of nations.[2] Here is the pillar called Absalom's Hand, and the sepulchre of King Uzziah.

In the neighborhood is also a great spring, called the Waters of Siloam, connected with the brook of Kidron. Over the spring is a large structure dating from the time of our ancestors, but little water is found, and the people of Jerusalem for the most part drink the rain-water, which they collect in cisterns in their houses. From the valley of Jehoshaphat one ascends the Mount of Olives;[3] it is the valley only which separates Jerusalem from the Mount of Olives. From the Mount of Olives one sees the Sea of Sodom,[4] and at a distance of two parasangs from the Sea of Sodom is the Pillar of Salt into which Lot's wife was turned; the sheep lick it continually, but afterwards it regains its original shape. The whole land of the plain and the valley of Shittim as far as Mount Nebo[5] are visible from here.

In front of Jerusalem is Mount Zion,[6] on which there is no building, except a place of worship belonging to the Christians. Facing Jerusalem for a distance of three miles are the cemeteries belonging to the Israelites, who in the days of old buried their dead in caves, and upon each sepulchre is a dated inscription, but the Christians destroy the sepulchres, employing the stones thereof in building their houses. These sepulchres reach as far as Zelzah in the territory of Benjamin. Around Jerusalem are high mountains.

On Mount Zion are the sepulchres of the House of David, and the sepulchres of the kings that ruled after him. The exact place cannot be identified, inasmuch as fifteen years ago a wall of the church of Mount Zion fell in. The Patriarch commanded the overseer to take the stones of the old walls and restore therewith the church. He did so, and hired workmen at fixed wages; and there were twenty men who brought the stones from the base of the wall of Zion. Among these men there were two who were sworn friends. On a certain day the one entertained the other;

after their meal they returned to their work, when the overseer said to them, "Why have you tarried to-day?" They answered, "Why need you complain? When our fellow workmen go to their meal we will do our work." When the dinner-time arrived, and the other workmen had gone to their meal, they examined the stones, and raised a certain stone which formed the entrance to a cave. Thereupon one said to the other, "Let us go in and see if any money is to be found there." They entered the cave, and reached a large chamber resting upon pillars of marble overlaid with silver and gold. In front was a table of gold and a sceptre and crown. This was the sepulchre of King David. On the left thereof in like fashion was the sepulchre of King Solomon; then followed the sepulchres of all the kings of Judah that were buried there. Closed coffers were also there, the contents of which no man knows. The two men essayed to enter the chamber, when a fierce wind came forth from the entrance of the cave and smote them, and they fell to the ground like dead men, and there they lay until evening. And there came forth a wind like a man's voice, crying out: "Arise and go forth from this place!" So the men rushed forth in terror, and they came unto the Patriarch, and related these things to him. Thereupon the Patriarch sent for Rabbi Abraham el Constantin, the pious recluse, who was one of "the mourners for Jerusalem," [7] and to him he related all these things according to the report of the two men who had come forth. Then Rabbi Abraham replied, "These are the sepulchres of the House of David; they belong to the kings of Judah, and on the morrow let us enter, I and you and these men, and find out what is there." And on the morrow they sent for the two men, and found each of them lying on his bed in terror, and the men said: "We will not enter there, for the Lord doth not desire to show it to any man." Then the Patriarch gave orders that the place should be closed up and hidden from the sight of man unto this day. These things were told me by the said Rabbi Abraham.

MYSTIC DRAMA OF JERUSALEM

The *Zohar*

The *Zohar* (The Book of Splendor; see "Mystical Understanding of Jewish Concepts") and other medieval mystical writings present a drama wherein the phenomena of life on earth serve as mere symbols of what takes place between the human soul and its Creator, between the Community of Israel and the Holy One. In this drama, Zion and Jerusalem play a significant role. Jerusalem's position in the past, its fall and hoped-for restoration, are intricately bound up with the destiny of Israel and of the world. The destruction of Jerusalem causes a critical disruption of unity in the whole of the universe; the restoration of Zion will bring about harmony even within the Deity. The following passages, culled from various parts of the *Zohar*, illustrate the drama of the fall and the return, which takes place simultaneously on two levels, one upper, one lower: a blend of the rational and the supernatural, the heavenly and the earthly, which is Jerusalem.

I

One day the friends were walking with Rabbi Simeon. He said: "I see all other nations raised and Israel humiliated. Why so? Because the King, God, has sent away the Queen, Israel, and has put the handmaid, the alien Crown, in her place." He wept and continued: "A king without a queen is no king; if the king is attached to the handmaid of the queen, where is his glory? The handmaid rules over Zion as the Queen once ruled over it. But one day the Holy One will restore the Queen to her rightful place; who shall then rejoice like the King and the Queen?— the King because he has returned to her, and has separated from the handmaid, and the Queen because she is reunited to the King. Hence it is written: "Rejoice exceedingly, O daughter of Zion" (Zech. 9:9).

II

The souls of the Lower Paradise at times go forth and roam about the world. They behold those suffering who have been afflicted for the sake of their belief in the oneness of God. The souls return, and report to the Messiah what they have seen. The Messiah weeps aloud; he enters the Hall of the Afflicted, and there takes upon himself entirely the pain and the sufferings of Israel. So long as Israel was in the Holy Land, the service in the Sanctuary and the offerings averted afflictions from the world; now it is the Messiah who spares mankind.

III

The Messiah shall reveal himself first in the land of Galilee: it was here in the Holy Land that the destruction began. All the rulers will gather to wage war against him, and even from among Israel some evil ones will join the battle against the Messiah. The Messiah lifts up his eyes and he sees the Patriarchs standing at the ruins of God's Sanctuary. He sees Mother Rachel with tears in her eyes. The Holy One tries to comfort her, but she refuses to be comforted.

The day will come when a fire shall flame in Great Rome [Constantinople] and it will consume the towers and turrets; many among the great and powerful shall perish in it. The rulers will take counsel together and issue decrees for the destruction of Israel. The Messiah sees an image of the destruction of the Sanctuary and of all the martyred saints. The saintly fathers will then rise and gird the Messiah with weapons of war—Abraham at his right, Isaac at his left, Jacob in front of him. Whereupon the Messiah will take ten garments of holy zeal and go into hiding for forty days; no eye shall be permitted to look at him.

The Holy One will behold the Messiah thus attired, and He will take him and kiss him upon his brow and crown him with the crown that He Himself wore when the children of Israel were freed from the Egyptian bondage; with this same crown will He crown King Messiah.

Then the Messiah will enter one of the sanctuaries and there see the angels who are called "the mourners for Zion" [8] weeping over the destruction of the Holy Temple. They will give him a robe of deep red that he may begin his work of vengeance.

After having been crowned on high, the Messiah will be

crowned on earth, by the grave of Mother Rachel, to whom he will offer happy tidings; now she will let herself be comforted and will rise and kiss him.[9]

His army will consist of those who are diligent in the study of the Torah, but there will be only a few of these in the world. Yet his army will gain strength: through the merit of the infants for whose sake the Divine Presence dwells in the midst of Israel in exile. It is the young who will give strength to the Messiah.

That day, the Messiah will begin to gather the exiles from one end of the world to the other. From that day on, the Holy One will perform for Israel all the signs and wonders which He performed in Egypt.

IV

After the destruction of the Temple, blessings were withheld from the world, both on high and here below, so that the baser forces were strengthened and could exercise control over Israel who had sinned. When the Temple was destroyed and the people driven into dispersion, the Divine Presence left her home to accompany Israel into exile. Before leaving, the Divine Presence took one last look at the Holy of Holies and the places where the Priests and the Levites worshipped.

Entering the lands of dispersion, the Divine Presence saw how the people were oppressed and tyrannized over by the heathen nations. But in the days to come, the Holy One will recall the Community of Israel, and the Divine Presence will return from exile. The Holy One will speak to the Community of Israel: "Shake thyself from the dust, arise, O captive Jerusalem" (Isa. 52:2). He will erect the Sanctuary, restore the Holy of Holies, build the city of Jerusalem, and raise Israel from the dust.

TEN KINGS

A Midrash

The Midrash known as *Pirke de Rabbi Eliezer* (The Chapters of Rabbi Eliezer), based on earlier materials but compiled no earlier than the eighth century (according to L. Zunz), contains this short sketch of a history of world dominions. But the original and only true lord of the world is God, and to him the kingdom will return. This Midrash was popular in the Middle Ages and in the early modern period. The first edition was printed at Constantinople in 1514; a Latin version, with an extensive commentary, appeared in 1644.

Ten kings ruled from one end of the world to the other. The first king was the Holy One, blessed be he, who rules in heaven and on earth, and it was His intention to raise up kings on earth, as it is said, "And he changeth the times and the seasons; he removeth kings, and setteth up kings" (Dan. 2:21).

The second king was Nimrod,[10] who ruled from one end of the world to the other, for all the creatures were dwelling in one place and they were afraid of the waters of the flood, and Nimrod was king over them.

The third king was Joseph, who ruled from one end of the world to the other, and the Egyptians brought their tribute and their presents to Joseph to buy [corn]; for forty years he was second to the king, and for forty years he was king alone.

The fourth king was Solomon, who reigned from one end of the world to the other, as it is said, "And Solomon ruled over all the kingdoms" (1 Kings 4:21); and it says, "And they brought every man his present, vessels of silver, and vessels of gold, and raiment, and armour, and spices, horses, and mules, a rate year by year" (10:25).

The fifth king was Ahab, king of Israel, who ruled from one end of the world to the other, as it is said, "As the Lord thy God liveth, there is no nation or kingdom, whither my lord hath not sent to seek thee" (18:10). All the princes of the provinces were controlled by him; they sent and brought their tribute and their presents to Ahab.

The sixth king was Nebuchadnezzar, who ruled from one end of the world to the other. Moreover, he ruled over the beasts of the field and the birds of heaven, and they could not open their mouth except by the permission of Nebuchadnezzar, as it is said, "And wheresoever the children of men dwell, the beasts of the field and the fowls of the heaven hath he given into thine hand" (Dan. 2:38).

The seventh king was Cyrus, who ruled from one end of the world to the other, as it is said, "Thus saith Cyrus king of Persia, All the kingdoms of the earth hath the Lord, the God of heaven, given me." (2 Chron. 36:23).

The eighth king was Alexander of Macedonia, who ruled from one end of the world to the other, as it is said, "And as I was considering, behold, an he-goat came from the west over the face of the whole earth" (Dan. 8:5). And not only that, but he wished to ascend to heaven in order to know what is in heaven, and to descend into the depths in order to know what is in the depths, and not only that, but he attempted to go to the ends of the earth in order to know what was at the ends of the earth.

The ninth king is King Messiah, who, in the future, will rule from one end of the world to the other, as it is said, "He shall have dominion also from sea to sea" (Ps. 72:8); and another Scripture text says, "And the stone that smote the image became a great mountain, and filled the whole earth" (Dan. 2:35).

The tenth king will restore the sovereignty to its owner. He who was the first king will be the last king, as it is said, "Thus saith the Lord, the King . . . I am the first, and I am the last; and beside me there is no God" (Isa. 46:6); and it is written, "And the Lord shall be king over all the earth" (Zech. 14:9).

THE SUFFERING OF THE MESSIAH

A Midrash

The concept of the redemptive quality of suffering, most profoundly expressed in the enigmatic "Servant of the Lord" sections in Isaiah (especially chapter 53), became one of the significant motifs in the talmudic and midrashic eschatological thought. We find records of this motif (some with reference to Isaiah 53) in the third century, but the idea may be even older. A fully developed statement is preserved in the *Pesikta Rabbati* (chapters 36 and 37), a midrash compiled probably in the ninth century. The version below is from *Bereshit Rab-*

bati, by Moses ha-Darshan of Narbonne (eleventh century), as quoted by the Dominican Raymond Martini of Barcelona in his *Pugio Fidei* (The Dagger of Faith).

Said Satan to the Holy One, blessed be he: "Let me accuse the Messiah and his generation."

The Holy One answered: "You cannot prevail against him."

Satan insisted: "O Lord of the universe, give me permission and I shall succeed."

But the Holy One answered: "I shall drive Satan from the world rather than allow one soul of that generation to perish."

Thereupon the Holy One turned to the Messiah: "Messiah, my righteous one, the day will come when the sins of those that are preserved near you will impose a heavy yoke on you. Your eyes will not see the light, your ears will hear the nations of the world emit invectives, your nose will smell decay, your mouth feel a bitter taste, your tongue cleave to the roof of your mouth, your skin shrivel upon your bones, your body languish in sighs and in sadness. Are you prepared to assume these burdens? If you take these sufferings upon yourself, well and good; if not, I shall eradicate those [future sinners]."

Answered the Messiah: "Lord of the universe, happily will I take upon myself these sufferings if I know that you will restore to life all those who have died since the days of the first man. And that all those should see salvation who have been devoured by wild animals, and all those who have drowned in oceans and rivers. And that your salvation be extended also to those who have been born prematurely and to those whom you plan to create but have not yet created."

Thereto the Holy One said: "So be it."

Then took the Messiah lovingly all the sufferings upon himself, as it is said: "He was oppressed but he humbled himself" (Isa. 53:7).

CREATION AND WORLD'S HISTORY

Moses Nahmanides

The concept that the history of the world is presaged in the Biblical story of the six days of creation occupied the medieval mind. This concept, in its manifold formulations, introduced order into the chaos of events and the promise of redemption and resolution of conflicts in a final, Sabbatical, era. The account that follows is from Nahmanides' Commentary to the Pentateuch (see "Has the Messiah Come?" and "The Creation of Man").

On the first two days [of Creation] nothing reached perfection, as the world was still full of water. This suggests that the first two thousand years of world history were marked with imperfection, as there was no one who proclaimed the name of God to the children of man. It is as the sages have said, "The first two thousand years were *Tohu* (unformed)." [11] Light, however, was created on the first day, which suggests the thousand years of Adam who was the light of the world, since he recognized his Creator.

On the second day God said, "Let there be a firmament in the midst of the waters and let it divide the waters" (Gen. 1:6); this indicates the division between Noah and his children on the one hand, and the wicked ones of their generation on the other.

On the third day dry land appeared, as well as all kinds of vegetation and fruits; these intimated the events of the third millenium which commenced when Abraham was forty-eight years old, at which time, according to tradition, he began proclaiming to the world the name of God. [12] This process continued until his descendants accepted the Torah at Mount Sinai, and the Temple was built. At that time all the commandments of the Torah which are "the fruits of the world" were proclaimed.

The fourth day which marked the creation of the luminaries, large and small, symbolized the fourth millenium in world history. It began 72 years after the building of the First Temple, and was completed 172 years after the destruction of the Second

Temple. This was the era when "the children of Israel had light in their dwellings" (Exod. 10:23), as the Glory of God filled the House. The smaller luminary, the moon, symbolized the era of the Second Temple, when the Light over it was smaller. Finally, the two luminaries disappeared. The Temple was destroyed.

On the fifth day—corresponding to the fifth millenium in world history—the waters began swarming with living creatures. This indicates the time in world history when power came to the new nations that appeared upon the face of the earth. It is the era when "men are made like fishes in the sea, like swarms without a chief" (Hab. 1:14).

The sixth day, corresponding to the sixth millenium marked two creations: in the early part of the day, before sunrise, the earth gave forth living creatures, and then man was created. This was an allusion to the fact that during a part of this millenium power will still be in the hands of the kingdoms which are likened to the beasts [in the vision of Daniel], but ultimately the redeemer, as symbolized by Adam, will come.

The seventh day, the Sabbath, suggests the world to come, "the day" that shall be all Sabbath and rest in a life everlasting.

MESSIAH THE TEACHER

The Messianic hope, which originated in Biblical times, developed in the course of the centuries until it encompassed the hope for individual, national, and universal redemption. Belief in the coming of the Messiah inspired fighters and dreamers, militants and escapists, rationalists and mystics; it gave meaning to martyrdom. Messianic impatience gave rise to nihilists and revolutionaries. Since there was no dogma to stabilize the functions and the features of the Messiah, many possibilities opened themselves to thought, imagination, and fancy. There was Messiah, the arbiter of the world, and Messiah, the miraculous redeemer. It is not surprising that among the Messianic texts there appear some that speak of him as a teacher and attribute to learned discourse a redemptive quality. The first selection below is from the early medieval *Alphabet of Rabbi Akiba;* the second selection is based on a medieval Yemenite manuscript. Compare also "The Sufferings of Messiah," "Mystic Drama of Jerusalem," and "Ten Kings."

I

At that future time, the Holy One, blessed be he, will sit down in the Garden of Eden and teach, and all the righteous ones will sit before Him. The Celestial Family will be present there: to His right the sun and the planets, to His left the moon and all the stars. The Holy One, blessed be he, will explain the principles of the new Torah which He is about to issue through the Messiah.

When He reaches the homily, Zerubbabel the son of Sealtiel [13] will rise and proclaim: "Exalted and sanctified be His great name." His voice will reach from one corner of the world to the other and all people will respond and say: "Amen!" Even those from among the Israelites and the heathens who are still confined in Gehenna, the place of punishment, even they will respond and say "Amen!" out of Gehenna, and their Amen will shake the world and will be heard by the Holy One, blessed be he.

The Lord will ask: What is this frightful voice which I have heard? The ministering angels will answer Him: Master of the universe, this was the voice of people in Gehenna, faithfully responding with Amen. Whereupon the Lord's compassion will be moved strongly toward them, and he will say: Why should I punish them beyond what they have already endured? The Evil Impulse caused them to fail.

In that hour will the Lord take the keys of Gehenna, hand them over to Michael and Gabriel in the presence of all the righteous ones, and say: Go and open the gates of Gehenna and let them come out. As it says: "Open ye the gates that the righteous people that keepeth faith may enter in" (Isa. 26:2).

Then go forth Michael and Gabriel, open the gates of Gehenna, grasp each person by his hand and lead him out of Gehenna, wash him, anoint him, heal him from the wounds of Gehenna, clothe him with beautiful and good garments, grasp each one by his hand and bring him before the Holy One, blessed be he, and before all the righteous ones.

Scripture says: "Let Thy priests, O Lord God, be clothed

with salvation, and let Thy pious ones rejoice in good" (II Chron. 6:41). By "priests" Scripture means the righteous among the Gentiles who serve God as priests in this world; by "pious ones" Scripture means those who formerly were wicked in Israel [and who have repented].

II

In the Messianic future the Holy One, blessed be he, will call the Garden of Eden "Zion" and Zion He will call Garden of Eden. The desolate places in Zion He will make bloom like Paradise. He will build a Jerusalem in Heaven and call it "the throne of the Lord." The just ones who remained in Zion and the pious ones who were found there will all be placed on thrones of glory, and a crown will be put on the head of every one, and the divine splendor will be reflected in their faces.

The Holy One, blessed be he, will write down the name of every just one for a good life, and for blessed years in the Messianic age, so that he may take part in the joy of Zion and the gladness of Jerusalem. As Scripture says: "Rejoice ye with Jerusalem, and be glad with her, all ye that love her" (Isa. 66:10).

The Messiah, son of David, will be given his seat in the Academy on High; they will call him "Lord" just as they call his Master, as it is written: "And this is his name whereby he shall be called, the Lord our righteousness" (Jer. 23:6).

And as the Messiah sits in his Academy, all the people will come and sit before him to listen to the new teaching and new laws and profound wisdom which he will teach Israel. Elijah the prophet—may he be remembered for blessing—will stand as an interpreter before the Messiah, whose voice will reach from one end of the world to the other.

What will come to pass in that hour? It will come to pass that Abraham, Isaac, and Jacob, Joseph and all the tribes, Moses and all the prophets, Aaron and all the Temple servants, Samuel and all the seers, David and all the kings, Solomon and all the wise men, Daniel and all the pious, Mordecai and all the sages, Ezra and all the scribes, the Hasmonean and all the heroes, Nehemiah and all the enlightened ones, yes, all the just ones, all of them will rise from their graves by the power of the Holy Spirit, and come and take their seats in the Academy of the Messiah and listen to his discourse on the Torah and the commandments.

And the Holy One, blessed be he, will reveal to them through Elijah—may he be remembered for blessing—laws of life, laws of peace, laws of zeal, laws of purity, laws of restraint, laws of piety, laws of justice. Whosoever hears the discourse issuing from the mouth of the Messiah, he will never forget it, because it is the Holy One, blessed be he, who makes himself manifest in the Academy of the Messiah, and it is he who pours from His Holy Spirit over all the human beings in that Academy so that the Holy Spirit rests upon each and every one.

In that Academy man's own reason will make him understand the commandments, the exegesis, the deliberations, the lore, and the traditions; each one will know out of his own knowledge; as Scripture says: "And it shall come to pass afterward, that I will pour out My spirit upon all flesh; and your sons and your daughters shall prophesy, and old men shall dream dreams, your young men shall see visions" (Joel 3:1).

Even men servants and maid servants which were bought from the heathen nations will be endowed with the Holy Spirit and be able to engage in a discourse; as it says: "And also upon the servants and upon the handmaids in those days will I pour out My spirit" (Joel 3:2). And each one will have a study room in his home, a room for the Divine Presence.

THE DANCE OF THE RIGHTEOUS

Judah Loew ben Bezalel

Concerning the author see "The Sabbath and the Days of the Week." The selection that follows is from his *Be-er ha-Golah,* Prague, 1598.

In the last paragraph of the talmudic tractate Taanit the following statement is made in the name of Rabbi Eleazar: "A time will come when God will arrange a dance for the righteous in paradise. He will sit in their midst and everyone will point a finger at Him, as it is written: 'Lo, this is our God; we have waited for Him, and He will save us; this is the Lord: we have waited for Him, we will be glad and rejoice in His salvation'" (Isa. 25:9).[14]

People point to this statement and say that it is against all reason to suppose that there could be young maidens and men dancing in a holy place like the world to come, detached as it is from everything material. One must, however, understand that those words are meant to reveal a great blessing reserved for the righteous, and that deep wisdom is contained in this saying.

The dance is specially suitable for young maidens, as it is written: "Then shall the virgin rejoice in the dance, both young men and old together" (Jer. 31:13). The dance is joy expressed through action, not joy remaining in the heart. Women, and especially young maidens, are less thoughtful than men, and thought keeps back the full expression of joy. Since one day joy will find pure expression in paradise, joy itself is called the dance of the righteous. This will be the joy in God, as it is written: "Rejoice in the Lord, ye righteous" (Ps. 97:12). Therefore it is said that God will sit in their midst and everyone will point a finger at Him. This means that the righteous have no other joy except in God. He is the perfection of themselves. So far there is a simple explanation of the words of the sages.

But one must understand also what really is meant by the dance. Joy is something psychical, it is the expression of a perfection in man which belongs only to the soul but not to the material body. The body has only potential power, but no independence. Without this there is no perfection. The body is kept down by the weight of nature; it is oppressed. When therefore a man dances he experiences a greater joy, because he feels the perfection of the soul as power. Therefore it is said that God arranges a dance of the righteous in paradise, because all that is depressing and material is taken from them and only the soul has power. When it is said that God is in their midst, it means that they are freed from the material, which formed a barrier between them and God.

The dance spoken of is not any kind, but a round dance, in a circle. Every circle has a center, equidistant from any point of the circumference. Therefore it says that God sits in the center of the righteous, as all points of the circumference are joined to the center by the radii, turned towards it and attracted by it. And just as the center is apart from the circumference, so He, the Holy One, remains apart, although in their midst.

The dance has to be a round one, so that no one can say that every righteous person adheres to God in his own manner. As the dance proceeds round and round, every righteous one is joined to God not from one place only, but from all places. Pointing a finger at God means that one points out something that is separate from the rest. The righteous learn to know wherein lies God's oneness and His difference from all else that is. The pointing with the finger is the recognition of this truth.

One can only write little about such mighty matters. The wise one will add to it out of his own wisdom and knowledge. May God forgive us and make us the last participants in this holy dance.

HAS THE MESSIAH COME?

Moses Nahmanides

The debate at Barcelona in 1263 was one of the major religious disputations between Christians and Jews in the Middle Ages. It was preceded by the debate at Paris in 1240, and followed by one at Avila in 1375; the most impressive—and longest—disputation took place at Tortosa, in 1413-1414. The aim of the Christian initiators of such public meetings was to demonstrate the superiority of the Church and to gain converts to Christianity. At the Barcelona debate an attempt was made for the first time to interpret talmudic-midrashic statements in support of Christian teachings. The initiative for this disputation came from Fra Paulo (or Pablo) Christiani, a converted Jew who had become a Dominican monk; some scholars assume that he taught the Hebrew Bible and rabbinic writings to the scholarly Dominican, Raymond Martini. The disputation was sponsored by King James I of Aragon and was attended by Raymond Martini, Raymond de Peñaforte, the King's confessor, also a Dominican, by the Franciscan Peter de Janua, and the aristocracy and representatives of the population. The spokesman for Judaism was Moses ben Nahman (Nahmanides, Bonastrug de Porta, 1195-1270), rabbi in Gerona, Bible commentator, and mystic. Upon the conclusion of the debate (that lasted four days) Nahmanides wrote a Hebrew report of the proceedings, in order to counteract a possible misrepresentation of his position in the discussion. Upon the intervention of Pope Clement IV, Nahmanides was banished from Aragon. He went to Palestine (1267), where he spent the last three years of his life.

Nahmanides' account appeared in print first in Wagenseil's *Tela ignea satanae,* 1681, together with a Latin translation; both text and translation are corrupt. A more reliable text appeared in Constantinople in 1710. The best edition is by M. Steinschneider (Berlin, 1860). The following are only selected parts from the report.

Our lord the king had commanded me to debate with Fra Paulo in his majesty's palace, in the presence of himself and his council, in Barcelona. To this command I replied that I would accede if I were granted freedom of speech, whereby I craved both the permission of the king and of Fra Raymond of Peñaforte and his associates who were present. Fra Raymond of Peñaforte replied that this I could have so long as I did not speak disrespectfully. [. . .]

Then Fra Paulo began by saying that he would prove from our Talmud that the Messiah of whom the prophets had witnessed had already come. I replied, that before we argued on that, I would like him to show and tell me how this could possibly be true. [. . .] Did he wish to say that the scholars who appear in the Talmud believed concerning Jesus that he was the Messiah, and that they believed that he was completely man and truly God in accordance with the Christian conceptions of him? Was it not indeed a known fact that Jesus existed in the days of the Second Temple, being born and put to death before the destruction of that Temple? But the scholars of the Talmud were later than this destruction. [. . .] Now, if these scholars had believed in the Messiahship of Jesus and that he was genuine and his religious belief true; and if they wrote those things which Fra Paulo affirms he is going to prove that they wrote; then how was it that they continued to hold by the Jewish faith and their original religious usage? For they were Jews and continued to abide in the religion of the Jews all their days. They died as Jews, they and their children, and their disciples who heard all the words they uttered. Why did they not apostatize and turn to the religion of Jesus as has done Fra Paulo who understands from their saying that the Christian faith is the true faith? [. . .]

Fra Paulo took up the debate and claimed that in the Talmud it was stated that the Messiah had already come. He brought forward that haggadic story, contained in the Midrash to the Book of Lamentations,[15] about the man who was ploughing when his cow began lowing. An Arab was passing by and said to the man: "O Jew, O Jew, untie your cow, untie your plough, untie your coulter, for the temple has been destroyed." The man untied his cow, his plough, and his coulter. The cow lowed a second time. The Arab said to the man: "Tie your cow, tie your plough, tie your coulter, for your Messiah has been born."

To this I answered: "I do not give any credence at all to this Haggadah but it provides proof of my argument." At this the fellow shouted: "See how the writings of his fellow-Jews are denied him!" I replied: "I certainly do not believe that the Messiah was born on the day of the destruction of the Temple and as for this Haggadah, either it is not true or it has another interpretation of the sort called the mystical explanations of the wise. But I shall accept the story's plain literal statement, which you have put forward, since it furnishes me with support. Observe then that the story says that at the time of the destruction of the Temple, after it had been destroyed, on that very day, the Messiah was born. If this be so, then Jesus is not the Messiah as you affirm that he is. For he was born and was put to death before the destruction of the Temple took place, his birth being nearly two hundred years before that event according to the true chronology and seventy-three years previous to that event according to your reckonings." At these words of mine my opponent was reduced to silence.

Master Gilles who was the king's justiciary,[16] then replied to me with the remark: "At the present moment we are not discussing about Jesus, but the question rather is: whether the Messiah has come or not? You say that he has not come, but this Jewish book says that he has come."

To this I said: "You are, as is the practice of those of your profession, taking refuge in a subtlety of retort and argument.

But nevertheless I shall answer you on this point. The scholars have not stated that the Messiah has come, but they have said that he has been born. For, for example, on the day when Moses our teacher was born he had not come, nor was he a redeemer, but when he came to Pharaoh by the commandment of the Holy One and said to Pharaoh, 'Thus saith the Lord, Let my people go,' (Exod. 8:1) then he had come. And likewise the Messiah when he shall come to the Pope and shall say to him by the commandment of God: 'Let my people go,' then he shall have come. But until that day comes, he shall not have come, nor [till then] will there be any Messiah at all. For David the king, on the day when he was born, was not a king nor was he a Messiah, but when Elijah shall anoint one to be a Messiah by the commandment of the deity he [the anointed one] shall be called Messiah and when, afterwards, the Messiah shall come to the Pope to redeem us, then it shall be announced that a redeemer has come."

Hereupon my opponent Fra Paulo urged that the Biblical section Isaiah 52:13 beginning with the words "Behold, my servant shall deal wisely" [17] treats of the subject of the death of the Messiah, of his coming into the power of his enemies and that they set him among the wicked as happened also in the case of Jesus. "You do believe," asked Fra Paulo, "that this section is speaking of the Messiah?"

I answered him: "According to the real meaning of the passage the section speaks only of the community of Israel the people. For thus the prophets address them constantly, as in Isaiah 41:8: 'Thou Israel my servant' and as in Isaiah 44:1: 'O Jacob my servant.'"

Fra Paulo then rejoined: "But I can shew you from the statements of the scholars that in their view the Biblical section is speaking of the Messiah."

I replied to this as follows: "It is true that our teachers in the Haggadic books do interpret the servant, in the Biblical section referred to, as indicating the Messiah. But they never assert that he was slain by his enemies. For you will never find in any of the writings of Israel, neither in the Talmud nor in the haggadic works, that the Messiah the son of David will be slain or that he will ever be delivered into the hands of his foes or buried among them that are wicked.

My opponent, Fra Paulo, returned again to the point discussed, with the assertion that in the Talmud it was distinctly stated that Rabbi Joshua ben Levi had asked Elijah when the Messiah would come and Elijah had given him the reply: Ask the Messiah himself. Joshua then asked: And where is he? Elijah said: At the gates of Rome among the poor. Joshua went there and found him and put a question to him, etc.[18] "Now," said Fra Paulo, "if what the Talmud here says be so, then the Messiah has already come and has been in Rome—but it was Jesus who was the ruler in Rome."

I said to him in reply to this: "And is it not plain from this very passage you cite that the Messiah has not come? For you will observe that Joshua asked Elijah when the Messiah would come. Likewise also the latter himself was asked by Joshua: when will the Master come? Thus he had not yet come. Yet, according to the literal sense of these haggadic narratives, the Messiah has been born; but such is not my own belief."

At this point our lord the king interposed with the question that if the Messiah had been born on the day of the destruction of the Temple, which was more than a thousand years ago, and had not yet come, how could he come now, seeing that it was not in the nature of man to live a thousand years?

My answer to him was: "Already the conditions of discussion have been laid down which preclude me from disputing with you and you from interposing in this debate—but among those who have been in former times, Adam and Methuselah were well nigh a thousand years old, and Elijah and Enoch more than this since these are they who [yet] are alive with God."

The king then put the question: "Where then is the Messiah at present?"

To this I replied: "That question does not serve the purposes of this discussion and I shall not give an answer to it but perchance you will find him, whom you ask about, at the gates of Toledo if you send thither one of your couriers." This last remark I made to the king in irony. The assembly then stood adjourned, the king appointing the time for the resumption of the debate to be the day after next.

On the day appointed, the king came to a convent that was within the city bounds, where was assembled all the male population, both Gentiles and Jews. There were present the bishop, all the priests, the scholars of the Minorities [i.e., the Franciscans] and the Preaching Friars [i.e., the Dominicans]. Fra Paulo, my opponent, stood up to speak, when I, intervening, requested our lord the king that I should now be heard. The king replied that Fra Paulo should speak first because he was the petitioner. But I urged that I should now be allowed to express my opinion on the subject of the Messiah and then afterwards, he, Fra Paulo, could reply on the question of accuracy.

I then rose and calling upon all the people to attend said: "Fra Paulo has asked me if the Messiah of whom the prophets have spoken has already come and I have asserted that he has not come. Also a haggadic work, in which someone states that on the very day on which the Temple was destroyed the Messiah was born, was brought by Fra Paulo as evidence on his behalf. I then stated that I gave no credence to this pronouncement of the Haggadah but that it lent support to my contention. And now I am going to explain to you why I said that I do not believe it. I would have you know that we Jews have three kinds of writings —first, the Bible in which we all believe with perfect faith. The second kind is that which is called Talmud which provides a commentary to the commandments of the Torah, for in the Torah there are six hundred and thirteen commandments and there is not a single one of them which is not expounded in the Talmud and we believe in it in regard to the exposition of the commandments. Further, there is a third kind of writing, which we have, called Midrash, that is to say sermonic literature of the sort that would be produced if the bishop here should stand up and deliver a sermon which someone in the audience, who liked it should write down. To a document of this sort, should any of us extend belief, then well and good, but if he refuses to do so no one will do him any harm. For we have scholars who in their writings say that the Messiah will not be born until the approach of the End-time when he will come to deliver us from exile. For this reason I do not believe in this book [which Fra Paulo cites] when it makes the assertion that the Messiah was born on the day of the destruction of the Temple."

My opponent now stood up and said: "I shall bring further evidence that the Messianic age has already been." But I craved my lord the king to be allowed to speak a little longer and spoke as follows: "Religion and truth, and justice which for us Jews is the substance of religion, does not depend upon a Messiah. For you, our lord the king, are, in my view, more profitable than a Messiah. You are a king and he is a king, you a Gentile, and he [to be] king of Israel—for a Messiah is but a human monarch as you are. And when I, in exile and in affliction and servitude, under the reproach of the peoples who reproach us continually, can yet worship my Creator with your permission, my gain is great. For now I make of my body a whole-burnt offering to God and thus become more and more worthy of the life of the world to come. But when there shall be a king of Israel of my own religion ruling over all peoples then I would be forced to abide in the law of the Jews, and my reward would not be so much increased.

But the core of the contention and the disagreement between Jews and Christians lies in what you Christians assert in regard to the chief topic of faith, namely the deity, for here you make an assertion that is exceedingly distasteful. And you, our lord the king, are a Christian born of a Christian and all your days you have listened to priests and they have filled your brain and the marrow of your bones with this doctrine and I would set you free again from that realm of habit and custom. Of a certainty the doctrine which you believe and which is a dogma of your faith cannot be accepted by reason. Nature does not admit of it. The prophets have never said anything that would support it. Also the miracle itself cannot be made intelligible by the doctrine in question as I shall make clear with ample proofs at the proper time and place. That the Creator of heaven and earth and all that in them is should withdraw into and pass through the womb of a certain Jewess and should grow there for seven months and be born a small child and after this grow up to be handed over to his enemies who condemn him to death and kill him, after which, you say, he came to life and returned to his former abode —neither the mind of Jew nor of any man will sustain this. Hence vain and fruitless is your arguing with us, for here lies the root of our disagreement. However, as it is your wish, let us further discuss the question of the Messiah."

Fra Paulo then said to me: "Then you do believe that the Messiah has come?"

I replied: "No, but I believe and am convinced that he has not come and there never has been anyone who has said concerning himself that he was Messiah—nor will there ever be such who will say so [concerning themselves]—except Jesus. And it is impossible for me to believe in the Messiahship of Jesus, because the prophet says of the Messiah that 'he shall have dominion from sea to sea and from the River until the ends of the earth' (Ps. 72:8). Jesus, on the other hand, never had dominion, but in his lifetime he was pursued by his enemies and hid himself from them, falling finally into their power whence he was not able to liberate himself. How then could he save all Israel? Moreover, after his death dominion was not his. For in regard to the Empire of Rome, he had no part in the growth of that. Since before men believed in him the city of Rome ruled over most of the world and after faith in him had spread, Rome lost many lands over which it once held sovereign power. And now the followers of Muhammad possess a larger empire than Rome has. In like manner the prophet Jeremiah declares that in the Messianic age 'they shall teach no more every man his neighbor, and every man his brother, saying, Know the Lord: for they shall all know me' (31:34), while in Isaiah it is written, that 'the earth shall be full of the knowledge of the Lord, as the waters cover the sea' (11:9). Moreover the latter prophet states that, in this time, 'they shall beat their swords into ploughshares . . . nation shall not lift up sword against nation, neither shall they learn war any more' (2:4). But since the days of Jesus up to the present the whole world has been full of violence and rapine, the Christians more than other peoples being shedders of blood and revealers likewise of indecencies. And how hard it would be for you, my lord the king, and for those knights of yours, if they should learn

war no more!" [. . .] Afterwards on the same day I had audience of the king who remarked: "The debate still remains to be
concluded. For I have never seen anyone who was in the wrong
argue so well as you have." Then I heard in the palace-court
that it was the will of the king and of the Preaching Friars [the
Dominicans] to visit the synagogue on the Sabbath. So I tarried in
the city for eight days.

When they came to the synagogue on the following Sabbath
I addressed our lord the king in words that were worthy of the
occasion and of his office. [. . .]

Fra Raymond of Peñaforte rose up and gave a discourse on
the subject of the Trinity and asserted that the Trinity was wisdom and will and power. "And had not also the master," he said,
"in a synagogue in Gerona assented to what Fra Paulo had said
on this point?"

At this I got to my feet and spoke as follows: "I ask both
Jews and Gentiles to give me their attention on this matter.
When Fra Paulo asked me in Gerona if I believed in the Trinity,
I replied: 'What is the Trinity? Do you mean that three material
bodies, of the sort that men have, constitute the Godhead?' He
said: 'No.' Then I asked: 'Do you mean that the Trinity consists
of three subtle substances such as souls or that it is three angels?'
He said: 'No.' 'Or do you mean,' I enquired, 'that the Trinity is
one substance which is a compound of three substances such as
are those bodies which are compounded of the four elements?' He
said: 'No.' 'If that is the case' said I, 'then what is the Trinity?'
He answered: 'Wisdom and will and power.' To which I replied
that I acknowledged that the deity was wise and not foolish, and
will without passibility, and powerful and not weak, but that the
expression Trinity was entirely misleading. For wisdom in the
Creator is not an unessential quality but He and His wisdom are
one and He and His will are one and He and His power are one
—and, if this be so, the wisdom and the will and the power are
one whole. And even if these were unessential qualities of God,
the thing which is the Godhead is not three but is one, bearing
three unessential qualities."

Then Fra Paulo stood up and said that he believed in the
perfect unity of the Deity but that nevertheless there was in that

unity a Trinity, and this was a doctrine very profound for neither
the angels nor the princes of the upper regions could comprehend
it.

My answer to this was: "It is clear that no person believes
what he does not know. Hence it is that the angels do not believe
in a Trinity." The associates of Fra Paulo made him remain
silent. Our lord the king rose up and he and those with him
descended from the place where the prayer-desk was, each going
their several ways.

On the morrow, I had audience of our lord the king whose
words to me were: "Return to your city in safety and in peace."
Then he gave me three hundred dinars and I took my leave of
him with much affection. May God make him worthy of the life
of the world to come. Amen.

A VISIT TO PARADISE

Immanuel ben Solomon of Rome

Immanuel ben Solomon ha-Romi (ca. 1270–ca. 1330) was born in Rome,
lived in various Italian cities, and is known in Italian as Manoello
Guideo. He wrote Biblical commentaries and poetry, occasionally in
Italian, but chiefly in Hebrew. Influenced by his country, he introduced the sonnet form into Hebrew poetry, but wrote also in the style
of the Spanish Hebrew poets. His themes range from the sensual and
frivolous to the lofty and religious, from witty satire to sublime prayer.
He collected his poems in a Diwan, entitled Mahbarot (Makamat, mis-
cellanies). The concluding poem (from which a section is here reprinted), a vision of the "world beyond" called Ha-Tofet ve-ha-Eden
(Hell and Paradise), is patterned on Dante's Divine Comedy. Guided
by Daniel (Dante?), Immanuel meets in Hell such men and women as
the daughters of Lot, the Biblical Pharaoh, the wife of Potiphar, Aristotle, and Galen. In Paradise he finds a throne prepared for "Daniel,"
another possible allusion to Dante. The Diwan was first printed at
Brescia in 1491. The author and his work are of interest as products
of their time and surroundings; in the history of Jewish thought Immanuel occupies a very minor place.

While we walked to and fro through the streets of Eden,
and looked upon the gallery of the men of wisdom, I perceived

men full of splendor and majesty, compared to whose beauty the sun and moon are dark; a place was given them in the world of angels. Not recognizing any one of them, I asked the man who talked with me, that I might know concerning them. And he said unto me: "These are the pious of the Gentiles, who prevailed with their wisdom and intellect, and ascended the degrees of the ladder of wisdom in accordance with their ability. They were not as their fathers, a stubborn and rebellious generation; but they investigated with their intellect as to who is the Maker, and who the Creator that fashioned them with His loving-kindness, took them out from nothingness to existence, and brought them to this world; and as to what is the purpose for which He created them. When they asked their fathers, and considered their answers, they knew that they were worthless; they despised their creed, and set their mind to investigate the creed of other nations.

"Having investigated all the creeds, and having found that the hands of each of them are steadfast in strengthening its own foundations and in disparaging other creeds, they did not say: 'Let us remain in our creed, for it has been handed down to us by our fathers,' but out of all creeds they chose those doctrines which are true, and concerning which the wise men did not differ; these doctrines they accepted, and to them they clung. But to those opinions which all nations disparage they turned their back, not their face. As regards God, they arrogantly call Him by a name at which our heart trembles and shudders, for every nation calls Him by a special name.

"We, however, say: 'Let His name be what it may, we believe in the truly First Existence, that produced life; that was, is, and will be; that created the universe, when His wisdom so decided; that is hidden from us through the intensity of His revelation; that faints not, and is not weary, and of whose understanding there is no searching; that has mercy upon His creatures, and feeds them, as a shepherd tends his flock; who will call us unto Him, when our end draws nigh, and whose glory will gather us together.' " [. . .]

[Then] I remembered the rank of Daniel my brother, who had led me in the right way, and directed my path, and who had been near me when I fled. He is the plate of the holy crown upon my forehead, the life of my flesh and the breath of my spirit. I thought of the full account of his greatness, of his generosity and excellence, of his prudence and understanding, of his humility and righteousness, and of his renown which fills the ends of the earth. I then said unto the man who held my right hand: "I pray thee, my lord, show me the place of Daniel and his habitation; what manner of house do ye build for him, and what place is his rest?"

And he said unto me: "Know of a certainty that his rank is very high, and that the ends of the earth are full of his renown; even thy rank is too low to reach him. 'For he bore the sin of many, and made intercession for the transgressors' (Isa. 53:12). But because the Highest Wisdom knew that without thee he would find no rest and no repose, it placed thy booth near his booth, though thy worth is less than his; for the Highest Wisdom knew that he will have delight in thy company: he would be Moses, and thou wouldst be Joshua unto him; in order that all may declare, as it is said: Your souls are united, they cling together, and cannot be sundered. 'Will two walk together, except they have agreed?' " (Amos 3:3).

There is nothing to marvel at that I was joyful, for I knew that my lot fell in pleasant places, being aware that I shall have redemption on account of him. And I said unto the man: "As thou livest, show me the splendor of his throne, where he rests. For I know that its height mounts up to the heavens, and its head reaches unto the clouds."

And the man said unto me: "Come with me, and I shall show thee his joy and the glory of his resting-place." So I went after him [. . .]. Angels kept on bringing material for the work, and were making pleasant and beautiful canopies that shone like the brightness of the firmament, whose covering was of every precious stone, and whose structure was of sapphire, and tables, lamps, thrones, and crowns for the pure souls. We saw there a big ivory throne overlaid with gold, which gave life to him that finds it, and health to all his flesh. Crown stones glittered upon it, and garments of blue and purple and scarlet were spread over it; they sparkled like burnished brass, the glory of all lands. Upon the top of the throne was a crown, the weight of which was a *kikkar* of gold, and a precious stone that cannot be obtained for fine gold, nor can silver be weighed for the price thereof.

A voice was saying: "Proclaim that the merchandise thereof shall be for them that dwell before the Lord." And the man that talked with me said: "Hast thou seen the crown and the lofty throne whereupon thy brother Daniel rises as a lion, and lifts himself up as a lioness? This is his resting-place for ever, and here shall he dwell, because he hearkened to the word of the Lord, and there is no sage or thinker like him in all the earth."

Thereupon I rendered praise and thanks unto my Lord, because He brought him to the rest and to the inheritance; and I said: "Blessed be the Lord who is one, and who has no second, because He has not forsaken His loving-kindness and His truth toward my master."

When we ascended to the higher steps of Eden, we saw a thing whereat we marvelled; for there we saw men who during their life were ravenous beasts, bad to God and bad to men; they died as wicked men the death of them that are slain; their blood was poured out as water, and their flesh as dung. When I saw them shine like the brightness of the firmament, their height mounting up to the heavens, and their head reaching unto the clouds, I said in my heart: "Behold, the Lord has forgiven the sin of many, and makes intercession for the transgressors." I then inquired of the man that talked with me, that I might know the reason why these men deserved this lofty rank.

And he said unto me: "These men sinned, dealt perversely, and transgressed; for their sin they perished before their time, and were filled with bitterness; they were delivered into the hands of cruel people, and fell wounded, having been pierced through, into the lions' dens and upon the mountains of the leopards; they were left together unto the fowl of heaven and unto the ravenous birds of the mountains. When they approached the bitterness of death, they recalled the wickedness they had done, and accepted the bitterness of death with love, knowing that it came to them as a just retribution. Death was more pleasant unto them than life, because they considered that

they deserved a greater calamity, and that through these sufferings they were redeemed from a severer punishment than death.
When at the point of dying they showed their joy and delight
with their mouth and heart; and because they had received part
of their punishment in the corrupt world, wrath was averted from
their souls. Their death having been cruel and bitter, it was accounted as a crown of glory and a diadem of beauty upon the
head of their souls. It is, therefore, because of their death that
they deserved this glorious rank."

THE MESSIANIC AGE

Moses Maimonides

Maimonides rejected the various popular conceptions of Messianic
Utopia that persisted for centuries and—in the concluding chapters
of the *Mishneh Torah*—presented a natural, rational, historical, political view of the Messianic era. In contradistinction from the Messianic
age, Maimonides defined the classical Jewish concept of "the world to
come" as a state of incorporeal, spiritual bliss into which the souls of
persons worthy of this state enter "after the life of the present world
in which we now exist with body and soul" (*Mishneh Torah, Hilkhot
Teshuvah* VIII). The Messianic age appears to him as a period of preparation for the life in the world to come. Compare also "The Event on
Sinai."

The Messianic king will in time arise and establish the kingdom of David in its former position and in the dominion it
originally had. He will build up the sanctuary and gather the
scattered of Israel. In his day, the laws will become what they
were in olden times. They will bring offerings, they will observe
years of release and years of jubilee, according to the commandment given in the Torah.[19]

The Torah testifies to the Messianic king, as it is written:
"The Lord thy God will turn thy captivity, and have compassion
upon thee, and will return and gather thee from all the peoples,
whither the Lord thy God hath scattered thee. If any of thine
that are dispersed be in the uttermost parts of heaven, from

thence will the Lord thy God gather thee, and from thence will He fetch thee. And the Lord thy God will bring thee into the land which thy fathers possessed, and thou shalt possess it" (Deut. 30:3–5).

Do not think, however, that the Messianic king must give signs and miracles and create new things in this world, or bring the dead back to life, and the like. It will not be so. For see: Rabbi Akiba, who was a great sage among the sages of the Mishnah, it was he who carried arms for ben Koziba,[20] the king, and it was he who said of him that he was the Messianic king. He and all the sages of his generation thought that this was the Messianic king, until he was slain in his guilt. And after he was slain they all knew that he was not the Messianic king. But never had the sages asked him for a sign or for miracles. The root of these things is the following: This Torah, its statutes and its laws, are for all times. There is nothing one could add to it, and nothing one could take away.

If a king should arise out of the house of David, one who meditates upon the Torah, and like his ancestor, David, occupies himself with the commandments according to the written and the oral law, who has bent Israel to go in the ways of the Torah and to restore its breach, and who has fought the battles of the Lord, then it might be presumed that he is the Messiah. If he has succeeded, if he has built up the sanctuary in its place, if he has gathered the scattered of Israel, behold, then he is surely the Messiah. He will perfect the whole world, so that all together may serve the Lord, as it is written: "For then will I turn to the peoples a pure language, that they may all call upon the name of the Lord, to serve Him with one consent" (Zeph. 3:9).

Do not think in your heart that in the days of the Messiah something will be changed in the ways of the world, or that an innovation will appear in the work of Creation. No! The world will go its ways as before, and that which is said in Isaiah, "And the wolf shall dwell with the lamb, and the leopard shall lie down with the kid" (Isa. 11:6) is but a parable, and its meaning is that Israel will dwell in safety with those who were lawless among the heathen, and all will turn to the true faith; they will not rob, nor destroy, and they will eat only what is permitted, in peace, like Israel, as it is written: "The lion shall eat straw like the ox" (Isa. 11:7). And everything else like this that is said concerning the Messiah is also a parable. In the days of the Messiah all will know what the parable signified and what it was meant to imply.

The sages said: "Nothing, save the cessation of the servitude to the nations, distinguishes the days of the Messiah from our time." [21] From the words of the prophets we see that in the early days of the Messiah, "the war of Gog and Magog" will take place,[22] and that before this war, a prophet will arise who will make straight the people of Israel and prepare their hearts, as it is written: "Behold, I will send you Elijah the prophet before the coming of the great and terrible day of the Lord" (Mal. 3:23). But he comes only to bring peace into the world, as it is written: "And he shall turn the heart of the fathers to the children" (Mal. 3:24).

Among the sages there are some who say Elijah will come before the coming of the Messiah. But concerning these things and others of the same kind, none knows how they will be until they occur. For in the prophetic books these things are veiled, and the sages have no tradition concerning them, save what they have deduced from the Scriptures, and so herein their opinion is divided. At any rate, neither the order of this event nor its details are the root of religion. A man must never ponder over legendary accounts, nor dwell upon midrashic interpretations dealing with them or with matters like them. He must not make them of primary importance, for they do not guide him either to fear or to love God. Nor may he seek to calculate the Messianic end. The sages said: "Let the spirit of those breathe its last, who seek to calculate the end." [23] Rather let him wait and trust in the matter as a whole, as we have expounded.

The sages and the prophets did not yearn for the days of the Messiah in order to seize upon the world, and not in order to rule over the heathen, or to be exalted by the peoples, or to eat and drink and rejoice, but to be free for the Torah and its wisdom, free from oppression and intrusion, so that they may become worthy of life in the world to come.

When that time is here, none will go hungry, there will be

no war, no zealousness, and no conflict, for goodness will flow abundantly, and all delights will be plentiful as the numberless motes of dust, and the whole world will be solely intent on the knowledge of the Lord. Therefore those of Israel will be great sages, who will know what was concealed and they will attain what knowledge of their Creator it is in man's power to attain, as it is written: "For the earth shall be full of the knowledge of the Lord, as the waters cover the sea" (Isa. 11:9).

Epilogue

THE HOLY ONE IS

WITHIN THEE

Eleazar ben Judah

Eleazar ben Judah of Worms, called also Eleazar Rokeah, *ca.* 1160–*ca.* 1230, talmudist, liturgic poet, moralist, is important chiefly as a disciple of Judah the Pious (see "Simple Piety") and, with him, promulgator of the mystic doctrine of the "Pious Men of Germany." His God "maintains His silence and carries the universe"; but He reveals himself through the appearance of His Glory (*Kavod*), which acts as mediator between Creator and Creation. Eleazar wrote *Rokeah* (Dealer in Spices), a treatise on Jewish teachings and laws (first appearance in Fano, 1505). The extract that follows is based on Hosea 11:9, "The Holy One is within thee."

Let thy life be one of holiness and self-denial. [. . .] Fix thy mind upon the Almighty when thou standest before Him in prayer; should some alien thought come to thee in thy devotions, be silent until thy heart is joined once more in reverence to thy Creator. Say to thyself whilst thou prayest, "How honored am I in being suffered to offer a crown to the King of Glory! In awe and humility will I enter the divine gates."

Love the Lord thy God. Let thy heart know Him, and declare His oneness. Do thy work until eventide; but remember to love Him at all times. See, He stands before thee! He is thy Father, thy Master, thy Maker, submit thyself to Him. Ah, happy is he whose heart trembleth with the joy of God and is forever singing to its Maker! He bears patiently the divine yoke, he is humble and self-denying, he scorns the world's vain pleasure, he lives by his faith, he has gentle speech for all, he rejoices in the joys of others, he loves his neighbor, and does charity in secret.

216

NOTES

I

1. Hagigah 15b.
2. Cf. Sifre on Deut. 11:22.
3. I.e., the universal soul, from which all human souls derive.
4. Cf. Num. 23:13.
5. I.e., God.
6. A play on words on Isa. 41:1; *bor* in Hebrew means both pit and purity.
7. The Soul emanates from the Intelligence, as the latter emanates from the Will (of God).
8. Cf. Isa. 30:33.
9. Cf. Job 33:6.
10. Cf. Exod. 25:11.
11. Cf. Job 13:15.
12. Cf. Ps. 73:24.
13. Cf. Isa. 12:1.

II

1. Sifre on Deut. 11:13.
2. Sayings of the Fathers I, 3.
3. Pesahim 50b.
4. Berakhot 54a.
5. Shabbat 30b.
6. Midrash Psalms 100:2.
7. Cf. Job 13:15.
8. Cf. Lam. 4:1.

III

1. Nedarim 62a.
2. Saadia Gaon (ninth–tenth century), religious philosopher, author of *Sefer ha-Emunot ve-ha-Deot* (The Book of Doctrines and Beliefs).
3. From the Additional Service for the New Moon.
4. The Day of Atonement.

217

IV

1. *Mishneh Torah,* The Fundamentals of the Torah II.
2. Berakhot 33b.

V

1. Horayot 13b.
2. Pesahim 50b.
3. Sayings of the Fathers VI, 4.
4. *Ibid.,* II, 21.
5. *Ibid.,* I, 15.
6. *Ibid.,* II, 5.
7. Erubin 55a.
8. Sayings of the Fathers II, 6.
9. *Ibid.,* IV, 12.
10. Taanit 7a.
11. Sayings of the Fathers IV, 7.
12. *Ibid.*
13. *Ibid.,* I, 10.
14. *Ibid.,* II, 2.
15. Gittin 67a.
16. Berakhot 63b.
17. Abodah Zarah 3b.
18. "The Son of Proverbs," aphorisms in the form of the Biblical Book of Proverbs, by Samuel ha-Nagid, Spain, eleventh century.
19. Jer. 35.
20. The system of critical notes on the accepted Biblical text.
21. Sayings of the Fathers I, 2.
22. *Ibid.,* I, 18.
23. Rashi: Rabbi Solomon ben Isaac (France, eleventh century), commentator of Bible and of Babylonian Talmud. Tosafot: Explanatory notes on the Talmud; the period of the Tosafists began immediately after Rashi. Both the commentary of Rashi and the notes of the Tosafists are printed on the margin of a typical page of the Talmud.
24. Our teacher; a rabbinical title.
25. Fellow; a title of distinction.
26. A difference in the point of view of two authorities.
27. Presentation, in four parts, of the rabbinic law, by Jacob ben Asher (Germany–France, thirteenth–fourteenth century).
28. Isaac Alfasi (North Africa–Spain, eleventh century), author of a compendium of the Talmud.
29. Central governing organization of Polish Jewry, from 1580 to 1764; the "four lands" were Great Poland, Little Poland, Red Russia (Podolia and Galicia), and Volhynia.
30. Rosh ha-Shanah 25b.

31. Fast day commemorating the destruction of Jerusalem.
32. Purim.

VI

1. Sayings of the Fathers II, 9.
2. Sotah 5b.
3. The *Kedushah*.
4. Ketubot 111b.

VII

1. Shabbat 156a.
2. Symbolically, the ancestors of Christianity and Israel.
3. Israel fell in 721 B.C., after the death of Shalmaneser V of Assyria.
4. Roman poet (first century); in his epic *Pharsalia* he described the civil war between Caesar and Pompey.

IX

1. "With ten words (sayings) the world was created" (Sayings of the Fathers V, 1).
2. Mekhilta on 15:2.
3. The center of emotion.
4. A compilation of the non-legal (aggadic) material from the Babylonian Talmud, by Jacob ben Solomon ibn Habib (Spain–Turkey, fifteenth–sixteenth century).
5. *See* note V, 23.
6. Moses ben Mordecai Galante (Rome–Safed, sixteenth century), talmudist and mystic, successor of Joseph Karo in the rabbinate of Safed.
7. A Tannaite.
8. Disciple of Rabbi Akiba (second century).
9. Disciple of Isaac Luria, head of the mystics of Safed.
10. Euphemistically so called because he was blind.
11. Bezalel ben Abraham Ashkenazi (sixteenth century), disciple of David ibn Zimra and his successor as chief rabbi in Cairo; author of *Shitta Mekkubetzet,* collection of talmudic annotations.
12. *See* preface to this chapter.
13. Predecessor of the Messiah, son of David.
14. Taanit 21a.
15. A part of the *Zohar*.

X

1. Numbers Rabba I, 6.
2. Genesis Rabba XXXIX, 1.
3. Mishnah Yoma VIII, 9.
4. *Ibid.*
5. Mishnah Terumot IX, 7.
6. Shabbat 30b.

XI

1. The Western (or "Wailing") Wall is a part of a wall surrounding the Temple Mount.
2. *See* Joel 4.
3. Part of its slopes were used as a burial field outside of the eastern wall of Jerusalem.
4. The Dead Sea.
5. *See* Deut. 34:1.
6. *See* II Sam. 5:7.
7. Name of various sects of men fasting and praying for the coming of the Messiah and the restoration of Zion.
8. *See* preceding note.
9. Cf. Jer. 31:14f.
10. Cf. Gen. 10:8f.
11. Sanhedrin 97a.
12. Genesis Rabba XCV, 2. *See also* "The Faith of Abraham."
13. Who once led the exiles from Babylon to Jerusalem.
14. Taanit 31a.
15. Lamentations Rabba I, 57.
16. The king's *justiciar* was, next to the king, the most important officeholder in Aragon; he presided over the *Cortes.*
17. Or, "My servant shall prosper."
18. Sanhedrin 98a.
19. Deut. 15:1-4; Lev. 25:8-24.
20. Ben Koziba ("Son of Lies") and Bar Kokhba ("Son of the Star"): names applied to the leader of the Jewish revolt against the Romans in 132 to 135.
21. Sanhedrin 91b.
22. Ezek. 38-39.
23. Sanhedrin 97b.

SOURCES

Prelude

KNOWLEDGE AND FAITH: Abraham ibn Ezra, Commentary on Hosea 6:3, tr. N. N. G.*; Joseph Caspi, *Sefer ha-Musar*, in Eleazar Ashkenazi, *Taam Zekenim*, tr. I. Abrahams, *Jewish Life in the Middle Ages*, London, 1932, p. 394; Solomon ibn Gabirol, *Choice of Pearls*, tr. A. Cohen, New York, 1925, pp. 45f.

I

THE ONENESS OF GOD: Maimonides, *Mishneh Torah, Hilkhot Yesode ha-Torah* I, 1–II, 2 abridged; the translations from *Mishneh Torah* throughout this volume are based on Moses Hyamson, *The Mishneh Torah*, New York, 1937, and Simon Glazer, *Book of Mishneh Torah*, New York, 1927.

KNOWLEDGE OF GOD: Maimonides, *Moreh Nebukhim* III, 51, tr. based on M. Friedländer, *The Guide for the Perplexed*, London, 1904.

IN THE PRESENCE OF GOD: Solomon ibn Gabirol, *Keter Malkhut* 1, 3, 4, 6, 29-32, 38, 40, abridged, tr. Bernard Lewis, *The Kingly Crown*, London, 1961.

LORD WHERE SHALL I FIND THEE?: My Thought Awakened Me: *Diwan of Jehuda Halevi*, ed. H. Brody, III, 65, tr. S. Solis Cohen, *United Synagogue Recorder* I, 1921, 3; With All My Heart, O Truth: ed. H. Brody, II, 221, tr. Judah Goldin, *Menorah Journal* XXXI, 1945, p. 196; Let my Sweet Song: ed. H. Brody, *Mivhar ha-Shirah ha-Ivrit*, p. 170, tr. Nina Salaman, *Selected Poems of Jehuda Halevi*, Philadelphia, 1928, p. 117; Lord, Where Shall I Find Thee: *Diwan*, ed. H. Brody, III, 150, tr. N. Salaman, *op. cit.*, pp. 134f.

II

"THOU SHALT LOVE . . .": Maimonides, *Mishneh Torah, Hilkhot Teshuvah* X; Bahya ibn Pakuda, *Hovot ha-Levavot* X, 1; *Zohar* on Deut. 6:5, tr. M. Simon and H. Sperling, *The Zohar*, London, 1934, V, pp. 357ff.

WHY IS MY LOVED ONE WROTH: Moses ibn Ezra, tr. S. Solis-Cohen, Philadelphia, 1934, p. 101.

* The initials refer to the editor of this volume.

THE UNIVERSALITY OF LOVE: Judah Abrabanel, *The Philosophy of Love* (Dialoghi d'Amore), tr. F. Friedeberg-Seeley and J. H. Barnes, London, 1937, pp. 188-191.

SAINTLINESS: M. H. Luzzatto, *Mesillat Yesharim* XIX, tr. M. M. Kaplan, Philadelphia, 1936, pp. 180f.

III

THE DUTIES OF THE HEART: Bahya ibn Pakuda, *Hovot ha-Levavot* Introduction, tr. M. Hyamson, *Duties of the Heart*, 1925, pp. 1-12, abridged.

THE SERVANT OF GOD: Judah ha-Levi, *Kuzari* III, 1-5, tr. H. Hirschfeld, London, 1905, pp. 119-124.

THE FAITH OF ABRAHAM: Maimonides, *Mishneh Torah, Hilkhot Abodah Zarah* I, 3.

DEVOTION: *Ibid., Hilkhot Tefillah* IV, 15-16.

THE SEVEN BENEDICTIONS AT THE MARRIAGE SERVICE: Prayer Book, ed. S. Singer, New York, 1915, p. 299.

IV

MAN—THE CENTER OF THE UNIVERSE: Saadia Gaon, *Sefer ha-Emunot ve-ha-Deot* IV, beginning, tr. A. Altmann, *Saadya Gaon, The Book of Doctrines and Beliefs*, Oxford, 1946, pp. 115ff.

ON CREATION: Maimonides, *Moreh Nebukhim* II, 25, tr. M. Friedländer, *op. cit.*

ON FREE WILL: Maimonides, *Mishneh Torah, Hilkhot Teshuvah* V.

THE CREATION OF MAN: Nahmanides, Commentary on Gen. 1:26; 2:7, 2:9; *Torat Hashem Temimah;* Commentary on Exod. 13:16, tr. Ch. B. Chavel, *Ramban,* New York, 1960, pp. 75, 78f.

ARGUMENT FOR THE IMMORTAL SOUL: Leone Modena, *Kol Sakhal* I, tr. Jakob J. Petuchowski, *Commentary* XX (1955), pp. 462f.

THE MAN AND HIS SOUL: *Midrash Yetzirat ha-Velad,* Jellinek, *Bet ha-Midrash* I, tr. N. N. G., *Commentary* XIV (1952), pp. 369ff.

THE BRIDGE OF TIME: Yedayah ha-Bedersi, *Behinat Olam,* quoted in *Judaism* II (1953), p. 224.

HEALING: Jacob ben Asher, *Arbaa Turim, Yore Deah* 336, quoted in Samuel S. Cohon, *Judaism: A Way of Life,* Cincinnati, 1948, p. 93.

THE END OF MAN: Prayer Book, ed. S. Singer, New York, 1915, pp. 317-324.

V

THE STUDY OF TORAH: Maimonides, *Mishneh Torah, Hilkhot Talmud Torah* I, 6-13.

IN PRAISE OF LEARNING, EDUCATION, AND THE GOOD LIFE: Judah ibn Tibbon, in I. Abrahams, *Hebrew Ethical Wills,* Philadelphia, 1926, III, abridged.

THE GIFT OF THE LAW: Obadiah ben Abraham, in G. Vajda, "The

Mystical Doctrine of R. Obadyah, Grandson of Moses Maimonides," *The Journal of Jewish Studies* VI (1955), p. 215.

PROPOSED JEWISH ACADEMY IN MANTUA: David Provenzal, in Jacob R. Marcus, *The Jew in the Medieval World*, Cincinnati, 1938, No. 78.

THE INNER LIFE OF THE JEWS IN POLAND: Nathan Hannover, *Yeven Metzulah* XVI, tr. A. J. Mesch, *Abyss of Despair*, New York, 1950, pp. 110-121.

THE HOUSE OF STUDY IN PADUA: Text, S. Ginzburg, *The Life and Works of M. H. Luzzatto*, Philaldelphia, 1931, tr. N. N. G., *Commentary* XI (1951), pp. 480-483.

VI

A POET'S ETHICAL COUNSEL: Solomon ibn Gabirol, *Tikkun Middot ha-Nefesh*, ed. and tr. S. S. Wise, New York, 1901, I, 1-3, III, 3 (pp. 58f., 61-64, 99); *Mivhar ha-Peninim*, tr. A. Cohen, New York, 1925, pp. 69, 78-80, 58f.

SIMPLE PIETY: Judah the Pious, *Sefer Hasidim*, quoted in S. Schechter, *Studies in Judaism* III, Philadelphia, 1924, pp. 19f.

A BRIEF SUMMARY OF ETHICAL RULES: Yehiel ben Yekutiel, *Sefer Maalot ha-Middot* XXIII, tr. N. N. G.

HUMILITY: M. H. Luzzatto, *Mesillat Yesharim* XXII, tr. M. M. Kaplan, Philadelphia, 1936, pp. 192-196, 204, abridged.

AT PEACE WITH THE WORLD: Joel ben Abraham Shemariah, in I. Abrahams, *Hebrew Ethical Wills*, Philadelphia, 1926, XXIII, abridged.

THE MIDDLE COURSE: Solomon Ganzfried, *Kitzur Shulhan Arukh* XXIX, 1-11, tr. H. E. Goldin, *Code of Jewish Law*, New York, 1927.

VII

THE GOD OF ABRAHAM AND THE GOD OF ARISTOTLE: Judah ha-Levi, *Kuzari* IV, 17-23, tr. H. Hirschfeld, *op. cit.*, pp. 196-200.

THE EVENT OF SINAI: Maimonides, *Iggeret Teman*, ed. A. S. Halkin, tr. B. Cohen, *Epistle to Yemen*, New York, 1952, pp. Vff.

THE PROSELYTE: Maimonides, *Teshuvot (Responsa)*, ed. A. H. Freimann, Jerusalem, 1934, No. 42, tr. N. N. G., in *Maimonides Said*, New York, 1941, pp. 57ff.

BENEDICTION WHEN FACING MARTYRDOM: Quoted in S. Schechter, *Studies in Judaism* III, Philadelphia, 1924, p. 17. The appended quotation: Meir of Rothenburg, *Responsa*, Prague, 1608, No. 517.

WHY CATASTROPHES COME: Solomon Alami, see preface, tr. N. N. G., *Commentary* XIX (1955), pp. 480-483.

THE PARABLE OF THE PRECIOUS STONES: Solomon ibn Verga, *Shevet Yehudah*, ed. Y. Baer, Jerusalem, 1947; tr. N. N. G.

EQUALITY: Jacob ben Abba Mari Anatoli, *Malmad ha-Talmidim*, Lyck, 1866, 28b; tr. N. N. G

THE HEBREW AMONG THE NATIONS: Simone Luzzatto, *Discorso circa il Stato degli Ebrei*, Venice, 1638, Considerations XVII-XVIII, tr. F. Giovanelli, *Commentary* III (1947), pp. 474-478.

VIII

SHIELD OF OUR FATHERS: Prayer Book, ed. S. Singer, *op. cit.*, p. 120.

THE SANCTITY OF THE SABBATH: *Zohar* on Exod. 20:8 (II, 88a-89a), tr. Simon and Sperling, *op. cit.*, III, pp. 268-273, abridged.

THE SABBATH BRIDE: Israel ibn al-Nakawa, *Menorat ha-Maor*, ed. H. G. Enelow, New York, 1930, II, 191, tr. A. J. Heschel, *The Sabbath*, New York, 1951, pp. 54f.

THE SABBATH AND THE DAYS OF THE WEEK: Judah Loew ben Bezalel, *Tiferet Yisrael*, Venice, 1599, X, tr. F. Thieberger, *The Great Rabbi Loew*, London, 1955, pp. 112f.

SANCTIFICATION: Prayer Book, ed. S. Singer, *op. cit.*, pp. 160f.

IX

MYSTICAL UNDERSTANDING OF JEWISH CONCEPTS: Body and Soul: *Zohar* on Lev. 19:2 (III, 80b-81b), tr. Simon and Sperling, *op. cit.*, V, pp. 91-94, abridged; The Ten Words: *ibid.*, II, 93b-94a, tr. *op. cit.*, III, pp. 280f.; The Poor and the Lowly: *ibid.*, III, 8b-9a, *Midrash ha-Neelam* to Ruth in *Zohar Hadash*, 94b, *Zohar* I, 168b, II, 61a, 86b, III, 85a, II, 198a, tr. in Y. Baer, *A History of the Jews in Christian Spain*, I, Philadelphia, 1961, pp. 263ff.; Material Wealth: *Zohar* I, 88a f., tr. Y. Baer, *op. cit.*, pp. 265f.

THE PRACTICE OF MYSTICAL MEDITATION: Abraham Abulafia, tr. from unpublished writings in G. G. Scholem, *Major Trends in Jewish Mysticism*, New York, 1954, pp. 134, 136f.

THE SEARCH FOR TRUTH: Solomon ibn Adret, *Sheelot u-Teshuvot*, Bene Berak, 1958, No. 548, tr. Gunther W. Plaut.

LIFE IN SAFED: Solomon Shloemel ben Hayyim Meinstrl, in *Sefer Taalumot Hokhmah*, Basle, 1629, tr. I. M. Lask, in K. Wilhelm, *Roads to Zion*, New York, 1948, pp. 57-64.

THE LIFE OF RABBI ISAAC LURIA: Solomon Shloemel ben Hayyim Meinstrl, *op. cit.*, pp. 37a-38b, tr. in Jacob R. Marcus, *The Jew in the Medieval World*, Cincinnati, 1938, No. 52.

IN THE PRESENCE OF THE DIVINE: Moses Cordovero. Who is a God Like Unto Thee? *Tomer Deborah* I, tr. Louis Jacobs, *The Palm Tree of Deborah*, London, 1960, pp. 47f.; The Disease of Pride: *ibid.*, II, tr. Jacobs, *op. cit.*, pp. 77ff.; Loving-kindness: *ibid.*, V, tr. Jacobs, *op. cit.*, pp. 90ff.

X

ISRAEL BEN ELIEZER, THE BAAL SHEM TOV: Legends: M. Buber, *Tales of the Hasidim: The Early Masters*, New York, 1947, pp. 35-78, selected; The Testament: *Tzavaat ha-Rivash*, tr. Sanford D. Shanblatt, *Judaism* IX (1960), pp. 282ff.

COMMUNION WITH GOD AND MEN: Abraham Kalisker, quoted in J. G. Weiss, "R. Abraham Kalisker's Concept of Communion with God and Men," *The Journal of Jewish Studies* VI (1955), pp. 89, 96.

THE TEACHINGS OF MENDEL OF KOTZK: M. Buber, *Tales of the Hasidim: The Later Masters*, New York, 1948, pp. 275-287, selected.

IN PREPARATION FOR THE DAY OF ATONEMENT: *Divre Torah*, Josefow, 1852, tr. M. T. Galpert and J. Sloan, in S. Y. Agnon, *Days of Awe*, New York, 1948, pp. 204-208.

DEATH: Louis Newman and Samuel Spitz, *The Hasidic Anthology*, New York, 1944, ch. XXIX, selected.

XI

JERUSALEM: *The Itinerary of Rabbi Benjamin of Tudela*, ed. M. N. Adler, London, 1907, pp. 22-25.

MYSTIC DRAMA OF JERUSALEM: *Zohar*. I: III, 69a; II: II, 212a; III: II, 7b-9a; IV: I, 134a, tr. *Commentary* XXI (1956), pp. 365f., based on tr. by Simon and Sperling (*op. cit.*).

TEN KINGS: *Pirke de Rabbi Eliezer* XI, tr. Gerald Friedländer, London, 1916, pp. 80-83, abridged.

THE SUFFERINGS OF THE MESSIAH: *See* preface; tr. N. N. G.

CREATION AND WORLD'S HISTORY: Nahmanides, Commentary on Gen. 2:3, tr. Charles B. Chavel, *Ramban*, New York, 1960, pp. 75ff.

MESSIAH THE TEACHER: I: A. Jellinek, *Bet ha-Midrash* III, Leipzig, 1853; II: Yehuda Ibn Shmuel, *Midreshe Geulah*, Jerusalem, 1954. *Commentary* XVIII (1954), pp. 466f.; tr. N. N. G.

THE DANCE OF THE RIGHTEOUS: Judah Loew ben Bezalel, *Beer ha-Golah* IV, tr. F. Thieberger, *op. cit.*, pp. 100ff.

HAS THE MESSIAH COME? *See* preface, tr. O. S. Rankin, *Jewish Religious Polemic*, Edinburgh, 1956, pp. 179-210, abridged.

A VISIT TO PARADISE: Immanuel ben Solomon, *Ha-Tofet ve-ha-Eden (Mahberot XXVIII)*, tr. B. Halper, *Post-Biblical Hebrew Literature*, Philadelphia, 1921, pp. 188-193.

THE MESSIANIC AGE: Maimonides, *Mishneh Torah, Hilkhot Melakhim* XI-XII, tr. N. N. G., abridged.

Epilogue

THE HOLY ONE IS WITHIN THEE: Eleazar ben Judah, *Rokeah, Hilkhot Hasidut*, tr. S. Schechter, in *Studies in Judaism* III, pp. 22f.

Acknowledgments

Thanks are due to the following authors and publishers for permission to use their translations referred to under "Sources": American Academy for Jewish Research for excerpts from *Moses Maimonides' Epistle to Yemen,* edited by Abraham S. Halkin, translated by Boaz Cohen (1952); *Commentary* for permission to reprint six "Cedars of Lebanon"; East and West Library, London, for excerpts from *Saadya Gaon: The Book of Doctrines and Beliefs,* edited and translated by Alexander Altmann (1946), and *The Great Rabbi Loew of Prague,* by F. Thieberger (1955); Philipp Feldheim, New York, for selections from *Ramban: His Life and Teachings,* by Charles B. Chavel (1960); Abraham J. Heschel and Farrar, Strauss and Cudahy for a quotation from *The Sabbath,* pp. 54f. (1951); the estate of Moses Hyamson for the use of his *The Mishneh Torah, Book I* (1937), as the basis for the rendition of the respective selections, and for excerpts from his *Duties of the Heart* (1925); The Jewish Publication Society of America for excerpts from *Selected Poems of Jehudah Halevi,* translated by Nina Salaman (1928), *Selected Poems of Moses ibn Ezra,* translated by S. Solis-Cohen (1934), *Mesillat Yesharim,* translated by Mordecai M. Kaplan (1936), *Hebrew Ethical Wills,* edited by I. Abrahams (1926), *Studies in Judaism III,* by S. Schechter (1924), *Post-Biblical Hebrew Literature,* edited by B. Halper (1921); *The Journal of Jewish Studies* for quotations from vol. VI (1955), pp. 89, 96, and 215; Bloch Publishing Co., for a selection from *The Hasidic Anthology,* by L. I. Newman (1944) and *Abyss of Despair,* translated by A. J. Mesh, ch. XVI (1950); Schocken Books Inc., New York, for selections from *Days of Awe* by S. Y. Agnon, translated by M. T. Galpert and J. Sloan (1948), *Major Trends of Jewish Mysticism,* by G. G. Scholem (1954), *Roads to Zion,* edited by K. Wilhelm, translated by I. M. Lask (1948), *Tales of the Hasidim* I-II, by M. Buber (1947-48); The Sonzino Press, London, for quotations from *The Zohar,* III, V, translated by Harry Sperling, Maurice Simon and P. P. Levertoff (1934, 1949), and from *The Philosophy of Love,* translated by F. Friedeberg-Seeley and Jean H. Barnes (1937); The Union of American Hebrew Congregations for passages from *The Jew in the Medieval World,* by Jacob R. Marcus, Nos. 52 and 78 (1938); University Press, Edinburgh, for the translation of the Barcelona Debate in *Jewish Religious Polemic,* by O. S. Rankin

(1956); Vallentine, Mitchell, London, for selections from *Solomon ibn Gabirol: The Kingly Crown*, translated by Bernard Lewis (1961), and *Rabbi Moses Cordovero: The Palm Tree of Deborah*, translated by Louis Jacobs (1960).

SUGGESTIONS FOR

FURTHER READING

(PB: *available in a paperback edition;* JPS: *The Jewish Publication Society*)

A comprehensive treatment of the history of the period is Salo W. Baron, *A Social and Religious History of the Jews* ("High Middle Ages, 500-1200," Vol. III-VIII, 2d ed., New York: Columbia University Press, 1957-58); briefer presentations are Solomon Grayzel, *A History of the Jews* (Philadelphia, JPS, 1947); and Cecil Roth, *A History of the Jews* (New York: Schocken Books, 1961, PB).

Good regional histories are: James Parkes, *A History of Palestine* (New York: Oxford University Press, 1949); Cecil Roth, *The History of the Jews of Italy* (Philadelphia, JPS, 1946); A. Neuman: *The Jews in Spain* (Philadelphia, JPS, 1948); Yitzhak Baer, *A History of the Jews in Christian Spain*, vol. I (Philadelphia, JPS, 1961); Cecil Roth, *The Jews in the Renaissance* (Philadelphia, JPS, 1959), and *A History of the Marranos* (Philadelphia, JPS, 1959, PB); Albert M. Hyamson, *A History of the Jews in England* (London, Methuen, 1928); and Simon Dubnov, *History of the Jews in Russia and Poland*, vol. I (Philadelphia, JPS, 1916).

The Jewish society and community life is discussed in Salo W. Baron, *The Jewish Community* (Philadelphia, JPS, 1942); Israel Abrahams, *Jewish Life in the Middle Ages* (London, Goldston, 1932); Jacob Katz, *Tradition and Crisis: Jewish Society at the End of the Middle Ages* (New York, The Free Press of Glencoe, 1961); and *Exclusiveness and Tolerance. Studies in Jewish-Gentile Relations in Medieval and Modern Times. Scripta Judaica III* (Oxford University Press, 1961, Schocken Books, 1962, PB).

Trends in Jewish thought are analyzed in Isaac Husik, *A History of Medieval Jewish Philosophy* (Philadelphia, JPS, 1958, PB); Alexander Altmann, "Judaism and World Philosophy," *The Jews: Their History, Culture, and Religion*, ed. L. Finkelstein, II (Philadelphia, JPS, 1949); Gerschom G. Scholem, *Major Trends in Jewish Mysticism* (New York, Schocken Books,

228

1961, PB); Abraham J. Heschel, "The Mystical Element in Judaism," *The Jews* II, *op. cit.*; A. H. Silver, *A History of Messianic Speculation in Israel* (Boston, Beacon Press, 1960, PB); Jacob B. Agus, *The Evolution of Jewish Thought* (London–New York, Abelard-Schuman, 1959); Shalom Spiegel, "On Medieval Hebrew Poetry," *The Jews* II, *op. cit.*; and various essays in *The Legacy of Israel*, ed. I. Abrahams and Charles Singer (Oxford, Clarendon Press, 1928).

Other collections of source material are Jacob R. Marcus, *The Jew in the Medieval World* (Philadelphia, JPS, 1960, PB); Franz Kobler, *A Treasury of Jewish Letters* (Philadelphia, JPS, 1954); Leo W. Schwarz, *Memoirs of My People* (Philadelphia, JPS, 1945, Schocken Books, 1963, PB); and N. N. Glatzer, *A Jewish Reader: In Time and Eternity* (New York, Schocken Books, 1961, PB).

Index